The New Operational Culture

Also by Beatriz Muñoz-Seca and Josep Riverola:

Problem-Driven Management. Achieving Improvement in Operations through Knowledge Management.

Transformando Conhecimento em Resultados. A gestao do conhecimento como diferencial na busca de mais produtividade e competividade para a empresa (in Portuguese).

The New Operational Culture

The Case of the Theatre Industry

Beatriz Muñoz-Seca and Josep Riverola
IESE Business School
University of Navarra
Barcelona-Madrid
Spain

First published in Spanish 2007
English edition published 2009 by
PALGRAVE MACMILLAN

Palgrave Macmillan in the UK is an imprint of Macmillan Publishers Limited, registered in England, company number 785998, of Houndmills, Basingstoke, Hampshire RG21 6XS.

Palgrave Macmillan in the US is a division of St Martin's Press LLC, 175 Fifth Avenue, New York, NY 10010.

Palgrave Macmillan is the global academic imprint of the above companies and has companies and representatives throughout the world.

Palgrave® and Macmillan® are registered trademarks in the United States, the United Kingdom, Europe and other countries.

ISBN-13: 978-0-230-22096-6 hardback
ISBN-10: 0-230-22096-7 hardback

This book is printed on paper suitable for recycling and made from fully managed and sustained forest sources. Logging, pulping and manufacturing processes are expected to conform to the environmental regulations of the country of origin.

A catalogue record for this book is available from the British Library.

Library of Congress Cataloging-in-Publication Data

Muñoz-Seca, Beatriz, 1953–
    The new operational culture : the case of the theatre industry / Beatriz Muñoz-Seca and Josep Riverola.
        p. cm.
    ISBN-13: 978-0-230-22096-6 (alk. paper)
    ISBN-10: 0-230-22096-7 (alk. paper)
        1. Teatro Real (Madrid, Spain) – Management. I. Riverola, Josep, 1940– II. Title.

ML1747.8.M32M86 2009
792.5068—dc22   2008030141

10 9 8 7 6 5 4 3 2 1
18 17 16 15 14 13 12 11 10 09

Printed and bound in Great Britain by
CPI Antony Rowe, Chippenham and Eastbourne

Contents

Part III   Unity

Preface

Welcome, dear reader. You are about to embark upon a fascinating adventure that combines the world of *theatre*, focusing on Opera, and the world of *business management*, focusing on Operations.

On this adventure we'll explore two difficult but very rewarding subjects; first, how to manage highly qualified staff, so-called *talent management;* and second we'll look at how to achieve *competitiveness* through the implementation of the 'Golden Triad' of Operations. In the course of our travels through these territories, we will be guided by an expert in the form of Problem-Driven Management, or PDM.

However, it is not our intention only to present an abstract discussion of these subjects. Indeed, there are other interesting books that do just that (the first that comes to mind is by the current authors, *Problem Driven Management* – a must for your bookshelves!) That is why we explore these subjects in the context of a service activity that is as old as civilisation, but no less relevant for that: theatre.

The fascinating world of theatrical Operations has been our major discovery of the past three years. Until then, we were mere onlookers from our seats in front of the stage. Over these three years, guided by excellent professionals from the Spanish theatre, we have been able to go backstage and discover a whole new world, a world not normally seen by mere mortals. With feelings of admiration and envy, we have seen that the way Operations are managed in some, if not all, theatres, is actually *much more advanced* than in most companies!

We see theatre as the Galapagos Islands of the corporate world; having drifted off from the mainland, it long remained separate and independent, isolated from the evolutionary currents that have shaped business management style. (This is where the analogy begins to seem a bit stretched, but please bear with us.) Over time both worlds evolved, each developing its own rules according to the necessities and demands of the time... until advances caused the two worlds to converge once again. The two have finally arrived at a similar place, but they've been on completely different journeys. A little explanation is in order.

On the one hand, we have the world of theatre. Throughout history, the only asset a theatre needed in order to be competitive was its peoples' *talent*. The Ancient Greeks, the Spanish Golden Age players, the British with their immortal bard – they all had wealth and possessions in varying degrees but, ultimately, they had to rely on their art in order to survive. This reliance on art produced artistic talents of enormous stature, from

Shakespeare and Cervantes, to the Pavarottis and Domingos of recent times, to name but a few.

Companies, on the other hand, evolved in exactly the opposite direction. The industrial revolution introduced repetitive processes, standardisation and the creation of a new social caste of *manual labourer* or *workforce*. An individual's talent was ignored (what was the use of that?) and only their motor abilities were appreciated. Some exceptionally sophisticated examples of companies based on this type of paradigm appeared in the course of this evolution, which continued until the globalisation of competition forced companies to realise that their competitive advantage is not, and cannot be, based on any of the resources they own except for one: *knowledge.* But knowledge is held by people. Thus, almost overnight, labour ceased to become a matter of hands, and became a matter of brains. Companies suddenly discovered the need to learn how to *manage* their people's *brains or talent.*

At the same time, the theatre, in its continual quest for new horizons of artistic expression – in a process paralleled by all the other art forms –started to explore the possibilities offered by technology and progress. Developments such as sophisticated props, dynamic lighting and audiovisual projections have helped pave the way. In the process, highly complex theatrical machinery has been created with processes that even challenge those of the most technologically advanced companies.

*   *   *

Although our background was in business, one of us had close family ties to the stage, so we knew this experience would be a lot of fun for us. We also knew that it would be rewarding, since the ideas developed within companies to overcome the *talent barrier* had long been known by 'theatre people' – those people, extremely professional, most of them highly talented, who are never seen on stage, but whose work is responsible for the memorable occasions enjoyed by their audiences.

We now want to share this experience with you, the reader. In this book, we try to combine what is known (or intuited) by people in business with what is known and practiced by the people in the theatre. The result, we believe, is a new and compelling insight into what should be the *Operational Culture* of any World-Class company in the twenty-first century.

We hope the reader will reflect on the many interesting subjects that are raised in these pages and will think about how he can *adapt* these ideas to his[1] company. We have thought about this long and hard but, while we can assure you that the results have been excellent, there is no better recommendation than personal experience. So we hope that you, dear reader, will think about putting into practice the recommendations that you'll find in

---

[1] We tend to use 'him' or 'his' when talking of anonymous or unknown people – it is purely a writing style, and no reflection on gender attitudes.

these pages and, in particular, that you think deeply about the challenges we set out.

So why the Teatro Real[2] in Madrid? Ok, we'll be honest. One of the authors, a long-time opera enthusiast (who frankly knew very little about theatrical Operations until he read a rather whimsical and sensationalist book on the subject) was trying to find a way to go the New York Met[3] and, to this admittedly self-serving end, proposed a case study about it. However, realising that his ulterior motive was perhaps too obvious, the author decided to lower his sights, and decided instead to contact an internationally renowned opera house closer to home. There were really only two choices: the Liceo in Barcelona or the Teatro Real in Madrid, and the decision was practically taken out of our hands by the wonderfully enthusiastic response received from the Teatro Real.

So, that is where we started our journey and met our *cicerone*,[4] Daniel Bianco, the Operations Director of the Teatro Real. Daniel undertook, with patient resignation, the enormous task of trying to make us understand what 'theatre people' are really like and how they are managed. He should really be considered a co-author of the book, as the reader will come to understand by reading the summaries in this book of our conversations with him over the past two years. By the last chapter, he'll be your friend too!

Daniel still thinks that we don't have the faintest idea about art ... and he's probably right. But after two years of working with us, he has come to realise that, in spite of our ignorance, we do want to understand, and one day we will succeed. Daniel has come many times to IESE to talk about his experiences in our educational programmes. And true to his good-natured modesty, he still remarks, 'I don't know why all these important people find what I say so interesting!' As he reads these pages, the reader will be able to judge for himself just how interesting the things Daniel says are.

The book follows a dual structure where a chapter with the summary of an interview is followed by another chapter of remarks, lessons and points for reflection ... and some criticisms too because, despite its reputation, the Teatro Real isn't an earthly paradise where nothing can go wrong!

We have sought to preserve the 'freshness' and dynamism of the original interviews. They were spontaneous interviews, not following any script, which often started in one direction and then took some unexpected turns as we realised where our thinking converged and where it differed. Of course, all of the interviews were focused from perspective of the authors'

---

[2] Meaning literally 'Royal Theatre', but we'll continue using the name in Spanish 'Teatro Real'.

[3] The New York Metropolitan Opera, created in 1883.

[4] *Cicerone* is an old term for a guide who explains matters of archaeological, antiquarian, historic or artistic interest.

business experience, which sometimes caused some perplexity among our interviewees; similarly, their ideas sometimes caused astonishment in us. We have edited them as far as possible to avoid repetition, but in some cases the same concept was linked to two different issues and an author cannot assume that the reader's memory is flawless. So, if the reader perceives some degree of repetition, it's because there is.[5] Our excuse is the intention to convey the interviewee's line of thought.

And finally, the thanks. Of course, Daniel Blanco is not the only 'star' in our story: also Miguel Muñiz, General Manager of the Teatro Real; Lluís Pasqual, the widely respected Stage Manager; José Lluís Tamayo, who knows more about backstage than most people have even dreamt of; and Maestro Jesús López Cobos himself, who kindly took the time to enlighten and fascinate us.

Sadly, it would take too long to list all the other people who have helped us in our work, but we would like to make particular mention of Leonard Garuz, the Operations Director at the Gran Teatro del Liceo; the Teatro Real's previous management team with Ines Argüelles at the helm; Emilio Sagi, the Artistic Manager; and Vicente Salgado, the Administration Manager. And, last but not least, all the members of the Operations Management team: Carlos, Daniel's assistant; Ignacio, who handles logistics (and a lot more); Marta Maier, who co-ordinates the Floor Managers; and all those who have taught us so much with their words and deeds. We thank them all for the support and enthusiasm they shared with those 'pains in the neck' from IESE.

Both authors usually blame the other author for any errors in the books they write together. But this time, we've got a better scapegoat. We can take advantage of the fact that Daniel hasn't worked with us before, and declare that any error in this book is clearly the fault of ... Daniel Bianco.[6]

---

[5] Guadalupe Moragues, the assistant of one of the authors, was entrusted with the mission of transcribing the interview tapes. Her most commonly heard remark was: 'Another one? My God!'. We like to think that it was her way of imploring God to help her do her job well ...

[6] OK, OK, calm down, we're only joking.

Overview

'Operations' are all those activities involved in delivering service to the clients. All companies, from service providers to industrial firms, have Operations at their heart. Operations include everything from design of products and procedures to quality control, production, logistics and after-sales service, and are crucial for three main reasons:

1. *The effectiveness of a company's Operations directly influences the quality of service experienced by the customer. Customer satisfaction is almost exclusively a function of Operations. Get it wrong, and you may lose a client.*
2. *Operations represent the lion share of costs in a P&L.[1] In fact, Operations can provide an index to calculating the firm's profit margin – the difference between sales and costs. Costs are incurred in everything from raw materials to labour and, generally, throughout the entire activity of a company.*
3. *Every department in a company has Operations. The Accounts department has its financial Operations, Sales and Marketing may have sales, marketing, PR and customer relationship Operations and so on.*

It's probable that 90 per cent of staff in an average company work in Operations, yet Operations management theory seems to have been left in the past. Indeed, in most companies it still appears to be based on business models inherited from the time of the Industrial Revolution. Manual labourers were not supposed to think; rather their lot was limited to obedience. Indeed the phrase 'manual labour' or 'work force' would seem to indicate that the most important thing about such workers is their hands; their manual abilities. This is completely at odds with the current situation, where the biggest challenge is not to manage hands, but to manage minds. Hands do not make a company competitive. Even skilled hands are, often literally, two a penny. What make us competitive are our minds and talents. Instead of workforce, we want brainpower. To incubate and develop talent, we need to embrace a different way of operating: a new Operational Culture. This is the key message of this book, the new Operational Culture of the twenty-first century: a culture that will help companies to become truly 'world-class'.

But what is this 'Operational Culture' we keep mentioning? It is the combination of rules and values that determine the manner in which different parts of an organisation interact in a work context in order to deliver customer service.

One must not confuse this Operational Culture, as we have defined it here, with the concept – poorly defined and oft-abused – of Corporate Culture. We're not even

---

[1] Profit and Loss Account.

sure what that really is, but Operational Culture is easy to define because of the following:

1. *We are talking about relationships within a work context; how people interact when working with a common purpose, what their responsibilities are and how they relate with those of other people.*
2. *They are explicit or implicit rules and values; explicit if they have been formally defined and implemented, implicit if they have arisen informally or organically and don't need formalising ('we've always done it like that'). Implicit rules almost always appear when explicit rules have been forgotten.*
3. *They are always aimed at delivering customer service. We are not talking about 'human behaviour' or 'employee relations' – we are in Operations and our purpose is to serve our customer.*

The Operational Culture that we propose is based on two central ideas. One is that a world-class manager should not DO 'but rather should make sure that others do'. This focus goes hand-in-hand with the second, namely that brainpower must be exploited and given every opportunity to function. To do this, we propose putting into practice the message: 'Don't bring me problems, bring me solutions'.

These two maxims succinctly express our Operational Culture proposal. Those managers who use them will be telling the organisation that people not only can but MUST think about, decide and implement decisions for improvement. And with that they will be creating a need for change that requires new organisational models.

The necessary management style that emerges is based on three criteria, summarised in what we call the 'Golden Triad'; three ways of running and appraising the organisation that are at once comprehensive, complementary and synergistic. The components of the Golden Triad are 'Efficiency', 'Attractiveness' and 'Unity'.

In this book we will look at how Operational Culture changes when it is supported by the Golden Triad, and what the necessary steps are for success. We believe that, for the majority of companies, it is not a matter of choice. We believe that if they do not change, especially along the lines we propose, they are dooming themselves to becoming uncompetitive and, sooner or later, to eventual failure; overtaken by companies better than them in almost every sense.

We start the book with a brief presentation of the Golden Triad and the basic components of this new Operational Culture.

1
The Need for a New Operational Culture

Introduction

The world of Operations, viewed from this early part of the twenty-first century, is in turmoil. Engineering firms with engineers in revolt, doctors who don't accept the authority of their hospital administrators, consultants who deliver only half-measures, line managers who don't contribute new ideas or improvements to their Operations... the list is endless. At the same time, many companies realise that they need to change but simply don't know how.

Nevertheless, this turmoil often leads them to consider new ways of working. Perhaps they realise they have to become competitive on a world scale, perhaps they accept the need for World-Class Operations, perhaps they even suspect that a *new Operational Culture* is needed... but how to achieve these changes?

Our proposed answer is Problem-Driven Management, or PDM.

PDM proposes that the *problem-solving process* is central to Operations Management. On the one hand, it leads to *improvements* in the firm and, on the other, to the *education* of its staff. Therefore, PDM incorporates *true knowledge management*,[1] dramatically transforms the classic approach and seeks to gain maximum leverage from the management of *'brainpower'*, or *talent*.

PDM has been developed over the course of 20 years' work by both the current authors, as consultants to many companies in the field of Operations, albeit with different approaches – one of the authors concentrating on the more quantitative part[2] and the other on the more strategic and qualitative part.[3] However, both have managed to agree on the design and approach of the new way of doing things in Operations.[4]

---

[1] Not that multitude of completely useless things propounded by some...
[2] Full of formulas that are unintelligible to the other author.
[3] Which the other author has always considered 'soft' and sometimes has called 'waffle...'
[4] Muñoz-Seca and Riverola. *Problem-Driven Management*, Palgrave, 2004.

Many of the basic concepts of this Operational Culture are expressed in what we call 'quotable quotes'; one-liners that are easy to remember and enable the reader to focus on the basic idea. To introduce this new way of doing things, we can think of no better way than to dive straight in with one of our most emblematic sayings: *'Don't bring me problems, bring me solutions'*.[5]

By just saying this simple (but magical!) sentence, the reader takes a big step towards doing away with Taylor's model of Operations[6] which was so much *en vogue* in the twentieth century. The sentence proposes that each person must bring solutions to his problems and, moreover, that he must also have the means to solve them, while at the same time bringing decision-making down to the staff strata closest to Operations and giving them the authority to improve.

To achieve this operating method, we need to properly integrate the firm's 'middle managers', the *line managers*. This is the level between senior management and the 'rank and file' and includes people like the warehouse manager, the bank branch manager, the Operations Manager in a hotel, the shop manager, the plant manager and so on. In other words, all the managers of departments, functions, sections and so on, who play a significant part in *what is done* and *how it is done*. This level or group has always been absent from Operations paradigms, but it is this group that holds the key to the firm's service. They can help service become excellent and keep it that way or equally can block any change if they disagree with the way things are done.[7] Thus is it also the group that has the greatest need of finding new ways of doing things to increase productivity. And, last of all, it is the group that has the least time – being focused on operating management – to think about how to do that. The world is shifting beneath their feet, they face new challenges every day, their Operational problems are increasingly complex, and many people at this level are not sufficiently prepared to cope with them. Nevertheless, they are the key elements in Operations and therefore

---

[5] It has given us great pleasure – and others a huge surprise – to see that many managers have put this motto on their office door. PDM is gaining ground...

[6] Fredrick Wilson Taylor's Theory of Operations, *The Principles of Scientific Management*, Harper & Brothers: Dover Publications, 1911.

[7] Many projects that were implemented during the past century under the umbrella of 'Quality' have been implicitly boycotted by this level. The reason for this is very simple. The Quality movement has striven above all to work with the top level of the company (to sell itself) and with the bottom level (to get results). But efforts have never been concentrated on the middle level. This has led some line managers to feel threatened and to subtly block the improvement process. A quality-derived approach, 6-Sigma, has made some effort in this direction by introducing the idea of 'belts', as in martial arts, using facilitators who are drawn from the middle level. But it does not seem to have been an integrative approach – rather it is often blamed for creating parallel actions and advisory structures.

they must be responsible for implementing and cascading each new model throughout the organisation.

In the course of our work as Operations consultants, we have always concentrated on changing how things are done at this level. And the results have always been excellent. Of course, to get these results, you first have to work with the senior management. Senior management must set the stage for line management – clear priorities and actions must be defined for the entire organisation. But the daily work of improving productivity and competitiveness is the line manager's responsibility. And this work is what makes a firm 'world-class'.

In a multinational Latin American company we have been working with for three years, the phrase 'don't bring me problems, bring me solutions' was initially viewed with trepidation. The line managers were used to their bosses giving them orders and providing solutions to problems. When the Management Committee adopted this phrase as their philosophy, the first reaction was scepticism. The second was despair. Because life is easier when you obey than when you think. And then, fearing failure, the third reaction was something like panic. However, assisted by *Opcoaching*[8] (our jargon for procedures aimed at developing confidence, knowledge and methodology), the line managers' full potential 'blossomed'. The senior managers encouraged them to propose action plans; they rose to the challenge and proposed them. There was no chaos. But there was a change in the way of operating, a change in 'Operational Culture'. Some may fear that if people *think* and are given the *power* to act on those thoughts, it may cause a 'May 1968' uprising,[9] but the results in this case proved exactly the opposite.

Even so, *prudence* is necessary. It should be made clear from the beginning that our aim is not to create acracy[10] or anarchy or within organisations. But there is a need for a new way of doing things. The old philosophy of 'I'm the boss: I think, you perform' is no longer tenable. First, because the boss usually knows less than his subordinate. Second, because the person who understands the problem best is the person who 'owns' that problem, not the boss.[11] That's why the best option is for the problem to be solved by the 'owner', since he will seek what is best for both the company and himself.

It's true that nobody really knows exactly what this best way actually is, or at least, there is no single answer. We are not dealing with a single

---

[8] Operational Coaching. Good word, eh?

[9] Student uprising in France, initiated in the Sorbonne, which lead to the fall of De Gaulle's government.

[10] Acracy (from the Greek α-, 'no' and κράτος, 'force, violence'), absence of coercion. It refers to the negation of rule, or 'government by none'. An acratist is a person who submits to no authority or who is his own authority.

[11] Of course, the boss has other problems that in turn his own boss does not understand...

assessment criterion that is applicable to all cases. An 'optimal' solution should bring *effectiveness* to the firm and *gain* to the individual. Don't make the mistake of thinking that the only possible gain is short-term material gain, which is to say profit. The crucial gain is that which brings profit in the long term, that is that which generates *learning*. The one great need of the modern manager is to learn continuously, and those who achieve it gain in personal competitiveness. And that leads to long-term profit.

It is an approach in which you win (you, the employee, learn) and I win (I, the boss, get solutions for my Operational problems). In other words, it's a 'win-win' approach. However, this in turn shows that there must be consistency between the two goals: what a person naturally and spontaneously wants to do should also be what the company wants him to do. And that's not just a tongue-twister. There needs to be a consistency of goals so that, in the end, everyone does what the group needs to get done to achieve its strategic goals. This isn't achieved by giving orders[12] but rather by implementing this new operating method.

The intervention levels for implementing the Golden Triad

Implementing this new form of operating requires three levels[13] of intervention, what we call the *Golden Triad*. These actions are complementary and synergistic, and their imbalance is the cause of many business disruptions.

The three levels are as follows:

- *Efficiency*: The degree to which the organisation solves its Operational problems well and achieves its goals. It focuses on the actions required to solve day-to-day problems.
- *Attractiveness*: The degree to which people are satisfied in the organisation, basically because of what they get from it. It focuses on taking care of the individual's learning process.
- *Unity*: The degree to which the organisation's members identify with its goals. It focuses on achieving a consensus on what the firm wishes to achieve.

Case: A Spanish branch of an NGO (non-governmental organisation) was faced with the challenge of modernisation and having to become the spearhead of the international organisation. Its Managing Director understood

---

[12] Are you aware that nobody obeys you? People do what you say must be done when they think you're right. Otherwise, they either don't do it or look for excuses to not do it.

[13] These three levels are taken from our colleague and friend Juan Antonio Pérez López's book *Teoria de la acción humana* ('The Theory of Human Action') Rialp. Madrid 1991.

that they had to establish a new way of operating. The management team fully identified with the NGO's principles, which they shared and advocated, and the degree of *Unity* was satisfactorily high. However, the management didn't work efficiently and was not achieving the levels of productivity required to progress. Investigating the matter further, they realised that what they lacked were working methodologies and processes. But they also discovered that the organisation was not paying sufficient attention to their learning, which made them feel as if they were going nowhere in their careers. The Managing Director's initiative in establishing a new way of operating not only focused on improving their level of efficiency, but also on learning to see themselves as better managers and to feel that they were progressing in their professional lives. The harmony now being achieved between the three levels has enabled the NGO to walk a far easier path in the search for competitiveness.

Let's take a closer look at the three criteria that form the Golden Triad.

Efficiency

Efficiency is focused on productivity. Productivity is not just a factor for a company's differentiation; it is a necessity for survival. No company can survive if it is not productive and, to achieve this, it needs to have an efficient Operational structure.[14] This requires adapting its Operations to the mission that the firm has designed.[15]

However, the pitfall that faces many firms is that they may become obsessed with this criterion alone. Concentrating solely on seeking efficiency in its Operations may paralyse the firm by destroying innovation – clearly, an obsession for today may sacrifice the future for the present. It's like a person buying a 4x4 off-road sports vehicle for €60,000 on a 15-year loan, even though he knows he'll change the car after 8 years because it will look old. He may be maximizing efficiency by taking out a low-interest loan, but he is also placing a heavy burden on the future: a loan which will have to be repaid long after the car has stopped bringing him any satisfaction. We must be productive and efficient both today and tomorrow, and this means promoting productivity without annihilating competitiveness. A company that is interested only in productivity runs the risk of becoming a 'zombie', not dead, but not really alive...

---

[14] How to do this is by no means a trivial question – as we shall see, a methodology is required. Such a methodology was implemented for one of the authors to gain a better understanding of how her Operations worked when she was Managing Director of a company... ironically, it was designed by the other author, even though the former is the one who believes most in its effectiveness!

[15] A little bit of advertising. If the reader is interested in finding out more about these concepts, we recommend reading the other books we've written on the subject, or take a course with one of us at IESE-Business School!

Attractiveness

It is vital that the efforts made to increase productivity are accompanied by actions that make the firm 'attractive' for the people who work in it. *Attractiveness* does not mean making the worker happy. This is one of the many absurdities advocated by some human resources textbooks and gurus. No, a company is not a charity. Its ultimate goal is not to make the worker 'happy', whatever that may mean. The company's goal is to provide goods or service, adding economic value and surviving indefinitely. Anything else detracts from its mission. But, and this is a big but, if 'the talent' does not feel satisfied with the firm, the talent will not perform. Therefore, we must ensure that the talent is satisfied with the firm, not out of an unwholesome selflessness but out of a beneficent selfishness. If the talent is not satisfied and the firm is not attractive to it, it will not work. End of story.

Attractiveness is basically achieved by enabling people to *learn*. How do adults learn? This question is at the heart of so-called *andragogy,* or adult learning,[16] and provides a very simple answer: *By solving problems.* If the problem poses a *sufficient challenge* to the individual, then the individual will learn, even as he is finding the best answers to his problems. However, if the challenge is too big, the individual may become frustrated and thus not learn.

What does the level of *challenge* depend on? On the stock of knowledge held by the individual. If solving the problem requires knowledge that the individual does not have, the reaction may be one of frustration. Challenges, problems and knowledge are closely interrelated. A problem produces effects (challenging, learning and so on) in an individual, and the nature and scale of those effects depend upon the knowledge he has.

Problem-solving is the foundation of both a company's Operations and its progress. If problems are allowed to take over, unmanaged, then the problems themselves will become the focus, rather than *problem-solving.* This then leads to a vicious circle, when what we want is a virtuous one – the individual needs to solve the problem that is bothering him but may not have the necessary knowledge and skills to find the solution. If he finally solves the problem, he will probably have acquired knowledge which will allow him to solve it again more efficiently in the future. But when he is solving it for the first time, the organisation must provide him with the means to acquire the basic material he needs. Thus, he will be able to find the desired solution in a process in which he will learn without frustration. The onus is on the

---

[16] 'Andragogy' is the process of engaging learners in the structure of the learning experience. The term was originally used by Alexander Kapp (a German educator) in 1833, and was developed into a theory of adult education by the American educator Malcolm Knowles, (24 April 1913–27 November 1997). He held that andragogy (from the Greek words meaning 'adult-leading') should be distinguished from the more commonly used pedagogy (Greek: 'child-leading').

organisation to facilitate this learning, this personal improvement, by focusing what will make problem-solving easier.

Unity

Finally, the third criterion for achieving this new Operational Culture is to get the entire organisation to identify with the firm's mission. To make every individual feel integrated with the collective goal and to assimilate the mission's values as if they were their own. An extreme but graphic example of a lack of Unity might be a vegetarian being forced to working in an abattoir...[17]

In order to achieve Unity, it is necessary to specify and clarify the *basic principles* that govern the business, and then to be *consistent* with them. 'Brainpower' requires above all else a consistent approach. The rules by which the organisation functions will be continuously analysed and evaluated. The greatest risk is if these values should be lost or lose substance; this would lead to a collective loss of direction, and individuals may not agree with the new course taken by the company.

There are firms that clearly state what their basic *values* are during the recruitment process and ask the candidate whether he agrees with them. Other companies give presentations during the induction process in which the goals are explained. Although we are not against these practices, we think that achieving Unity requires a much more constant and subtle process.

What is the process of achieving this Unity, this identification and even empathy with the company? We believe that a starting point is to concentrate on *getting others to 'do'*. Pulling together and having clear criteria are indispensable in this. Unity is achieved only when the world is viewed with the same values, and thus must necessarily involve allowing others to solve and to do. But, as one manager confessed to us, 'It's very hard to do, it's very stressful.' Yes, it's easy to feel that your role is diminishing because you're letting other people solve problems instead of you; yes, it can seem as if you're letting go of the reins...it is not an easy journey, but things will get better.

Conclusions

In this chapter, we presented the basic elements of our proposal for achieving world-class Operations. PDM requires acting on the Golden Triad, and this leads to the following:

- Solving problems that enable the improved productivity of Operations. In other words, *doing* efficiently.

---

[17] In the course of our work as business consultants, we have seen many types of Operations. However, one of the authors vividly remembers her tour of a pig-processing plant...particularly the part of the process where the animals were slaughtered. She still shudders at the thought of it...

- Providing a continuous learning process in which both the individual and the organisation gain. This means *progressing*.
- Enabling each individual to fully identify with the firm's priorities and values. This leads to *belonging*.

We close this chapter with a few reflections that the reader should ponder.

- Have you considered that those productivity gains you are seeing in your company might actually be to the detriment of your competitiveness?
- How attractive is your company to its people?
- Is learning considered important in your company?
- Do your people identify with the company's priorities?

II
The Teatro Real de Madrid

In Chapter II, you'll meet the book's protagonist, Madrid's Teatro Real – the Royal Theatre of Madrid. You'll get to know its various components, the key players, how it's organised and its structure. We'll present a summary of the operations that must be undertaken in order to produce an opera, and of the people responsible. If you're not familiar with the Teatro Real or with the wonderful world of opera, then you mustn't miss this chapter! Well, nobody should miss any chapter – they're all important ...

The Teatro Real is a very old theatre inaugurated in October 1850; extensively renovated in the 1990s, it remains one of the world's finest opera houses. It has a relatively small auditorium, with 1,700 seats of various types and prices. The acoustics are exceptionally good throughout, but the horseshoe shape means that certain positions suffer from a restricted site-line to the stage.

The Teatro Real operates as a foundation, *Fundación para el Desarrollo del Teatro Lírico* (Foundation for the Development of Musical Theatre), of which 75 per cent is held by the Spanish government's Ministry of Culture and the remaining 25 per cent by the Community of Madrid (the autonomous region in which Madrid the capital, logically, is to be found). The foundation's governing body meets twice a year to establish the general characteristics of and approve the budget for the Teatro's services and productions. The theatre has, as part of its statutes, the objective of developing and promoting Spanish music. This means not only producing or performing the Spanish operatic repertoire but also commissioning new works by Spanish authors. Sometimes this even means excursions into the 'smaller' genres, such as *zarzuela*.[1]

---

[1] *La zarzuela* is a musical show in which a set of musical numbers is set to a conventional libretto or book, often in verse. There are many types of *zarzuela*, from the *zarzuela 'grande'* (big), typified by works such as *Doña Francisquita* or *Los Gavilanes*, to *'chico'* (small), with major works (normally in the form of comic farce) such as *La*

Currently, the Teatro Real has an annual budget of around €45 million, of which some 25 per cent comes from box office, 25 per cent from sponsorship and the rest from contributions from the Ministry of Culture and the Community of Madrid, in the same 75/25 proportion as mentioned above. As with the majority of the world's opera houses, the Teatro Real runs at a loss and needs public support in order to sustain.

The average ticket price for the Teatro Real is about €60, which is clearly aimed at a relatively well-to-do social sector. Nevertheless, the spectators receive an indirect subsidy from public funds of double the ticket price. The Director General of the Teatro Real, Miguel Muñiz, has developed a long list of initiatives to help drive the Teatro Real and, at the same time, to bring it closer to the people.

In the past 15 years, opera has come back into fashion, as a result of which the demand for seats has boomed. Tickets sell out almost immediately, regardless of the artistic content of the production. The Teatro Real programme functions throughout the entire season; specifically, for the 2005–2006 season, 54.5 per cent of all the productions were operatic (97 productions out of a total of 178), with the rest being concerts and musical evenings.

The Teatro Real is one of the most modern opera houses in the world, featuring all manner of technical-artistic advances.

An operatic production

An opera is a complex show in which a large number of people participate. A complicated opera may require the following: the orchestra, made up of some 110 musicians; the chorus, another 60 people; the singers, perhaps a dozen or so; the corps de ballet of perhaps 20 principals; and more than 100 people performing the additional, and no less essential, tasks such as stage and scenery decoration, lighting, sound, costume, make-up, stage management, and so on. This veritable army of staff must act with a high level of precision, and the majority of them must do so invisibly and, literally, behind the scenes, with all the glory and recognition going to the singers and the conductor, who always get the applause.

Curiously, the theatrical quality of many operas is, by the standards of the twenty-first century, pretty poor: mediaeval knights, hunchbacks, damsels, gods and various other 'normal' characters are regularly to be found embroiled in staggering tragedies, submitting to their destinies while

---

Revoltosa o *Agua, Azucarillos y Aguardiente*. Typically, the *grande* needs performers who can combine acting ability with a very high level of singing ability. The tenor's role in *Doña Francisquita* is not easy and is beyond the reach of most amateurs. On the other hand, the *chico* type can usually be sung by almost anyone with a decent ear for music.

shouting at the top of their voices. As the presence of such grand music necessarily limits the time available to develop the story through action, there is no room for the protagonists to develop subtle sentiment or nuances in their relationships. For this reason, the story is usually portrayed in a very simple form, in pompous declarations that, thanks to the alchemy of the music, are turned into beautiful arias. At this point, we should stop to take a breath and remember the play by Pedro Muñoz-Seca,[2] *Los extremeños se tocan*, a delightful *zarzuela* without music.

To stage an opera, a production, which is the total of all the necessary visual parts for the performance (thus distinguishing production from the direction, which includes the music) is required. The essential components of the production are, then, the set and the costumes. The most important person in the production design is the Stage Director, which is why he is usually a permanent member of staff. The Stage Director may be considered analogous to the director of a film, or the principal artist on a work of art. Stage Directors work independently and have the freedom to create. They are celebrities in the show-business world, and each has his/her own style and, indeed, peculiarity. One of the most popular Stage Directors is the Italian Franco Zeffirelli.[3] His productions for the New York Metropolitan are renowned for their scale, often with more than 300 extras onstage, and employ all manner of scenic tricks and devices, such as rotating platforms, lifts, projections, mobile sets and so on.

There are three basic methods of obtaining a production. The first is 'renting' a pre-existing production. The sets and costumes form the basis of the transfer, even though the 'rental' comes with the people who created that particular production. The average price of a rented production is between €7,000 and €12,000 per performance. This method has its advantages in being relatively low cost; however, it also brings with it some notable disadvantages – the artistic originality of the theatre is obviously

---

[2] Pedro Muñoz-Seca is, among many other glorious claims to fame, the paternal grandfather of one of the current authors, as may be guessed from the surname. He was one of the inventors, with Jardiel Poncela, of the '*astracán*' or astrakhan, which, in its time, was considered a minor comic genre. But time puts everything in its place and Muñoz-Seca's works, when contrasted with other minor works, are considered to be comedies of the highest order, for their originality and theatrical quality. In Spain it would be difficult to find many people who hadn't heard of him, his work, or some of his memorable lines.

[3] Assumed name of Gianfranco Corsi (b. 1923). A director, designer and producer of film, opera, theatre and television, Zeffirelli is characterised by the simultaneously monumental and yet delicate touch he brings to his work. He is probably best known, internationally, for his 1968 film version of Romeo and Juliet, but he is a regular at the New York Met. One of his more recent films was *Callas Forever*, a biography of his friend Maria Callas built around a fictional production of Carmen which, curiously, Callas never appeared in. The critics were not at all kind to the film, but the visual style is gloriously typical of Zeffirelli.

impaired, and numerous adaptations will be necessary to accommodate the production as no two theatres have the same dimensions or facilities. The sets may be too big for the stage and thus require modification or, conversely, too small and would look 'lost' on a big stage. A similar set of considerations pertains to the costumes because, in general, they are not designed to be readily reusable and need the attention of the theatre's Costume department.

The second method is home-grown production. This usually takes between four and six months, and the total cost can go up to €600,000, meaning that the cost is never going to be covered by the income from the box office. It is can therefore be justified only for artistic reasons, the fame and acclaim garnered in the theatrical world and the possible sales later (as in the first method). In general, Artistic and Musical Directors of theatres prefer to develop their own productions.

Certain key decisions in the production have a considerable impact on the cost and on its potential for later sale. Clearly, big productions are unlikely to sell to small theatres. Conversely, a minimalistic production, relying heavily on hi-tech lights and projections, could be staged in, and therefore sell well to, theatres of almost any size, although obviously the pricing structure would then be different.

And finally, the third method, co-production with another theatre. This is the most common method these days, for obvious reasons of cost- and risk-sharing. For example, the Teatro Real has entered into an agreement with the Los Angeles Opera, whose Artistic Director is Placido Domingo, to co-produce various works in forthcoming seasons. This results in relatively low costs, although the theatre that is central to the production is the one that contributes most and, justly, obtains the greatest renown from the product.

A production culminates in the performances, of which there are typically between 8, for a little-known opera, and 16 for a popular opera; for instance *La Bohème*[4] in the 2006 season ran for 16.

---

[4] *La Bohème*, by Giacomo Puccini (1858–1924), a piece of 'veristic' theatre (of the Italian Verismo style), and one of the pinnacles of Puccini's art. The first thing that anyone does, upon entering the world of opera, is get to know *La Bohème*. Its first act is musical gold but, of course, the libretto is so twee and prissy you'll be hard-pushed not to giggle. A young girl, Mimí, who makes flowers in an attic in the Latin quarter of Paris, gets to know her neighbour, Rodolfo, who is a poet (could he be anything else?). Throughout four acts of glorious music, and much warm fuzzy feeling on her part and hunger and passion on his, she returns to the attic just in time to die in the arms of her lover. It's hard to keep the popcorn down. Nevertheless, this is a moment that beings a lump (of a different kind) to the throat of many an opera lover, when Rodolfo's anguished cry announces the death of Mimí (a peaceful death, surrounded, as she is, by a 120-piece orchestra).

The management structure

A typical theatre has to balance artistic demands with its economic needs. Tradition has it that excellence in the artistic field should always be given priority and, from this point of view, one would expect a certain budgetary freedom when programming productions. The objective of the management is to balance these artistic and economic needs in a coherent programme that, while providing artistic satisfaction, does not lead to unmanageable financial deficits. In the Teatro Real's organigram there are certain key positions:

Miguel Muñiz de las Cuevas has been the General Manager of the Teatro Real since 2005, when he replaced the previous incumbent Ines Argüelles. He is the most senior person in the Teatro Real, answerable only to the shareholders.

Alfredo Tejero Casajús is the Administrative Director responsible for the economic and administrative functions of the Teatro Real. He has approximately 60 people under him, covering functions such as Human Resources, IT, Finance, Contracts and various others necessary to the daily running of the Teatro Real.

Daniel Bianco is the Operations Director. Daniel, in his fifties, is a true theatre man. Before becoming the Operations Director of the Teatro Real, he was in stage design. The operations team, under Daniel, is the biggest in the Teatro Real, with approximately 250 staff.

The Operations department is in charge of the operations necessary for a performance and the necessary design preparation beforehand. They design detailed processes for each production; processes which they then carry out. The Teatro Real is normally open from 8:30 a.m. until midnight, and this requires three shifts. The operations staff are a mixture of people, some with art or craft-related professions, such as painters, carpenters and electricians and some without professions but with extensive experience in theatre.

Antonio Moral is the Artistic Director. He proposes the production plans for each season to the management, attends to the artistic demands for each production. The Artistic Management enjoys, in this respect, complete autonomy. The management always limits itself to approving their requests, the only negotiation being over the permissible budget.

Jesús López Cobos is the Musical Director. He's the Director of an internationally renowned orchestra, and a master of all things operatic. Maestro López Cobos works with Antonio Moral in defining the season's musical programme as well as in selecting the singers and Musical Directors.

Programming the season

Each season is planned four years in advance, which means that the Artistic Director maintains a three-year rolling plan. Though this sort of advance planning may seem excessive to some, it is absolutely necessary in order to be on time with the co-productions. If a theatre stages an existing production, it can have very little say in the matter. But if it is involved in a co-production from day one, it has the opportunity to leave its mark on the production. Singers are also contracted well in advance, but with sufficient flexibility to take into account the latest fashions, stars, values and trends that might change year to year; this would simply not be possible if the entire casting process were completed too far in advance.

When planning the season, the Artistic Director tries to anticipate the 'end-product' of each production. The structure will be fundamentally determined by the choice of Stage Director. If he chooses, for example, Franco Zeffirelli, he will probably[5] end up with a massive production, with immense sets and lots of movement of people. Choose Robert Wilson,[6] on the other hand, and he'll more likely end up with static, abstract and stylised sets relying heavily on the lighting. Clearly, these choices not only affect the artistic side, they also have a significant impact on the total cost of a production.

After the Stage Director, the two other key players in production planning are the Musical Director and the singers. Therefore, the Artistic Director has three key decisions to make for every production and these are, in order of importance, Stage Director, Musical Director and singers. With those decisions made, to use the words of Caesar, 'alea iacta est'.[7]

The operating structure of the Teatro Real

The stage covers an area of 1,430 sq m, opening to the theatre through a proscenium 18 m wide by 14 m high. Even so, perhaps the least showy and flamboyant feature of the theatre is, in fact, the stage. Everything ends up happening there, but seen up close it appears to be remarkably simple. One would have no idea, just from looking, that it is in fact a huge movable platform, capable of being moved horizontally and lowered by as much as 14 m!

Surrounding the stage, and unseen by the public, is an incredible installation. High above the stage, almost disappearing from view, is the 'launch zone' or fly tower, where pieces of the set are kept ready to be lowered down to the stage when required during the performance. Its height is much greater than that of the stage, as it needs to be capable of hiding the entire

---

[5] We say 'probably' because the artistic inspiration of such people is, predictably, unpredictable.

[6] Robert Wilson (b. 1941) a very *avant garde* North American Stage Director, perhaps best-know for *Einstein on the Beach*.

[7] 'The die is cast'. The reader must excuse us but, as we're so immersed in the world of culture, it's a weakness (an affectation?!) to leave such token references scattered here and there.

set. The ceiling cannot be seen from the stage, given that it is 40 m above it and hidden by the grid, on which the fly pulleys are mounted.

Beneath the stage, and extending behind it, there are five empty, open spaces, of approximately the same size as the stage. The floor of each of these spaces is a mobile platform that can rise and shift individually and, in each one of these five spaces, a complete set can be built[8] and later brought up to the stage to be finished off in detail. The time required to change sets is, as may be imagined, studied down to the smallest detail. The Operations Director told us, 'In a set change, using all possible resources available, we managed to reduce the time from 1 hour 11 minutes to 31 minutes.'

Of course, not all the machinery necessary for this can be managed manually and the entire theatre is connected via fibre optic cables, linking a series of computerised control centres to the various elements, allowing the operators to control everything remotely. Lighting or extinguishing a spot is a simple matter of pushing the right button in the control centre. A more complicated operation, like a lighting transition, requires a program that controls the various elements.

Above the stage are various catwalks at different levels, and these allow operators to move about to any position without being seen and without intruding on the performance. In our first visit to the Teatro Real, we chatted with a Stage Manager, who proudly showed us his hi-tech control post. It looked to us like an air traffic controller's post. 'We call it the Pope mobile', he said, 'because it's a carriage which, with all the computers and me inside, moves on wheels across the whole level, allowing it to be placed in the best position at any moment during the performance.' While he was telling us this, the Head Stage Manager, the most senior member of the technical management, who was also accompanying us, looked on proudly with a very satisfied expression.

Complementing the set installations are a series of enclosures that are used in the performances or the rehearsals. These are the set rehearsal areas, which duplicate the characteristics of the stage floor and, thus, allow 'laboratory' studies of everything that will later take place on the real stage.

Everybody in the theatre is very young; the average age must be about 35, with a very small number of people above that age.

At a more operational level, the Teatro Real has workshop departments for Props, Hair and Costume which are used to create and maintain the required elements for each production.

The Props department, staffed by four young artisans, makes all the furniture and moveable objects required for a performance. They make all manner of things, from mediaeval armour made of injected plastic that

---

[8] For example, in the production of *Tosca* during the 2003–2004 season, the three sets (the church of Sant' Andrea de la Valle, the Farnese palace, and the Castle of Sant' Angelo) were prepared simultaneously: one on stage and two in the areas beneath. These latter two were then ready to be raised to the stage at the appropriate moment.

looks remarkably like steel to dozens of Egyptian lances. When we visited the workshop for the first time, they were just finishing some mannequins that represented the jail inmates of the last act of *Tosca*.[9] Each figure was made from an industrial mannequin or shop dummy, dressed in rags and arranged in humble poses. There was also a cardboard characters being spray-painted by the artisan who had created it. Another was sculpting a metre-high crucifix, from expanded polyurethane, which he would later finish and decorate by hand with extreme precision. The Operations Director told us, 'Care in the details is fundamental. We prefer to make a crucifix rather than borrow one from a museum – less responsibility, and an opportunity for the craftspeople to express themselves.'

The made-to-measure wigs for the singers are made in the Hair department, with its staff of about ten people. The Teatro Real maintains a database of all the anatomical details of the possible participants in a given work, and this responsibility lies with the Head of Production. The wigs are made from natural hair, not with synthetic fibres. 'It's more expensive, but it looks authentic, and the people can tell', Daniel told us.

Last minute changes to the costumes are done in the Costume department. In general, the creation of the costumes from the designer's sketches is subcontracted and made from high quality material such as velvets, satins, and the like. They are also made to last, which is essential if the production is sold to another theatre. About 15 people work in the Costume department, including the sub-department of washing and ironing which cleans and prepares all the necessary costumes for the chorus and the soloists before every performance.

The Teatro Real doesn't have a set department, nor does it store the sets anywhere on-site. Previous productions' sets are stored in containers, in an owned warehouse in Siete Iglesias, a small town on the outskirts of Madrid.

Operations

A performance is a project that must be managed with incredible precision, and with a very high level of synchronisation between the various necessary activities. Everything, from moving the set to changes and transitions, is carefully rehearsed and planned, with the timing measured in tenths of a second.[10]

---

[9] Another of Giacomo Puccini's top works. This one is about revolutionaries, a singer who is quite a character, a painter who is her lover (and a bit bland) and Baron Scarpia, governor of Rome and a very powerful, but repulsive, man. As Tosca says, after having stabbed and killed him, 'È avanti a lui tremava tutta Roma!' – 'Before him all of Rome trembled!'

[10] The reader might like to think for a moment about the effect of a delay, of even one second, in moving the follow spot on the soloist about to sing her great aria, with the

In fact, the Teatro Real is conceptually a project company. At any given moment, there are a certain number of projects under way, each in a different phase of its life-cycle. Nevertheless, two essential peculiarities differentiate the theatre from other companies of this type:

1. The projects terminate at a predetermined time, without possibilities of delays or advances. On a stipulated day and hour, the curtain is going to rise, whatever condition things are in. There are simply no excuses. In an expensive production and in a theatre of the first order, nobody can fail, otherwise the reputation of the theatre, cast and crew will suffer from the disaster.[11]
2. As we've already noted, when planning the season, the Teatro Real elects those projects it's going to pursue, as a function of both the artistic message that it wants to convey and the budget available.

Designing a production

In brief, the process of a production, from its conception until it reaches the theatre, is as follows:

1. *Take the artistic decisions.* These are taken, usually three years in advance, by the Artistic Director in accordance with the board of the Teatro Real.
2. *Prepare the budget.* This is done by the Budget department, collaborating with the Head of Production, one year in advance.
3. *Present sketches and mock-ups by the Set Director.* In phase 1, the Set Director was given the task of creating the production and, now, he must present the budget to the Teatro Real.
4. *Discuss feasibility and analyse value/cost of the set.* This is done by the Operations Director, the Set Director and the theatrical designer. Between them, they will reach a consensus in line with the budget.
5. *Prepare the tender for contracting the sets.* This is done by the Operations Director and must be in line with the basic contracting laws of the state.
6. *Award the contract.* This must be done for set construction.
7. *Construct the sets.* In the subcontractor's workshop, they will build and partially mount the sets. The mounting progresses until it is seen, beyond doubt, that there are no problems in finishing the job.

---

rest of the stage in darkness. In fact, it is said that, in the New York Met, a lighting crew member deliberately did something very like that to a very conceited *prima donna* who had treated him particularly badly in the rehearsals.

[11] This even extends to the singers. Many performances have been deemed 'failures' because of the classical 'false note' caused by the voice breaking on a high note, when the rest of the performance might have gone perfectly.

8. *Design and contract the costuming.* Some 20–25 days before the opening, the costumes are created for the chorus and, at the end of the process, when the soloists have arrived in Madrid, their costumes will be finalised.

9. *Hairdressing.* All the wigs are made and maintained by the Teatro Real's own Hair department.

10. *Design and organise the props.* All the objects and furniture necessary for the production are bought, assembled or modified by the Props department.

The cost of a production

In a new production, the set construction represents a major part of the total design cost. In a recent production of *Macbeth*,[12] the set budget was some €240,000. Even though the initial estimate by the Stage Director was substantially higher than that amount, the Operations Director managed to reduce the cost through various cost and value analyses.

The costumes can also be a significant cost. For an opera such as *Tosca*, around 250 costumes were made. With the average cost of a costume being e around €1,500, the total cost can easily amount to about €375,000.

The props, all the items additional to the set, vary greatly in cost from production to production. To use *Tosca* example again, the production called for reproductions of works of arts, including Michelangelo's *Pietà* in fibre glass (costing some €30,000) and a version of his *Last Judgement* (from the Sistine Chapel) in almost full size.

The singers' professional fees are the largest of the variable expenses in any production. The Teatro Real long ago introduced the idea of capping the maximum fees for any singer. This currently stands at €18,000 per performance, although only a few top singers in the opera world can command that sort of fee. The rest of the singers must be contracted at a lower fee, with each person covering his/her own costs of travel and lodging. Higher professional fees can be found at other theatres but, with their lower prestige, they have much less appeal for the professional singers.

With these cost schemes, then, the variable costs depend hugely upon the type of opera. A simple opera, such as *Tosca*, with essentially only three protagonists, is far cheaper than, for example, *Don Carlo*, in which there are

---

[12] By Giuseppe Verdi, it is one of the lesser-known, but still very interesting, works. Based on the play by William Shakespeare, it tells the story of Macbeth, the Scottish noble who, after killing the king, ascends to the throne, only to be haunted by regret, remorse, and a ghost or two. Some witches (as we said before, opera is full of such 'normal' characters) predict that 'nobody born of woman shall harm [Macbeth]'. Finally, he's struck down and slain by Macduff who, in a well-known twist of pedantry, was taken, by caesarean section, from the womb of his dead mother.

seven protagonists. Similarly, a performance of the dual *Pagliacci-Cavalleria Rusticana*[13] is hugely expensive because two top tenors are needed, one for each opera, and each charges the complete fee, regardless of the length of the work. All of these fees are fixed at the time of deciding the productions for each season.

The rest of the company, excluding the orchestra, chorus and ballet, costs relatively little – for example, an extra can expect somewhere around €180 per performance (including rehearsals).

Setting up

Once the sets are complete, the Teatro Real organises their collection and transport to the theatre. Typically, this involves a fleet of 13 or 14 lorries bringing their bulky cargo to the centre of Madrid, much to the joy of the other road users in this already-jammed city. Most of the lorries unload their cargo in the areas annexed to the theatre, but some reach as far as the actual stage.

Once the lorries have arrived with the sets, work begins on setting them up, a process that will culminate in the public performance. At this time, and during the process of mounting the sets, two additional parallel processes also commence which will finally converge into one: the staging and musical processes. The first consists of preparing for all the stage movement during a performance, and the second in developing the form which the supporting music is going to take. All of this is done through rehearsals. In fact, to begin these rehearsals, it is not strictly necessary to have the presence of the sets.

---

[13] Two short operas that are usually performed together, because they are both similar and in the 'veristic' or 'verismo' style. The first, *Pagliacci* (Clowns) was written by Ruggero Leoncavallo (1857–1919). It is about the eternal drama of the Commedia dell' Arte. The clown continues to laugh while the tears of pain flow because his wife, Nedda, playing Colombina, is cheating on him with Silvio, a villager. At the end, the clown stabs his wife, presumably to cheer himself up.

The second opera, *Cavalleria Rusticana*, is by Pietro Mascagni (1863–1945). It's a Sicilian drama of, you guessed it, honour and passion. A youth, Turiddu, is in love with Lola, a married woman of the village. Not sufficiently plot-laden already, we then also have to deal with Santuzza who, in her turn, is in love with Turiddu. The drama reaches its climax when Lola's husband has a few words with the lad, which results in him being sliced up with a few knife strokes. Needless to say, Turiddu dies.

Both authors are today known almost exclusively for these two short operas, which are excellent examples of 'verismo'. It is very rare to find anyone who can name another opera by either of the two. Curiously, Leoncavallo wrote a Bohème that nobody remembers. Somewhat better known are the works of Mascagni, although only experts are likely to be able to name more than one.

There are two types of rehearsals – stage rehearsals and musical rehearsals:

1. *Stage rehearsals*: Before casting for the show, the senior Stage Manager and his team meet periodically with the Stage Director. From the preliminary production data they will continue adjusting, in the rehearsal room 'laboratories', the stage movements of the production. All the necessary activities are designed and documented carefully, minutely and precisely detailing the exact moment in which the different events must take place. Each event, which in the internal jargon is called a *top*, is assigned a number which identifies it from that moment forwards.[14] The process of tops will continue to be refined throughout the rehearsals, until it is time for the actors to arrive. Before the first actor's rehearsal, all the tops are precisely sequenced and each one is associated with a precise moment in the production, which is noted in the score.
2. *Musical rehearsals*: These run simultaneously with the stage rehearsals, with the music is being continually adjusted, working intensively with the Musical Director. The rehearsals begin with the orchestra, but without singers, who only appear in the production about one month before the first night, and generally will remain performing there for about a month. Once the singers arrive, they begin to work accompanied only by a piano. Finally everything is put together with the participation of everybody involved.

The general rehearsals are performances of the complete opera, including with an audience. The singers generally sing their entire work, but occasionally omit the most difficult bits. The audience is made up of employees, collaborators and other people related with the theatre, who are under strict instructions not to get involved, in any way, whether positive or negative, during the rehearsals.

The first performance generally takes place once the general rehearsals are over, and after two days of rest.

In a performance, it is the Stage Manager's role to sequence the action. Sitting at his table and armed with TV monitors that show everything that's happening on stage and in the surrounding areas, he follows the score that was previously annotated with the tops, and thus is able to alert the various operators several seconds before something that they are in charge of needs to happen. He usually does this by using the phrase 'top XXX ready in YY seconds'. When the critical moment arrives, he gives the order to action by using the monosyllable 'tops!' Absolutely nothing is left to chance. Everything goes through an internal wireless system, which makes sure all

---

[14] Some examples of tops include a character's entrance onto the stage, bringing down a light, or moving a piece of the set.

the orders of the operations personnel are sent and received, while everybody works in perfect silence.

The result is that the rhythm and sequence of actions comes from the direction of the orchestra, and it is they who marked the basic time of the event. As the music unfolds, the events on stage and off are triggered in a co-ordinated manner, and this gives rise to the performance itself. Curiously, the annotated score does not form part of the production when sold, meaning that every theatre must realise its own sequence. The reason would appear to be that the method of generating the sequence of events depends heavily on the technology present in each theatre.

Production leadership

In an operation like Teatro Real, it is necessary to work with people who have egos of magnitudes bigger than normal. Singers, conductors, designers, painters and everyone else are characterised by an infinite variety of obsessions and peculiarities. The late Luciano Pavarotti used to demand a suite in a five-star hotel with his own private kitchen installed, since he liked to prepare his own plate of spaghetti every night. Of course, the necessary ingredients had to have already been bought and placed in the kitchen. Similarly, in his dressing-room there must be two apples, two pears, a banana, hot and cold tea, and these must be constantly replenished as necessary.

All of this generates a constant stream of incidents and events that need to be dealt with, and that interrupt the normal flow of operations. To minimise the effects of these on the production process, and to minimise the possibility of unforeseen problems, the theatre has an operational post whose job it is to deal with all these incidents. This is the Head of Production.

Reporting directly to the Artistic Director (in practice so does the whole world) the Head of Production prepares all budgets, supplies the extras, prepares and signs the contracts with all participants, sources all additional material, attends to all the personal and artistic problems, and co-ordinates the use of all equipment and installations.

The greatest skill of the Head of Production is problem-solving. Typically it is the singers who are the major source of these problems. Even though there are relatively few *prima donna* complexes, the profession is still replete with some people who are quite odd and sometimes insecure about their voice and their readiness.

For example, the singer in the lead role of *Manon*,[15] decided that the range of one of her *gavottes* was too high for the condition of her voice, and asked

---

[15] Jules Massenet (1842–912) is the author. A French opera, and thus of a markedly different style from Italian opera; much more refined and sensual. Manon is a young girl of 16 who, en route to Paris to join a convent, decides to forget about the convent and go off with the knight Des Grieux, who convinces her they'll have much more

for it be brought down a semitone. This required the transposing[16] of all the orchestral parts and the supply of completely new scores.

Another example is that of *Osud*,[17] an opera sung in Czech. The text of the chorus is also (obviously) in that language so, given that the chorus didn't know any Czech, they had to find a translator to transcribe the text using Spanish phonetics, which allowed the singers to approximately pronounce the words, even though they didn't know what it meant.

The Head of Production has four assistants, three of them in charge of individual productions, and the other providing general support.

His job requires very clear separation of what can and cannot be organised and programmed. To clarify this, the Operations Director prepares a work programme, but he maintains in spreadsheets available to the whole company, in which is listed all the activities of all the areas of the theatre, and their place in time. Included there is the transport of the sets, complete with the exact time and date of its rival, and a rehearsal plan, with the movement of all the people involved.

This entire framework needs to be specified in great detail for the staging of a show. How this is done is the object of detailed analysis contained in the following chapters.

---

fun together. They live together for a while, but she remained tempted by the attractions of the licentious life and become an illustrious entertainer, leaving the poor Des Grieux as the one who now takes holy orders. He's getting ready for this, delivering a sermon at the church of Saint Sulpice in Paris, when Manon appears in his plans get messed up. The two dedicate themselves to the life of gambling, but they get caught cheating and are detained. Manon is sent to Louisiana, like all the loose women that they seemed to have so many of in France, but she dies on the way in the arms (of course!) of Des Grieux. The opera has a soprano aria in the form of a *gavotte* which is the one referred to in the text.

[16] To transpose, in music, is to shift the entire piece up or down on the musical scale.

[17] Osud is a very little-known opera by Leŏs Janácek. Is it is a rather experimental opera in which the composer puts to the test some of his theories about music being associated to language. The girl in the piece is married to one man but in love with another. They meet in a spa and decide to live together. But they commit the error of taking her mother with them, which finally provokes a conflict resulting in the death of the mother and daughter. Years later, the protagonist is recalling this episode in his life, and collapses when he sees a vision of his old love in a storm.

Part I
Efficiency

The next six chapters will try to explain the way of achieving Efficiency in Operations, which is the first concept of the Golden Triad.

The first step, indispensable for meeting targets that we have set ourselves, is to clarify the company's mission. We are not proposing a strategic exercise here, but rather the contrary. Our objective is to make things clear, to make the mission operational and to avoid the pompous statements that work just as well for a garage as for a hospital. We also want to prioritise the elements of the mission, obtaining what we call the 'Promise' of the company. The Promise of a company is that which we try to ensure is going to happen when the client enters into contact with our Operations to obtain the service they desire.

To make this clearer, we talk to the General Manager of the Teatro Real, Miguel Muñiz, who decides the strategy and the priorities for the future of the institution he directs. Finally, we briefly state the principles necessary for you to be able to undertake an exercise to formulate the Promise of your company.

Part 1
Efficiency

III
The Mission of the Teatro Real

In this chapter, we give a summary of an interview with the General Manager of the Teatro Real, Miguel Muñiz, appointed in November 2004. This summary will help us with the first stage in the analysis of Efficiency, namely the clarification of the 'Mission' or the company's 'Promise'. The Promise is the realisation of the Mission, and must be used to prioritise those critical elements that guide the development of Operations.

What is the strategy that you wish to follow in the Teatro Real?

MM: When they made me the General Manager, I found myself in a very young theatre, only seven years into its 'current' history, and in a cultural project of extraordinary dimensions and complexity. At that time, they had achieved an image of being elitist, expensive and, worst of all, inaccessible.

Our primary objective, therefore, was to do away with that image and to get to the point where the opera was open to the whole of society. To make this happen, which sounded to many like little more than a pipe-dream, one could choose between various basic models of operatic theatre. One was the model that they use in Germany, which consists of programming 30 or 40 operas which get repeated over a long period of time, with very easy access for the public. In this case, the efforts are more directed towards facilitating this accessibility than the quality of the artistic proposition.

The second model consists of far fewer operas – between 8 and 10 per season. Each one of these needs a month of rehearsals and tends to have a very complex stage design which seriously complicates any attempts to alternate with another show. In this model, the efforts are clearly directed more towards the quality.

Our wish is to opt for the type of theatre that maintains the level of quality that we currently offer, but at the same time to advance towards becoming open and accessible to the widest cross-section of society. To achieve this, I would like to manage 12 headline productions every season, and break the barrier of 100 shows in a year. Our strategy, then, is fundamentally based on striving to achieve this goal: significantly increasing (although within reason) the number of shows and operas. Thus, as well as maintaining an optimal quota of season tickets, we will also considerably increase the non-member offerings.

We want to make quality opera, but opera that is also directed to the public. We want to make it form part of our national heritage, like the Prado Museum, or Don Quixote. To achieve this, it's essential that the public consider it to be something 'close' and within reach.

Another objective that we've identified is to convey what an opera theatre really is, to make it understandable and to show what it's like to actually work in such a place. There is a general impression, to an extent understandable, that an opera theatre is simply a place where the public can go to watch a show; but behind the curtain there exists another universe! The Teatro Real has about 300 people doing a wide variety of jobs, as well as more than 100 professionals who make up the orchestra and more than 60 in the chorus. In this extensive and varied group, one inevitably finds two things co-habiting: the discipline of a normal company coupled with the special buzz of delivering a show. Each opera requires, in addition, the incorporation of new and cosmopolitan extras, dancers and singers, and this represents an enormous physical and cultural mobility.

What is the role of the General Manager of the Teatro Real?

MM: In an opera theatre, the General Manager is the person ultimately responsible for everybody but at the same time, paradoxically, he has power over nothing. He can only say 'this is the project, do you all agree?' and, if his Artistic and Musical Directors do, then it will happen. The freedom that they have to work in is total. So that this works with the necessary harmony, I absolutely cannot stick my nose into their work.

The General Manager is the person who sketches out the big picture. It is he who says, to offer an example, the number of performances that he believes should be reached in a season, and the various channels in which the theatre should be selling tickets for them; if these criteria are met, then the artistic form those performances will take is the responsibility of the other guys. Well, having said that, once we've sketched out each of the aspects that come together to make up the season, there has to be a consensus among the whole team. A lack of agreement is the primary source of conflict, and very common in opera theatres throughout the world.

As General Manager, I dedicate a lot of time to following every detail of the events we put on. From the seat or up on stage, I actively help out in the majority of them. From there, behind the scenes, is where you'll see the incredible level of professionalism, and the intense concentration that the technical guys achieve in the course of their work. Everything is measured; in barely 40 seconds they can manage changes of extreme complexity without rushing or making a fuss. You see occasions that remind you of Formula 1 wheel changes. Everything in this behind-the-scenes world is the theatre; as much as everything that goes on in the visible part of the stage.

Content

Are you going to change the content?

MM: We want to fill the theatre with not only opera, but also with other types of artistic and cultural events. In fact, the productions for young people and children are awakening an enormous interest.

On the other hand, we will always have to programme a 'super-production' to satisfy the public's taste and keep the theatre people happy. Our intention is not to put on any *'prêt a porter'* or 'off-the-shelf' works, which is the typical practice in Germany, where the same productions are done year after year in the same way. To put on a repeat performance is much simpler because all the rough edges have already been smoothed, and much less time is needed to get everything ready. By contrast, if you put on an opera that, for example, the orchestra has never played before, the director will need twice the number of rehearsals.

Nevertheless, when we're programming shows we always have to keep in mind the physical limitations we'll run up against. We could do with some smaller rooms, and the main theatre has a very small capacity. At the Paris Opera House, for example, they have 2,700 seats; that's about a thousand more than we do, which makes Paris a much more profitable venue. In addition, with the Teatro Real being built in the form of a horseshoe – the traditional Italian floor plan – the visibility from about 500 of the 1,700 seats is not so good.

The stalls area is very small; much smaller than the Liceo in Barcelona, and this is even further reduced if the production demands it. If the orchestration needs the participation of an increased number of maestros in the orchestra pit – something which is the order of the day in operas of the twentieth and twenty-first centuries, even in some from the nineteenth – then we have no choice but to remove some rows of seats. The special characteristics of some of the staging can also oblige the Operations Director to take some space away from the seating; for all of these eventualities we have to look at a number of suggestions and possibilities, perhaps by making the productions slightly simpler, but, and this is key, never allowing that to adversely affect the quality.

Customers

Who are the customers?

MM: Our customer, first and foremost, is the season ticket holder. With the season ticket, we can propose and develop a cultural programme, which gives us much more freedom to programme operas of different eras and styles. With this system, the customer buys the ticket for the whole season, and this guarantees that they get the best seats. This also allows us to programme in operas from the twenty-first century, with their bold stage designs. Sometimes you can opt for a modernisation strategy that on occasion might raise objections, but that still helps to create a culture and a viewing habit in the ticket holder.

Then there are the shows not included in the season ticket, and these are very different because the audience control what we put on. If you offer an opera by Janácek,[1] it's possible that you'll fill only half of the theatre, but, by contrast, if you programme *La Boheme*, there's no doubt that you'll fill the house. We have to work on finding more of these 'non-season ticket' productions. To achieve this, I'd prioritise these sorts of openings. We also want to reintroduce special tickets within the reach of the fans, like the 'twentieth century ticket', which included three operas.

We're also going after the university students, by offering them cheaper prices, and creating special youth tickets, which would include last-minute tickets. With these sorts of tickets (which are those left over unsold, or returned by the season ticket holders) young members of the audience (up to 26 years old) can benefit from discounts as high as 90 per cent off the usual ticket price. With this initiative, we've already attracted more than 1,000 young people, many of whom got seats in the best areas of the theatre.

We've also just put together the Opera XXI association, which unites the opera theatres, festivals and seasons, and features members such as the Liceo of Barcelona, the Maestranza of Seville, Campoamor in Oviedo, as well as us and 25 other members. The idea is to promote opera, by giving it its full weight as a genre; a genre which, according to data provided by the SGAE (the Spanish Society of Authors, Composers and Publishers), had a total paying audience of around a million people.

People say that the Teatro Real is a closed and exclusive place, that it's impossible to get tickets. There might be some truth in that, but that's not

---

[1] Leŏs Janácek (Hukvaldy, Morovia, 1854–1928), the most important of the Czech composers. He was a tonal composer, inspired in large part by the Czech folk styles and the structure of the language. His best-known operas include *Jenufa* and *The House of the Dead*, the latter based on a novel by Dostoyevsky.

the whole story. For *La Traviata*[2] or *Don Carlo*,[3] we programme between 10 or 12 performances. Our auditorium, as I said, has 1,700 seats. Therefore, an average of 17,000 people attends a single opera. There is no other cultural show seen by such a large number of people. It must also be remembered that by the end of a season more than 100,000 people will have visited the Teatro Real.

The price of tickets is, to be honest, expensive, and that's why we have to constantly look for ways to offer them at special cut-prices. The idea is to popularise, in the best sense of the word. It's obvious that this type of culture will never be truly mainstream, but we're trying to take this minority, the minority that is interested in opera and gain cultural 'nourishment' from it, and make it every day a larger one.

---

[2] *La Traviata* is to Verdi what *La Bohème* is to Puccini. One of the best-known and beautiful of Verdi's operas, it is based on *La Dame aux camellias* by Alexandre Dumas (fils). And, of course, the protagonist, Violetta Valery, is a woman of easy virtue who abandons her 'pleasures' for the love of Alfredo. The father of Alfredo, a mischievous man and lifelong right-winger, convinces her to leave his son to avoid damaging the reputation of the family. Alfredo, who is his father's son and a bit spineless, having offended Violetta, leaves her in the hands of her various lovers. When he finally decides he loves her (and the father decides that she might be ok after all), they rush off after her... only to find her breathing her last. It's one of the most representative operas, perhaps exceeded only by *La Bohème* and *Rigoletto*, the latter also by Verdi. It was, curiously, a notorious failure on its opening. For the first time on stage people appeared dressed in normal clothes, rather than as mediaeval knights, minstrels or troubadours. And, moreover, the protagonist was a loose woman!

[3] *Don Carlo*, by Giuseppe Verdi, takes place in the court of the Spanish King Felipe II. It tells the story (apocryphal) of his son Carlos, and is based on the tragedy by Schiller. Carlos is in love with his step-mother, Isabel de Valois. At the same time, he hatches a plot with the Flemish against his father. Carlos considers that Felipe is obsessed with religion and a visionary. After many incidents, Carlos is jailed, and his best friend and fellow conspirator, Posa, is killed. There are at least three versions of the same work. One of them, in French, premiered in Paris, another had its debut in Italian at La Scala, and yet a third at Módena. It would appear that Verdi was unsatisfied with all three, even though the third seems to be the most representative. Don Carlo contains one of the most impressive scenes in the whole of opera: the infamous scene for bass 'Ella giammai m'amò...' ('She never loved me...') in which Felipe II describes his relationship with his wife and his vigils in El Escorial, alone and unable to get to sleep because of his immense power.

IV
The Mission's Concepts

First of all, we'd like to highlight something that Miguel Muñiz said in the previous chapter; something that has a bearing on a recurrent theme of this book: 'He [the General Manager] can only say "this is the project, do you all agree?"'. These words confirm our ideas about how to manage brain force. Of course, in the theatre the talent has to be 'managed' according to very different standards and norms than those of a traditional company: Muñiz cannot *order* people in the Teatro Real. How can he give orders to people like Jesús López Cobos, someone whose musical talent is universally recognised? Or Antonio Moral, the Artistic Director, who Muñiz appointed precisely because he is a leading authority in opera? It would not only be absurd, it would also be destructive. You do not, Muñiz tells us, *order* people of talent. You give them objectives, and then you leave them free to achieve them.

Once Muñiz had confirmed our position in this matter, we could get on with the details of the subject that concerns us. In what follows, we will try to demonstrate how to achieve clarity and operational realisation of the *Promise* of a company. Using the conversation we had with the General Manager as a starting point, we will revise the concepts most relevant to our theme.

The need to pin down the Promise of a company, and put it into practice

When the General Manager said that he wanted to open up the theatre to society, or popularise opera, that message was at an intellectual level, still barely operational. It tells us where he wants to go, but it doesn't establish *milestones for the journey*, so that the Operations can achieve the desired result. It's something similar to when a company says it wants to be environmentally conscious, or exercise corporate social responsibility. It's all very commendable, but it's not very operational.

> **Is your company's mission specifically defined and prioritised?**

To provide clarity of objectives from the strategy is one of the critical functions of senior management. Companies must be very specific about their strategy, to be able to prioritise the problems, identifying those most critical for the fulfilment of their *Promise*.

When Muñiz says 'we have to constantly look for ways to offer [the tickets] at special cut-prices' we can begin to understand his wishes at an operational level. But it is still not sufficient to apply action criteria to Operations. We need to go deeper. Miguel Muñiz says that he doesn't want to follow the German model of *prêt a porter*, but that he does want to increase the number of operas. Now is when he begins to send a *clear message*, and this becomes a *specific objective*. He wants 12 operas representing 200 performances. In addition, he specifies that among those there should only be some 'super-productions', that please and 'exercise' the theatre. But the rest can be more normal ones, or equally co-productions or bought productions. With all this, he has clearly defined the portfolio of products that he needs to manage.

> **Don't try to increase efficiency without having first prioritised your mission.**

Beginning an efficiency exercise without having scrupulously defined the *Promise* can lead to contradictions. Do we need to use wigs made from natural hair? Not really? Ok then, we'll use synthetic fibre, because it's cheaper. But Muñiz has not said that the *cost* is the priority, he has only said that he wants 200 shows within the current annual budget. Thus, the important thing is not the fixed costs; it is the variable costs that are crucial – the costs that depend directly on the number of shows. As a consequence, Operations must pay particular attention to this type of cost, without worrying too much about trying to reduce the fixed costs per production. And if, by trying to reduce costs by using synthetic wigs, the quality of service – which Muñiz has said must be of the highest level – will suffer (just think of the gossip in other theatres... 'Ooh, the Teatro Real uses synthetic wigs; they really make your head itch!'), Operations would be sacrificing a key point of the Promise, quality, in the interests of cost, which has not been deemed a priority.

In many companies, the typical *example* of this (false) *dilemma* occurs in the Purchasing department, and can be summed up as false economy. How many times has the obsession to save a few pennies later cost a lot more money, perhaps due to loss of quality, delivery delays or the loss of productivity? Countless times, surely! And the blame, if it belongs to anyone, is not with the Purchasing department, it is with the General Manager, who didn't know how to properly specify the priorities and have not made the Purchasing department aware of the consequences of, say, a delivery delay.

Our message is simple. Hold a meeting with your management team and try to establish the precise perception, reflected in operational criteria, of each person with respect to the service they provide. For this, use some method of scoring and evaluating, and see what you find out. We know many high-level directors who are emphatic that their team knows perfectly well the priorities of the Promise of the company. And we always challenge them to prove it empirically. The result is almost always the same. There is never more than the barest concordance; each member of the team has his or her own view of the common objective, and the vision of the management team and the boss rarely coincide. Does this ever happen to you?

So, use whatever form you wish, but send clear messages to the whole organisation. You must convey, with clarity, exactly what you expect, and make sure that everyone clearly understands what the final result should be. Everyone should be playing from the same score.[1] Break down your mission into specific criteria and prioritise them so that the whole organisation can focus on the results.

In the next section, we propose a simple *method* to define your company's Promise. It's a proposal, nothing more. If you have another method, then great! The method is, after all, irrelevant. What is crucial is sending a clear message. How you do it is not so important, but (as a certain sportswear company put it so well) just do it!

A method of evaluating your company's Promise

We present five *criteria categories* that must be considered to specify, and make operational, the Promise of a company. Each category represents a *dimension* of service, and can be further broken down into different constituent *attributes* of that dimension. Well, that sentence is one you can try repeating to your friends! Don't worry; we'll see how it works in practice… which is much simpler than we suspect we've made it sound.

The five dimensions are as follows:

Cost containing all the criteria related to the efficient use of resources in order to provide a service. A typical criterion of this dimension is net margin. In the Teatro Real, the difference between income from ticket sales and the direct cost of a function is a more specific criterion, and a variety of net margin. They say that the most important thing is to not exceed budget, because there simply isn't any more money. This is surely a universal message, not only in public institutions but also in the majority of multinationals.[2] You have your budget; don't' exceed it. And don't come in

---

[1] An appropriate analogy, don't you think? Opera, score… We do our best.

[2] Quite often, intelligent and wise directors accuse public companies, like the Teatro Real, of throwing other people's money around. But in the majority of large companies, it's the same, sometimes almost worse, because it's often hidden behind the disguise of efficiency. In companies, they often throw the shareholders' money

under budget, many people would add, because if you do then the budget for the following year will be cut by 20 per cent.

Time is made up of all the criteria that include magnitudes of time; for example, response time or delivery time. In the Teatro Real, the delivery time is explicitly set by Muñiz – he says that the theatre should put on 200 shows per year. That means to prepare each show takes 365/200 = 1.8 days per show. And we already know, from Chapter II, most of this process is sequential. There is not much parallelism. And, if they have to do ten productions per year, then the *cycle time*, the time between particular scenes in two successive performances, is 36 days. Consequently, if we need more time we have to have two or more productions in the pipeline simultaneously, this gives 72 or 108 days to prepare a production. And this means we need two or more production teams. With all this analysis, Operations already knows a lot more about what we need to fulfil the Promise.

Amplitude are the criteria related to the variety of serviced provided by the company to its clients. In the Teatro Real, Muñiz says that he essentially wants operas, children's opera and other events. This last concept is of course a little too undefined, and probably should be made clearer by enumerating these 'other' services. Perhaps they're concerts, or operas in concert version, or singing master-classes or even gala balls for introducing Madrid's affluent debutantes into society (as they do in the Vienna Opera). With this additional specification, Operations can have the necessary data to design flexibility.

Innovation. This includes all the criteria related with the capacity for introducing changes that enhance your service. Muñiz partially explains this criterion. He tells us that he wants to bring in at least one 'super production' per year, and that he wants to continue introducing works from the twenty-first century and increasingly bold sets and stage designs.

Consistency. This considers the spread of the diverse service components. Muñiz doesn't really pin this dimension down, perhaps because he takes as read the need to continue providing the same service level as now: an excellent level of service, with no failures.

Each company must begin the exercise of translating their Promise into criteria for each dimension, criteria adapted for each company's particular reality. Once the translation is done, it's useful to think, in numerical terms, the importance or weighting of each dimension. One simple way of doing this is to allocate a total number, 100 for example, between the five

---

around. Meeting budgets tends to be a common objective, even though this is often inefficient and gives a distorted view of things. To understand what we mean, the reader needs to only think of the 'cushion method' that is almost always used when preparing a budget – think of the number, and then add 10 per cent in the full expectation that the budget will be reduced by 10 per cent anyway.

dimensions. The score of each dimension will indicate the priority that senior management assigns to it. We didn't perform this exercise with the General Manager of the Teatro Real, but we can speculate a possible weighting array of (5, 15, 20, 25 and 35). These priorities would indicate very clearly that, for the fulfilment of the Teatro Real's mission, the dimension *Consistency*, with no failures, is much more important than possible reductions in cost. And indeed, the Teatro Real does not try to compete on cost, trying to offer services at a lower price, but rather it competes on quality, offering an extraordinary service at an increased price.

Designing service

From the point of view of the customer, and in much of academic literature on services,[3] four of the five previous dimensions tend to be included in one single concept: the 'Value' of service. These are the dimensions of time, amplitude, innovation and consistency. This simplification is interesting because with two dimensions it's possible to analyse the balance, or trade-offs, more simply than with the full set of five. It's not necessary to assign weightings, because having two dimensions makes it easy to perform a straight comparison, even in graphic form. Of course, the resulting description is less complete and therefore less powerful.

Value and cost of service allow us to synthesize the result of a service operation. With the help of a cause-and-effect model, it's easy to manage this pairing to achieve an appropriate *balance*. Each pair of values for these two dimensions determines a separate service operation. Of two companies that provide the same service, that which has lower costs will be the *competitive* one and, clearly, the other will not. For the Teatro Real we could specify this idea with the instruction: 'with the budget I give you (cost), get the best customer satisfaction (value)'. Although, to go further than that, we'll eventually have to break down that value into its components.

> **Designing services: stick everything in, take stuff out later!**

Above all, this methodological principle is an important idea in the design of services. In industry it is less-widely used and, generally, the value-cost pairing is substituted by a single principle, the principle of Parsimony: use the *fewest elements possible* to achieve the desired *function*.

Why is there this difference between industry and service? Some think that the value of a product is more difficult to define than that of a service, because the proximity to the client, to the service, is much lesser. What is the value of a rifle? Or a hammer? And, without doubt, there has long existed

---

[3] Heskett, J.L., Sasser, W.E. and Hart, C.W., *Service Breakthroughs. Changing the Rules.* Free Press: New York, 1990.

in industry a school of specialists in Value Analysis, specialised in trying to increase the value of a product without increasing its cost.

Our opinion is that, in the background, there are underlying reasons of knowledge. In industry they work much more with structured knowledge; knowledge than can be managed in a logical form. If I manufacture a screw with a 10 mm section, it will take 1,000 kg, according to the resistance tables of steel. Full stop. Design is through engineering; practical science. In any case, structured knowledge allows us to more easily analyse the final effect of a product's components.

We believe that the situation in services is different. What would be the difference between the replica of Michelangelo's *Pietà*, used in *Tosca*, being 2 or 5 m high? Who knows! The proof of the service pudding really is in the eating. This is why, when designing services, it's always prudent to follow a strategy of elimination. First we (mentally) add everything, and then we take bits away. The fundamental idea here is that it is far worse to leave something out than to add it in unnecessarily, even if this means dealing with the added complexity or cost of additional variables. As we don't really know what the key service components are going to be, we stick them all in and later we can take them out (again, mentally!)

Flexibility and cost

Another pairing that can complement the five basic dimensions is that of *flexibility* versus *cost*. Flexibility and cost have always been thought of as two opposing concepts. If you're flexible, you're expensive; if you're rigid, you're cheap. And this still appears to be the thinking in the world of theatre. The reality is that every day these concepts are becoming less opposing and even becoming closer, even a necessity. In today's world, if you're expensive and someone else discovers a way to be as flexible as you but cheaper, then you are done for. You'll end up with no clients. This is why flexible companies must force themselves to be *potentially* cheap. By potentially, we don't want to say that you necessarily have low prices, but rather that you must have the *potential* to lower them if necessary. Nevertheless, you should never ever actually lower your prices. Prices have to increase always – lowering them, competing on price, is *destructive*.

What theatre still hasn't discovered is that which is most relevant when organising: Operations – it's the way that every company, every theatre, competes. You can compete on price, being the cheapest, you can compete by being the most flexible or the most innovative, or even by having the widest range of services related to your core activity. And for every way of competing, Operations must be configured differently.

In the Teatro Real they have arrived at their current Operations structure in an iterative and intuitive manner. Of immeasurable importance has been the participation of some incredible experts such as José Luis Tamayo, with whom we'll talk later. He, and pioneers like him, are undoing the old given that 'good service must be expensive'. We don't mean to say that the productions of the Teatro Real are the lowest in its field. Nevertheless, and given the level of service that they must attain (that is, their way of competing), the Teatro Real must always be efficient. And this signifies that it must be difficult to achieve the same result at lower cost; if you wanted to reduce the cost, then you'd have to give a different service.

Conclusions

The mission of a company must be clearly specified and made operational. This means that it must be understandable for the entire organisation. To achieve that, general management must undertake an exercise of reflection, applying clear criteria that convey the stated priorities. In this chapter, we have presented a way of doing this. You can choose this way, or another, but the important thing is to get it done.

We'll end this chapter with a few questions that you can use to help you reflect on your own company's position:

- What are the components of your mission?
- How are they specified?
- Prioritise them (give them weightings!)
- Have you clearly conveyed them to all the levels of your company?
- Have you analysed how your way of competing influences the structure of your Operations?
- Who designs your services?
- What basic principles are employed in this design?
- Are you making unnecessary balances and trade-offs?
- Be daring, always ask for the impossible!

V
The Protagonists

The time has come to meet our hosts. Every opera has its protagonists; opera *means work in Italian, and so this book, our work, is no different.*

In fact, it is our protagonists who bring about the staging of an opera. In this book, some will appear identified by name, some not. But every one of them is essential to the final outcome. One of these protagonists is the Operations Director of the Teatro Real, Daniel Bianco. He is the person ultimately responsible for having introduced into the Teatro Real the operating culture that interests us. As we'll see, this would not have been possible unless the rest of the team had been in agreement with this culture, and had actively collaborated in it, thus achieving Attractiveness and Unity.

How does one become an expert in one of the theatrical arts[1]? How does one combine the knowledge with the talent? The next two chapters are dedicated to these questions and, to this end, what better way than to ask our protagonists. We provide a formal introduction of who is who in the Operations department of the Teatro Real, together with their origins and profiles. Using these interviews, we try to better understand their management style. As we see, for them, managing Operations efficiently is fundamentally resolving problems. Efficiency develops if we know how to emphasise this aspect. These people put into practice our maxim 'don't bring me problems, bring me solutions', but they have discovered it, them or their theatrical antecedents, surely without being taught, but through evolution and selection. They call their style 'theatrical common sense', but this is not normal common sense (if you see what we mean). In a Technical department like this and, by extension in the whole of the world of theatre, 'common sense' is the stock of knowledge necessary to resolve the basic problems of Operations, with a very clear objective: the success of the show. This common purpose guides all their actions.

---

[1] And we use this word 'art', as in the root of the word 'artisan'. This is a similar meaning to when we talk of, for example, 'the art of fishing'.

In the next two chapters, we explore, these questions, and we take the opportunity to present some basic ideas about knowledge and its relation with problem-solving.

The technical area of the Teatro Real is made up of more than 250 people. In this chapter, we're going to meet some of them, and we'll look at the paths they took on their journey that has led them to where they are now. This will help us to understand the areas of knowledge that are needed to manage a company of this type.

The Operations Director

We'll start with Daniel Bianco, Operations Director of the Teatro Real. In his fifties, Daniel is a man in great physical shape and talks with a faint accent that reveals his Latin-American origins – although because he's lived in Spain for so long, it's impossible to pinpoint where. Daniel is a born communicator, capable of conveying all sorts of sensations with facility and speed. In tenths of a second, and with great ease, he is able to pass from candid innocence to a complicit wink.

Daniel, how does one learn to be a man of the theatre?

Well, I don't know that very well – the truth is if you're asking me the question, I'm going to have to ask myself that first! The theatre is a legacy of history; it takes in all cultural spheres. I can't talk about all of it, so I'll concentrate on what I know best. I don't come from a theatrical family; I come from a family of painters; my father, my uncle. I have a family mixture of Italian and Spanish, even though my education is Spanish, since I've had much greater contact with that side of the family. My father painted pictures; pictures that he really couldn't stand, but that paid for his sons to go to university and thus gave them a head-start in life. When he retired, he said 'I'm never going to paint these ugly things again'!

I remember that in our house there was always some palette, loaded with many colours, but there was never any family relationship with the theatre. Although I must say that family sagas are very typical in the theatre. But I'm sure that this must happen in families of doctors, lawyers, dentists... but in the theatre people say 'you were born in a set' or that 'you've cut your teeth on the stage'.

Do you have to have started out on stage to be a man of the theatre?

No, you don't need to. Nevertheless, it helps to understand, by certain nuances, whether somebody can or can't work in this profession. Often they're silly things, but important silly things, like knowing that one always comes on stage in silence, that you don't drag your feet because this makes a noise ... you don't eat on stage ... you don't keep change in your pockets ... and common sense, knowing how to behave on stage, is important.

Have you ever been present at a lighting rehearsal? There is silence. Yes, to sort out the lights you need silence! Noise really disrupts things. It sounds stupid, but that's the way it is. You can't sort out the lights while people are making a noise.

But to get back to our theme ... how did I get into all of this? Let's see, when I finished college, I did a vocational test and it turned out I should study dentistry ... and I hate everything to do with teeth! Why did the test turn up dentistry? I remember perfectly, because they explained it to me – it was apparently because I had a great capacity for craftsmanship and artisanal things.

Of course, in the end, I didn't study dentistry. I did a bit of teaching – sociology, psychology ... but I had one thing very clear: art interested me a lot. Always, always, since I was old enough to even think about it, I'd loved going to the theatre. In the same way that other families took their kids to see a football match, in my house we went to the theatre. Don't ask me why, it was just a regular thing. My parents went out every Saturday night with their friends to see a play or a film, and then have dinner with them. And one Sunday a month, I'd say, we went as a whole family to see some show.

When I was very small, they took me to see a play at the Teatro San Martin de Buenos Aires. Now they'd call it a theatre city – six auditoria and a huge central one. It was entirely red, the theatre. When we were waiting for the performance to begin, I'd ask my father 'When's the bride coming?' because, seeing it all red and so pretty, I thought there was a wedding on and the couple hadn't arrived yet!

I've always had it clear that, whatever I studied, my work, my vocation, would have to be something related with people, and the organisation of these people. I had this very clear from day one. I always thought that managing a group of people would come easily to me. Anyway, one day I just went and signed up for a university course ... I really don't know why, honestly I don't ... I remember a great friend once said to me 'look, you don't think about the big decisions, you just make them' and, well, I went and signed up for Fine Arts, specialising in Set Design!

There's a Set Design specialisation in Fine Arts?

In Argentina there was. Now there is in other places. In Argentina, the course was very famous. I think Argentina is a country which took in a lot of people during the world wars. People were fleeing their own countries and went there. This helped Argentina a lot, this huge movement of people ... and while I studied Fine Arts and Set Design, which is a four-year course, I worked.

Were all the teachers you had at university 'theatre' people?

Yes, in a course on 'Set Design in Television, Cinema and Theatre' there's a very large technical part, and you learn to draw like an architect or draughtsman. But there's also a very large part about artistic development. While I studied I began to work as assistant to Hugo de Ana, who was my tutor on the course, on a theatre production he was doing. Back then, it didn't even occur to me that I might get paid, or that the theatre could help me at all financially. To me, just being a part of it was reward enough. When I entered that world and I saw it close-up for the first time, it was like I'd know it all my life. It appeared to me absolutely normal to be looking for a pair of period shoes for the lead. I felt important doing so.

I was in that job for two or three months. And in that time, doing this thing, something grows inside you, something that you can't explain, but then you start to get involved in all the theatre productions you can, you start to see everything from the point of view of the theatre. You know? You walk down the street and you start to see set designs. I suppose it must happen in all walks of life – when you get your leg put in plaster, you suddenly see lots of people in plaster casts. The same thing happens in the theatre, you start to see everything theatrically. Luckily, very soon after, there were a couple of places available working at one of the most important theatres in Buenos Aires, and I started there as a set builder. Well, I started there washing brushes.

What is a set builder?

They are the artisans, smiths, carpenters ... everyone who makes a set. It's an activity that has many specialities. There's an ironworker, someone who works with motors, a painter, a seamstress, a carpenter with all his wood-working, and I was in painting. But, of course, they don't let you start painting on the first day. All you get is 'Boy, clean the brushes!' which is the worst bit about painting. Washing brushes is horrible! I was there for the last two years of my degree course. I had left teaching, and I combined working with studying. If any production came up that needed somebody to do something, I'd get involved. But always, always, backstage – absolutely always. This gave me several years of incredible learning. In the theatre, there is a very oft-used aphorism: you have to be in the right place at the right time. For me, this was the right time. Maybe back then, and I'm talking 30 years ago, everything was more vocational.

I finished my studies and worked as a Set Designer for theatre and television. But I began to specialise more and more in managing the people who design the sets. I'll give you an example; there's me, 19 or 20 years old, and I put myself forward for a TV set design position. They gave me a call to do a morning magazine show. I had to be on set at seven in the morning to build the set. To do the set, to think about it and sketch it wasn't difficult, but to turn up at seven in the morning, 20 years old, a hippy, and find yourself with 50 people staring at you and asking 'ok, son, what do you want us do now?' ... well, it was hard work! But from the first moment, I just twigged to it, and I realised that I appeared credible to these people, that I was organising things – things that sometimes even I had no idea why – and it was all turning out ok. In the theatre, you have to have an answer, even if you've no idea. The biggest mistake you can make is to keep quiet. It's always better to answer something, anything. I did that and, I don't know how, I got it right.

That's how I started to realise that what interested me most was *making something possible*, more than sitting at home thinking about *how* to make things possible. I've received prizes for my stage and set design, but it's not as satisfying, and it doesn't give me as much pleasure as *getting people to do things*.

Later I came to work in Spain. I worked here as a Set Design Assistant, and I noticed a big difference in the training of the people who worked here. There was a lot of eagerness and enthusiasm, but they just hadn't had the specialised training.

And then happened something extremely lucky for me. By coincidence, Gerardo Vera,[2] who is today the Director of the National Drama Centre, had to do a set design for the María Guerrero Theatre. He called me to be his assistant, to sketch it and solve the technical issues. I did so, and when I'd handed it in to him, he studied it very carefully. That same day he was supposed to deliver that project to the directors of the theatre, but he said to me 'Look, I can't go. Why don't you go instead, deliver the project, and I'll go later?' And I went, and met Lluís Pasqual (a famous Stage Director) who was then Director of the theatre, and José Luis Tamayo (the brains behind the future reforms of the Teatro Real) who was then the Operations Director, and Isabel Navarro, who was Management Assistant. I arrived, delivered the entire project to them and left. That afternoon, a place came up as Artistic Co-ordinator and they called and asked if I'd like to work there. I accepted.

But was it because you got on with them well, or they received good reports of you, or...?

I suppose it's because they saw my work was good. I don't know, maybe they saw I had control of the situation; I was in control of my work. I dunno, I can't really say. But I believe that if a person is right for the theatre, it's immediately apparent. For example, I've just given an opportunity to a young lad. I recommended him to Gerardo Vera as a wardrobe assistant on *Macbeth*, because I think this lad's got talent, and Vera has confirmed to me that yes, he has. I don't know why, but I think this guy will be a great costume designer.

---

[2] (Born, Miraflores de la Sierra, 1947) Vera is a director of cinema, theatre, opera, *zarzuela* (Spanish light opera), stage designer and costume designer. He's considered to be one of Spain's most multi-talented creative people. In 1988, he received the coveted *Premio Nacional del Teatro*.

What does it mean to be an Artistic Co-ordinator?

In reality they themselves didn't know how to define it. From that point, I made the most of the situation and defined it myself. I thought, ok, Artistic Co-ordinator is an assistant to the Operations Director, so I said *I'm going to make things happen*, and I got stuck right in. Later, when Tamayo left the theatre, they named me Operations Director. Then, when there was a change of management, I left the María Guerrero Theatre but later still, when there was another change of management, I returned to the same post in the same theatre and stayed there for another three years.

Where did you get people for the Teatro Real?

From the open market. We were looking for managers, more than anything. There are many people with experience, but what happens is there's so much activity and turnover these days, you can only get youngsters with no experience; they don't know anything. There are 90 scene-shifters just in this theatre. In the María Guerrero with the general wage agreements, they went from 10 to 30. There comes a time when the professionals among them who you've known all your life just aren't there anymore. You have to bring in new people; kids who you know love the theatre and are available. And once you've got them in the Teatro Real, you help to set them on the right path.

If someone really wants to learn the trade, they will. If you're standing by the side of a scene-shifter, of a set builder, you'll learn the trade. And in part, this helps to nurture the theatrical common sense.

I don't know if you can teach a profession. I think that you learn depending on who you've worked with. IT's a trade. When I arrived in Spain, apart from working a lot with the maestro Hugo de Ana, I worked absolutely loads, and still do, with Lluís Pasqual, one of the most seasoned people to run a theatre and, additionally, an excellent Stage Director. I also worked with Fabià Puigserver, a great Set Designer from this country who died young. I believe that yes, you can learn many things. But above all, I believe in practical application. I reckon you can take a group of people, work with them and they'll learn the theatre that way.

You have to go through all the processes; you have to learn the basics before you get on to the complex stuff. People often start to work with a very small theatre group, perhaps from their town or village. And they learn, bit by bit. For example, no class in the world can teach you how to lay a ballet floor. A ballet floor is made up of metre-wide strips of lino laid in parallel. The advantage over a wood floor is that there are no splinters, and it doesn't slip. The joint between the strips is covered with tape, to avoid tripping. But you mustn't put tape around the edge of the floor; otherwise you end up with bumps. The air doesn't escape, it forms bubbles and this makes your floor bulge. You only learn that kind of thing in practice!

Ok, so should these lino strips go vertically or horizontally across the stage? According to the American Ballet Company, putting them vertically causes problems. When a ballerina who dances on point reaches stage centre, she can end up doing a pirouette on the join. For this reason, they say horizontal. But then along comes another company that doesn't care about that, and they want the strips vertical. What have you learnt? It's very simple. Every time you're putting on a ballet, you must ask 'And how would you like your ballet floor?'

These are the things that you capitalise on, the things that give you the advantage. But you can't give a methodology for that. You can show people other things, you can show what a counter-weight is, you can explain the electrics, you can teach the sound, you can demonstrate how to nail the wood, how to build … but the reality, the practice, is that you have to actually do it, hands-on, in theatres. And then, that's where you say to yourself 'I've got the knowledge, I'm ready and I'm a sponge, so now I'm going to do it in the theatre'.

If you arrive with the trade already learnt, you turn yourself into a sponge, then you learn, you learn the ins and outs, the customs and practices. You must have a good memory and remember everything. Just remember that, until fairly recently, each company's choreography could be reproduced only thanks to the memory of one dancer!

Er … what do you mean?

Exactly! How do you record choreography, right? Well, now there's video, but until only a few years ago that wasn't an option. All the companies had a repertory ballerina, usually a veteran, who could, from memory, reproduce ballets. Sometimes they'd sketch them, but it's a difficult thing to draw, right? They'd draw how to position and move each leg, but only one person could understand and interpret it, and that was the person who'd drawn it. There are many things that have to be recorded or remembered. This must happen in every company – you want to capitalise on experience. But what happens here is that the experience is very enriching. And very varied, because you deal with so many things. If things happen to you, you remember; if they don't, you don't. Snow is made using a 'drop' with holes in, you fill it with little pieces of paper, you move it as if sifting flour, and … snow falls. You know this. You study this, it's in a book. But if you find yourself in a place where they've never made snow before, you'll never know how to position the drop so that the snow can best be seen. Nor will you know that you have to mix white and grey paper, otherwise it won't be seen at all.

Carlos, Senior Technical Management Assistant

Carlos is a man of about 45, with a ruddy complexion, and he looks at you straight in the face when answering questions. With his ponytail, he has an air of sincerity, and his answers are simple and direct. He's worked with Daniel for 20 years, and they know each other perfectly. Quite often, before answering a question, Carlos looks at Daniel in some unspoken, informal communication, with never a word being uttered.

Carlos, how did you come to be here in the Teatro Real?

Well, I'm the Technical Management Assistant. I come from a family from the entertainment world; my parents and even grandparents were in theatre. My parents worked in revue; my father was a chorus-boy with Celia Gámez and my mother was one of the ballet girls. They started in 1937. Back then, the world of acting was pretty complicated. After leaving the revue, my mother was a circus hostess, a circus of which my father was the ring-master. Later on he became the agent and manager of the circus. It was the circus of the Aragon[3] family. I'm a relative of the Aragon family, which is the most powerful circus family in Spain. In my family there's a bit of everything, a ballerina, actors, well, practically my whole family is involved in showbiz in some way. Eventually my father had to leave his job and they offered him the job of concierge at the María Guerrero Theatre with live-in quarters; so we all moved there. I was four, and living on the fourth floor of the theatre. My mother used to sew there. The first few years were a very strange experience for me, living in the theatre.

We had the flat above what is known as the auditorium ceiling. Back in the glory days it was the house of María Guerrero herself. The ceiling of the theatre was made of wood, with beams and crystal chandeliers. My play room was María Guerrero's old greenhouse, annexed to the flat. That was my world. From there I could reach the stage. I knew absolutely everybody, the scene-shifters, the props people...I started to see up close how props worked. In school, my reports were always mediocre, but in the crafts or 'shop' subjects, I always excelled. If I had to make a periscope, I'd pop down to the workshop and they'd make me a periscope and, when I turned up at school with a periscope, I'd be triumphant. I was living in the theatre until I was 15, and then I went to work as a mail boy in an office. I'd deal with messages, letters, everything. I worked there for a year. I have a sister who was working in the circus, and she said she wanted me to go and audition with them. I was there a year and a half, working on sound and lighting.

---

[3] Important members of the Aragon family included the three brothers, Gaby, Fofó and Miliki, famous television clowns who, in the 1970s and 1980s delighted all Spaniards (not just the children) in their Saturday morning TV shows. Many Spaniards now in their thirties and forties continue to sing the songs that they created and popularised. Two of their sons, Fofito and Milikito, continued the family tradition working as clowns, but Milikito later gave up his stage name and his clown's costume, and became Emilio Aragón, who went on to become one of the most widely respected TV personalities in the Spanish-speaking world.

I learned to be in another world, I learned to survive, and I learned how to handle animals. Looking after them was a wonderful experience. Then I was called up for military service and, once I got out, I met José Luis Tamayo and Daniel, and started to work in the Operations department at the María Guerrero. Then, in 1997, they called me to come here, to be Technical Management Assistant.

So Tamayo called you too?

Yes, first it was to be Set Director, a position that they invented. For them, a Set Director is like an Operations Director, but locally, for one opera. In a big ship like this, there's an Operations department and the boss is very high-level. But on the stage, there needs to be an Operations Director of the company, who deals with the details of a production, of an opera. I had to see an event through from start to finish, in such a way that the higher-up directors weren't needed except in extreme cases. Let's say that on a scale of 1 to 10, from 7 to 10 the directors would get involved, but from 1 to 7 it was me who had to sort it out and co-ordinate with all the other sections.

And did this require you to know about music?

Not in my case, luckily, because it's something I know nothing about. For the musical bit there's the Stage Manager; we're complementary. You don't need to know about music to put on a production, nor is it needed when you want to make a change, because the Stage Manager's there to lay down the rules. What you do need to have is direct contact with the Stage Director.

Later I became Technical Management Assistant, a position that has much more power. The basic idea was to have an Operations Director, an Assistant and a Project Head for each production. What Daniel and I have done is to integrate the different functions in parallel. Daniel talks to the Set Designer, and while they're developing the idea, the Assistant is developing the operational project, translating what Daniel and the Set Designer agree on into processes. Finally, the draughtsmen and women arrive at the detailed plans of how it'll all come together. So, I have a general vision of the project, and at the same time I have the authority to pass the processes on to the senior heads of each section. Contact is much more direct, and information is shared very rapidly. At the same time that we're creating, we're also giving the section heads work on the production.

And do you feel that you're in charge of any project?

Yes, all of them. Right now there's *Don Giovanni, The Magic Flute,*[4] *Don Carlo* ... in fact Daniel says to me that if I'm not fully involved with 11 operas, I'm not doing my job properly. I have to get into bed with 11 operas.

---

[4] *The Magic Flute*, or *Die Zauberflöte*, was the last opera by Mozart, and features the best example of *singspiel*, 'song-play'; the German-language operatic genre. We doubt

How do you organise yourself to manage five 'live' projects?

Well, it's easier than it might seem, because what has been managed here exceptionally well is a work dynamic, and when there is that dynamic with *common sense*, things pretty much do themselves. Here *common sense* means that when an opera project arrives in front of me, I immediately think of a few *basic things*. Let's see, does it fit or not? And I say 'yes, it fits'. Fine, 'can I make the change?' Yes or no. Common sense is knowing the six questions that you have to formulate to be able to continue forwards, to be able to say yes or no. One has a kind of structured checklist in one's head, and you go down the list of things tick, tick, tick...

I have some rules for working that I drew up myself. I don't really know where they come from, but I've learnt them; we've talked about them. They're logical rules. The theatre has certain dimensions, certain possibilities. You have to synthesize and understand why you can't study every project in-depth. If when you want to buy a production, they send you four, you have to make the decision in a fortnight. With these norms, these rules, you see what is possible, what you can move and what you can't, and what you can arrange. All in broad strokes. In the background, you have to resolve the problem of feasibility. Can I do this? Is this opera compatible with the other? Could I do a concert if I'm doing this opera?

With common sense, you solve this problem on four levels, using the general structure; you don't need to see every detail.

You imagine, for example, when there's a strike. Another example: with the *Marriage of Figaro*,[5] the lorries were coming from Vienna, there had been

---

that anyone has ever managed to understand the libretto of *The Magic Flute*. Apparently, Mozart took this infamous libretto, in which were mixed bird-hunters, a sorceress who turns out to be a sister of mercy, someone who appears to be bad and turns out good, and other various strange characters, to create a Masonic allegory. Back then, Mozart had joined the Masons and was an active participant. The entire opera is a hymn to Brotherhood, Reason and Wisdom. But all of this is by the way, because *The Magic Flute* features some of the most sublime music in the entire history of opera. The music keeps the action together, and says much more than the words (which are, at times, contradictory) that the protagonists say. Some experts are of the opinion that this is a magnificent example of singing without lyrics. But perhaps this is too harsh. Either way, if there were some bizarre cosmic cataclysm and only one opera could be saved, this is the one that the present authors would probably choose.

[5] Another opera by Mozart. It is a kind of sequel to *The Barber of Seville*, which was written 13 years earlier. The characters are the same as the original play by Pierre Beaumarchais, but now we find Rosina as the wife of Count Almaviva and living in Seville. Susana, Rosina's maid, is going to marry Figaro, and they're going to live in the count's palace. But the count, who is a very sly and crafty old warhorse, remembers his *droit de seigneur* and that this, logically, includes Susana. The action stops here, but it becomes an amusing vaudeville, with entrances, exits, hide-and-seek and crossed loves, including that of the 15-year-old Cherubino, around whom is woven

snow and, of course, the lorries didn't arrive. The other day something arrived by DHL, I paid a fortune for it to be here in 24 hours and it took eight days. I have to think about this too but, you see, all of this is, for me, common sense. I have to think 'right, if something happens, can the show still go on?'

Oscar, Stage Manager

What is your job?

I'm the Stage Manager. They assign some operas to me, and the Operations Director and the Technical department supply me with information with as much notice as they think necessary and according to how the show is going. I have to study all of this information and make it happen on the stage.

The Technical department lays down some rules but, of course, they don't specify where every last nut and bolt is going. That's what I and the rest of the team are here for. For all the 'unforeseens' that come up, if I'm here, I evaluate them and decide what to do. If for any reason I need to, I can consult the Operations Director, but I am really the Operations Director of the show. Of course, it's all supervised by the Operations Director, but the person who does, decides and organises is me.

And when you decide, what decision criteria do you use?

Those of my trade, my work and those of the situation in every moment.

How did you learn to be a Stage Manager?

It's in my family. My grandfather worked in this. In my house we used to eat, sleep and drink theatre. My father was a painter; he worked in a production workshop, Viuda de Enrique López. In my house we've always talked about theatre. I have a scene-shifter sister, who also works here, brothers-in-law, my uncle, my cousins, my great-uncles... My great grand mother

---

three of the best musical moments of the opera. These are the aria of Figaro 'Non piu andrai' (no more gallivanting) that describes the charms that awaits Cherubino when he joins the army, and the two arias of Cherubino 'Voi, che sapete' (you ladies who know) in which Cherubino asks advice of the maids because they know 'what love is', and 'Non so più cosa son' (I no longer know what I am), in which he's seen disturbed by the amorous sentiments that are overwhelming him and he barely understands. In the last act, Susana and Rosina prepare a trap for the Count, which his wife takes advantage of to bring him into line. At the end, everybody ends up happy and content. The entire opera is an exquisite jewel, comparable with its sisters *Don Giovanni* and *Cosi fan Tutte*. The three are known as 'da Ponte' because the librettos were written by the same man, Lorenzo da Ponte.

sewed stage curtains! It runs in the family. Your family usually tries everything to keep members from working in the theatre, but we always end up here ...

How did you train for this?

Well, I got the BUP, which is a secondary school (14–17) certificate. But this job you learn by doing, there's no school, no trade as such. I worked in the workshop with my father. I've painted; I've washed glue bottles every morning; I've warmed bottles; I've patched curtains. But I've seen myself *advance* in this world, day by day, working. To this day, there isn't a school for this business.

Before working here, I was in the Theatre of the Zarzuela in the opera seasons, and in the Spanish Theatre, at the same time – in the workshop in the morning and doing performances in the afternoon. The Teatro Real reopened in 1997, and many people applied for the interviews. I applied as a scene-shifter and got in on 11 October 1997. From shifter I became Assistant Head, from there to level 1 Head, from level 1 to Head of Machinery, and from there to Stage Manager.

So you kind of picked it up as you went along?

Not really. This theatre, in particular, gives you the means. They give you the resources and let you participate. He who participates, organises well and gets stuck in is the person who has most chances to learn.

What we all do, at the end, is *common sense*, doing the job well with common sense, managing the organisation with common sense. In the end, everything's simpler than it looks.

What's the attraction of the theatre for you?

I would say that I get up in the mornings, I come here and I enjoy my work. I have the *capacity to decide* within my work, my category and my status. I do, and I undo, of course following some guidelines, I don't go mad! Of course, I know my business and I know my job, and that's common sense. But day to day in the theatre, you're never good enough; you're conscious of the many problems and you monitor them, but the 'unforeseens' are constant. And nothing, absolutely nothing, is the same as the day before.

Ignacio, Technical Management Assistant

Ignacio is a young man of 30-something, with curly hair and a face that is at once affable but bursting with energy. He speaks hesitantly and thinks carefully before answering our questions.

What's your background?

Well, I studied the normal stuff that everyone does at school, but what happened was I felt there was much more to do. I started taking various additional courses, such as English, and I started to get interested in sound. And I said 'I want to be a sound technician'; but when I started working as a sound technician, and I saw how that was, I began to like lighting and imagery more. I started working as a photographer's assistant, and doing lighting design for theatres. From there I went into the theatre proper. But even so, I wanted more. I tried to combine it with other things, such as stage management. And I began to take responsibility for entire prose theatre companies. While touring with the companies, I'd occasionally do renovations and installations in theatres in Madrid. And one fine day I found myself in a national theatre that paid more for less work. Until then I'd had to work 24 hours straight, alone, in a grotty theatre, lost to the world. And suddenly I was there working with people from the national theatres. Someone tipped me off that one of the national theatres was going to start a recruitment process. Even though I had all sorts of problems, by pure luck I managed to get an interview at El Clásico Theatre. Daniel was there and he interviewed me for 20 minutes, then we started working together and got on great. When he came here to the Teatro Real, he called me and here I am.

And what do you do?

I think in a normal company I'd be considered Head of Logistics. I always repeat the explanation that Daniel gave me about the purpose of technical management: 'This theatre is a big engine, and we're the oil that allows it to run'. My job is to be the oil. And apart from that I look after the logistics of the containers, the backstage areas, sharing out the work among the technicians, the box office, storage...

Right now we have about 295 containers and two large warehouses where all the spare props and material go. I have 250 technicians. And I also have to put up with Daniel and Carlos, as well as try to be a bit of a jack of all trades. Finally, I'm in charge of the parallel activities that we do on the sixth floor, and all the concerts that we put on the main stage.

What are these 'parallel activities'?

Everything that isn't an opera is a parallel activity, typically taking place in the *Café de Palacio*. For example, we might get 200 people together and do a piano recital. Well, I'd be in charge of that, of these kinds of shows.

And are you a theatre man? Were you born into a theatre family?

Nope, nobody in my family has anything to do with the theatre. But my wife worked in the afternoons as an usherette, because her mother and grandmother had been very well-known theatre ticket clerks in Madrid. My wife isn't a big theatre fan, but we did meet there. She was working in the mornings at Renault, and in the afternoons in a theatre I ended up at, and where I was the Head Technician.

And does the theatre world fascinate you or is it just another job?

I reckon it's the be-all and end-all; I'd almost pay to work here! It must have something going for it, because at the premieres I sometimes find myself crying backstage. It's just too beautiful. To be a part of all this is somehow like magic ... it's difficult to explain.

What I do in the shows I have assigned to me is try to take the problems away from Carlos and Daniel. To deliver the finished product the next day. To say to them, 'look, the concert yesterday turned out well' and that's that. On a small scale, it's the same as they do, but a very small version ... The ultimate responsibility is with logistics. If one o'clock tomorrow morning we need to have six trucks here with 18 people to load and unload, then I'm in charge of making sure that happens smoothly. If an entire production of *Carmen*[6] has to go to Tel Aviv or Los Angeles, I have to make that happen, make sure it arrives where it has to go.

This is essentially fitting together pieces; our needs with the needs of the intermediates. A little while ago we sent a *Carmen* to Los Angeles and it arrived two days late, because of the hurricanes. This almost caused the other theatre to bring a lawsuit against us, but when they sent everything back by their own channels, it arrived 24 *days* late! On the one hand, there's the stage, but on the other there's the sheer rush of doing things efficiently – in other words, *Carmen* really did arrive in Los Angeles and we did a good job.

---

[6] An opera by Georges Bizet. One of the most popular French operas, it is based on the story by Prosper Merimée. Stereotypically Spanish, with bullfighters, cigarette makers and bandits from the mountains; the whole lot set in Seville and a fascinating protagonist who seems to be the epitome of Spanish clichés. The authors manage to make Carmen a prototypical woman, which for some people is a symbol of liberation and for others is an unscrupulous villain. But Carmen is a libertarian, aware of the power she holds over men and unafraid to use it. She twists them round her little finger. She takes a fancy to them, falls in love, and then throws them away like a Don Juan, but without his promiscuity. It's also they who do all the chasing. Carmen sets her hopes on Don José, a fainthearted soldier who rejects the gentle love offered him by Micaela to be seduced instead by the maelstrom of Carmen. After an episode with the authorities, provoked by her disregard for them and egged on by the cigarette factory workers ('L'amour est un oiseau rebelle', 'love is a rebellious bird'), Carmen is captured, but convinces Don José to let her escape, and that he should flee with her. Don José, who's a bit naïve and not too bright, agrees. He also becomes a bandit for her, up in the mountains (of course) and spends his time singing dreamily to the flowers. Carmen quickly realises he's a bit boring and gets tired of him (you would, wouldn't you?) and instead falls in love with Escamillo, a very successful bullfighter. But Don José chases after her, imploring her to return to him. Imploring Carmen, however, is never going to be a winning formula. She needs dominating, and Don José simply hasn't got the necessary. When Carmen laughs at him, Don José becomes a tragic figure and stabs her in the back, the swine, while in the background can be heard the sounds of Escamillo triumphing in the bullring. Phew!

Yes, the luck I have is that Daniel doesn't tell me how I have to do things and he never has, maybe because that's where we might have clashed, because my working style would have clashed with his. For example, he might be able to come up with solutions that are quicker or more efficient, but if I don't arrive at solutions by my own means, that I believe are faster or more efficient, then I won't identify with them and I can't do it.

Daniel says that I get too closely involved with my work, but as long as things arrive perfectly on the right day and at the right time, then that's my problem.

VI
Understanding Our Protagonists

In the previous chapter, we met four characters with unique histories; histories that help to explain their methods of doing things and proceeding. We'd like to highlight those elements that made us stop and think, and that might help the reader to consider some critical themes relating to his or her company. To achieve this, we're going to concentrate, in this chapter, on four questions:

1. What do our protagonists do, and what do the people in your company do?
2. How should your people be best prepared to solve problems?
3. How do you focus on your daily responsibilities; do you do, or do you *get people to do*?
4. What is a company's *common sense*?

We'll tackle these one by one, commenting on the remarks made by our protagonists and highlighting those ideas that we think most relevant.

What do our protagonists do, and what do the people in your company do?

First of all, think about what each one does. They are very different tasks, but all of them have a common denominator: *solving problems*. Each one has his own set of problems, but by resolving them and adapting, they are providing *global solutions*. Each one has his area of responsibility perfectly identified, and each one provides his own solutions. Carlos struggles with the problems of the workshop, does it fit or not, what do I have, what information must I give to the first-level bosses so they can start their work, how do I organise all this and so on? Ignacio is concentrating on the logistics and one of those problems is how to lay a ballet floor.

But there doesn't appear to by any sensation of chaos. On the contrary, all of them seem to have it very clear what they want, and they even enjoy it a lot! Remember what Ignacio said: 'I'd almost pay to work here!' Is there anyone in your company who'd say that?

Solving problems is nothing new, it's something ordinary. But solving problems in an individual, but at the same time in a collaborative manner, looking for synergies and with a common purpose, is something very different. And the people at the Teatro Real seem to have achieved it. Why? It appears that all of them have a purpose, all of them know what problem-solving is for and they all provide support to the smooth running of the Teatro Real.

How did they manage this? This requires *coordination*, the existence of a common sense mechanism (dare we say, an Operational Culture?) that helps each one achieve his personal working style without ever losing the *global sense*.

Coordination. What is it and how do you achieve it? As an example, we can look at the Research and Development activities of your company. R&D is a field in which you absolutely must achieve coordination between many talented people who have initiative and want to exercise it in the interests of a common purpose: create and deliver a new service or product. Over the years, various methods have been identified by which this can be achieved. One is called *sequential processing*. Each person does one thing, and, when finished, it's passed to the next person in the chain and the first person forgets about it. The reader might remember that Carlos said this was the original idea they had, but didn't follow it through. Instead they opted for the alternative, the famous simultaneous design. All the activities are done in parallel, without waiting for one to completely finish before the next can be set in motion. The advantage is that the subsequent activity can form a part of the previous, to help understand the problem better and to reach a provisional solution that best fits each activity. The down-side is a certain amount of duplication. The up-side? At the Teatro Real they discovered that this simultaneous processing is the only way to co-ordinate a large number of uncertain elements, especially when the people involved are highly qualified and capable of working with a healthy dose of initiative.

Who's looking out for your company's sense of purpose?

If we analyse the interviews, we notice that there is a constant reference made to *mutual relations* in the context of service delivery; a clear indication that the method of proceeding later *directs the entire process*. All of this makes us see the necessity of a tremendously important function that all management should aim for. We're talking about creating an environment that provides a sense of *purpose* to an organisation. Daniel Bianco knows how to engender this purpose in his people. How you do it is one of the fundamental subjects of this book and will be discussed in later chapters, especially in Chapter XIX. But we'd like to introduce the idea here, right at the start, by asking you a question: in your company, who provides the sense of purpose? If there is nobody watching out for your people, making sure there is this sense of purpose, the result can be disorientation and chaos. Fire-fighting has no purpose. When

> **The essential function of a manager is to solve problems, but problems with purpose, that look for synergy to achieve excellent service.**

a company is fire-fighting, it's just attacking problems in the order they appear, with no sense of progress. To find solutions, one needs a clear sense of direction; where are we going, and what do we want?

One moment. Now look at yourself. What do you do in your working day? Pour oil on troubled waters? Dodge the boss? Maybe both, but beyond that, and occupying the major part of your time, we'd be willing to bet that you *solve problems*. Some of them yours, some not, but they land on your desk ... particularly after the invention of e-mail. Now it's common practice that when somebody received a problem by e-mail, they immediately fire off copies to all the bosses and several other people who aren't even involved. It's a common way to cover your back. But this doesn't happen to you, does it, because your boss has been reading this book and has seen the light: 'Don't bring be problems, bring me solutions'; 'don't bother me with stuff you can sort out – just get it sorted'. For a boss to act like this, he or she has to be very self-assured and sure of you, too. But you're also capable of doing it. You don't think so? Trust us; the only thing you need is to be given the initiative, the support and the right purpose. And then, when something *unforeseen* arises, *the blame won't be yours*. In short, when somebody finds a *problem*, they won't also find a *culprit*.

So, we propose (to put your mind at rest) that what you do is the respectable *function of problem-solving and creating a context in which others can solve theirs*. This phrase could be simplified to 'help solve problems and get things done' or '*do and get done*'. More details on that in a few paragraphs.

This is the critical function of the new Operational Culture. The essential function of a manager is to *solve problems*, but problems with purpose. That is, problems within the *framework* of the company's *priorities*; priorities that *have meaning* for every one of the collaborators, in such a way that the solution *provides service value*, or even better still, *fulfils the promise of the company*. Carlos, Ignacio or Daniel all know that every solution is a piece of the puzzle of the final service: the success of the opera. Their people understand that and the complementary nature of different solutions.

How should your people be best prepared to solve problems?

Is a university degree necessary in order to occupy a position of responsibility in a first-class opera theatre? Or in your company? Education is (should be) the transmission and acquisition of knowledge. We're all probably in agreement that knowledge can help to solve problems; indeed, we would say that knowledge is simply the capacity to find solutions to a problem. Therefore, why does the Teatro Real, which must constantly solve problems, not place any great importance on people attaining a sophisticated or high-level education before they start their careers?

> **Knowledge is the capacity to solve a certain type of problem.**

One of the main reasons is that traditional education places the emphasis on formalised knowledge, while in the theatre there is no body of formalised knowledge that covers the relevant spectrum of problems. It is said that university teaches one how to think. In a certain sense, those that think that are right, but more than think, we'd say it teaches you to *reason*. And formal knowledge has an important characteristic: you can increase the range of problems that you know how to solve simply by … reasoning.

Let's return to the ballet. If we know something of basic physics we see that if we have space, hermetically sealed by an elastic membrane – a ballet floor – and we push on it, by treading on one side, then the pressure will increase and deform the surface of the other side. *Et voilà!* Someone who knows nothing about ballet, but can recognise the problem, could reach the conclusion, if he knows how to reason, that the solution is to *not* seal the floor. Nor are we going to leave it open in the middle, because that's full of ballerinas jumping about, and we don't actually want to kill anyone. We've managed to arrive at the same conclusion that Daniel referred to, simply by reasoning. Is this 'common sense'? We'll see in the next point. For now we'll just note that human beings are capable of obtaining new knowledge (things you didn't know you didn't know) simply by using the brain to reason. You don't actually need experience. Full stop.

> **A large part of knowledge useful for solving a company's problems is knowledge that cannot be formalised and thus very difficult to pass on by conventional means.**

There is formalised knowledge within companies. Accounts, for example, is a formalised body of knowledge that, once established in the basics, continues to grow by reasoning. Formalised knowledge is relatively easy to pass on by the traditional teacher-pupil, master-disciple channel.

Ok, so apparently in the theatre there is very little formal knowledge to pass on. But what about in your company? What are the 'pieces' of knowledge that your employees most frequently manage? Don't worry, we'll give you the answer, even though we're sure you already suspect the answer. The knowledge that is most frequently managed is informal knowledge; something very general in the world of business. A large part of knowledge useful for solving a company's problems is knowledge that cannot be formalised and, to this end, very difficult to pass on by conventional channels, courses, conferences and so on. Again, let's go back to the ballet. To lay a floor, the best option is to ask the company how they want it. You might say that this is easily taught by explaining it to the student, and that's that. Imagine a course titled 'Theatre Maxims for Beginners' in which the whole course consists of the teacher giving advice like the foregoing. Not only would nobody 'internalise' the knowledge, but the teacher would also be in fear of sustaining bodily harm, probably by the second class. No, this could not be taught by classic means.

Thus, when dealing with the sort of knowledge useful in the theatre, or in your company, *rules-based* training is of relatively *little use.*

So, why do Training departments, perhaps even your own company's, engage in the organisation of such typical teacher-led courses? Why have a teacher giving out 'the usual spiel' to his students, for whom the class often has little or no interest, and who only go to class 'because they have to go'? Shall we tell you? Our analyses of various Training departments have led us to believe that the answer lies in the fact that this is simply the easiest method, the easiest way to do things.

> **People in companies need *Just In Time* training; just in time to solve the problems that are worrying them.**

To run conventional training courses, you can always find teachers. It's easy to organise a course, and it's cheaper. In short, what's important is that people have the sensation that we're training them. Whether they learn or not is, sadly, another matter entirely.

People in companies require *Just In Time* training; just in time to solve the problems they face. If instead of this, they receive (as is often the case) *Just In Case* training, and then when the day comes and they need this knowledge, they'll probably remember nothing they learnt, let alone where they put their notes.

This is wrong. This is a complete waste of time and money. We need to radically change the role of training in companies. The role that training plays in increasing the competitiveness of a company is, in the majority of companies, practically nil. We know that *knowledge*, the most important asset of a company, is only *accumulated* as a result of the *processes leading to problem-solving*. How should we, then, focus the training? Should we leave people to learn by themselves? Should we forget courses and save money? Can we see anything in theatre that might give us an idea?

Consider the histories of our protagonists. None of them has been hired by Human Resources, nor has any Training department taught them anything. They were chosen and trained by the very people who will be working along-side them, the workers themselves. Compare this with companies, and don't tell us you don't have time to recruit your colleagues. This is probably the most important tasks that you can have. Well, one of the most.

Daniel tells us that his development began with Hugo de Ana, but Hugo de Ana did not give classes. Instead, he gave him brushes to wash and put him in situations that needed sorting out. Something similar also happened to the others; they started in local theatres, later moving on to bigger theatres, until finally 'graduating' at the Teatro Real. And in this process they've had to gain the confidence of those who have the ultimate responsibility for actually getting the job done, and in turn they have continued promoting and developing them.

Does the answer lie in bringing back the apprentice system?

Ok, yes, all the pedants out there score a bonus point – this is an extra question, but it's still really part of the previous one.

If you have a few, or many, grey hairs then perhaps you'll remember when there existed in companies a system of apprenticeship; a system that had as its head, the Apprentice Master. One of the current authors spent a summer in apprentice school of a mechanical firm. They tried to teach him how to polish. That is, to polish with a file, not a machine. And almost nobody polishes with a file, but polishing well is an art. To end up with a beautifully smooth surface, buy using a file, really requires you to know 'how to polish' well! The typical problem for a beginner is that after a little while the surface starts to exhibit all sorts of curves and bumps, and these tend to get worse the more you try to fix them.

To learn how to polish, nobody gives you a lesson. When you arrive they give you a lump of iron which is roughly parallelepiped (lovely word, and so much more impressive than 'cube'!) and the master says 'turn this into a perfect parallelepiped'. He had trouble just saying the word 'paralleled...' but you know what he wanted of you.

And you start. And the master comes over now and then, and corrects you. 'Get your elbow down!' was his first observation to this author.

Can you recognise this focus in the learning experience of our protagonists? Daniel himself acts like a master to his apprentices, and all of them do the same with their colleagues.

> We propose adapting the apprentice system to the twenty-first century company. Make every boss an educator.

'Apprentice: a person who learns an art or trade' says at least one dictionary. Nothing wrong in that, but 'art or trade'? Not maths, not physics. Someone who *learns to do*! The method required to learn to do something has always been different from the method needed to learn to reason.

Disgracefully, many companies (the vast majority) have done away with this apprentice system. It's expensive. In an investigation that we carried out some years ago for the European Union, we identified that one of the reasons why a German company had lost some of its competitiveness was the abandonment of this apprentice system. And why did they drop it? Because it was very expensive.

In the apprentice system, there is no economy of scale, whereas in the traditional teaching system, there are. The cost (salary) of a teacher is spread between the 30, 40 or however many students that make up the course. In contrast, the apprentice system is Socratic. It's the apprentice system that Socrates described some four thousand years ago. Slow and expensive. But also the only way that really guarantees that one learns to actually do something.

And what conclusion does all this bring us to? That the bosses should also be educators in order to teach their people how to do things. How is this method managed in the theatre? Each person becomes an Apprentice Master for every person they work with. Simple, but effective.

How do you focus on your daily responsibilities; do you do, or do you *get people to do*?

One of our protagonists literally said: 'Yes, the luck I have is that Daniel doesn't tell me how I have to do things and he never has, maybe because that's where we might have clashed, because my working style would have clashed with his.' Does 'get people to do' mean leaving each person to do what they like? Not at all; note that our protagonist is only speaking about his method of working, not about the objective of his work.

Management is there to support, to train and to co-ordinate, but the individual must decide how to go about his or her tasks. There is no control over the process; there is only control over the results.

Recently, we have begun to notice the return of a certain anxiety that we thought had disappeared, among management over *controlling the details*. It's possible that this stems from the widespread use of the mobile phone. Have you noticed that managers have an obsession with talking on their mobiles? They either have it constantly in their hand or carry it strapped to their belt like a gun in a holster, ready to draw at a moment's notice. Also, when in meetings, they leave them on the table and sometimes switch off the ringer. We don't know what's worse, though, because if there's a call the phone starts vibrating on the desk and making the most appalling racket. If you try to ban the use of mobiles in meetings, then the moment everybody leaves the meeting they've got their mobiles glued to their ears as though the world might have forgotten how important they are. And the worst of it all is that the purpose of the majority of these calls is simply to check up on people; to control.

This control is destructive. The result is that people become inoperative and don't make decisions. 'I'm not sure... so the next time he/she calls,' thinks the employee, 'I'll ask them instead. They'll tell me what to do, and then I can't have got it wrong.' This goes completely against the principles of this book. Forget control; work towards results. Controlling gives a false sense of security, and covers up the insecurities of management. It's a phantom that must be exorcised. *Support* your people if they get stuck, find them ways to acquire the knowledge they need to solve their problems, but don't waste time trying to control them. *Invest your time in supporting and educating.* That's *getting people to do.*

As Daniel says, what's most important is getting results, making things happen. There's nothing worse than the sense of impotence that grips some managers when they see that nothing they wanted to happen is happening. Accept the facts: nobody obeys orders that don't coincide with their own interests. Your role as a manager is not to order. Your role is to *make sure that things get done.*

> **Getting people *to do* is the cornerstone of learning to think.**

What is a company's *common sense?*

One of our protagonists says, '*What is common sense? I can't define it. But in this work you need lots of different abilities; communication, willingness, ability to translate requirements into actions. Here common sense means that when an opera arrives in front of me, I immediately think of a few basic but important things. Of course, I know my trade and I know my job. All of that is common sense.*'

Obviously, the 'common sense' referred to here is not the same thing that you, or we, commonly understand by the term. Luckily, they call it 'theatrical common sense' which perhaps gives it enough of a nuance to make the idea more understandable.

We'd like to relate a story that has nothing to do with the theatre. It's about NASA; specifically, about mission control. In *Failure Is Not an Option*, a very interesting book but one somewhat marred by its overbearing American style, Gene Krantz, the legendary mission controller and flight director for the Apollo program, tells us in great detail of his experiences in this programme (as well as two others, the Mercury and Gemini programmes, but this anecdote refers only to Apollo). Exactly what mission control is, and how it's done, is something that Krantz had to come up with during his long and distinguished career in NASA. And, in his case, the answer was that mission control was in charge of all decisions about the development process of each flight.

For example, one of the most important decisions of mission control is whether or not to abort the mission. And it's a decision that has to be taken in a millisecond. Not aborting can lead to the deaths of the crew. On the other hand, aborting when you didn't need to costs a fortune and gets the story in all the papers; something that Krantz's boss hated. Moreover, even Krantz himself realised that the judgement over such a critical situation, necessary to take any decision, should not reside with any one person. A whole host of information must come together to make an informed decision, and one single person is incapable of managing it all. For this reason, he decided to split the decision between various controllers who were in charge of discrete sub-systems. One had responsibility for Saturn (the rocket), another was responsible for achieving orbit and so on. Now, how can they achieve a shared point of view, a common way of solving problems that guarantees coordination?

> **Common sense is the stock of knowledge necessary to solve "the majority of problems" that arise in the operation of a system.**

Krantz decided to create an *operating culture* based on *processes* that specified, as far as possible, what needed doing. This meant training the controllers to be in a state of readiness to anticipate, evaluate and take the right decision in the short period of time that they'd have in the event of an emergency. All of these processes culminated in a 'black box' called 'Decision', within which was hidden the process of arriving at a solution. Inevitably, to arrive at that decision – the solution – relied upon the 'common sense' of each of those highly trained controllers.

Can you see the relevant parallels with our theatre? Common sense is the *stock of knowledge* needed to face 'the majority of problems' that can arise in the operation of a system, whether that system is called Theatre or Space Flight. Notice that we said 'face', not 'solve' – we're not dealing with knowledge of control, but of *methodology*. As Carlos called it, *'a kind of structured checklist in one's head...'*

All companies have their own 'common sense', their kit of methodologies that the participants must take with them wherever they go in order to deal with their work in a coordinated and satisfactory manner.

Conclusions

In this chapter, we have seen that an essential function of a manager is to *solve problems* and to create an environment in which everybody can solve them with a common purpose. That's how you're going to get everybody to do what we've called *'getting people to do'*.

We've defined *knowledge* as the capacity to resolve a certain type of problem. We've proposed JIT training (*Just In Time*) focussed on gaining knowledge to look for specific solutions, and we've also proposed bringing back, albeit modified and adapted, the Socratic apprentice system.

Finally, we've defined the 'common sense' of a company as the stock of knowledge necessary to coordinate the solution to many of the problems that can arise in the normal, and abnormal, course of business.

We'll finish this chapter with a few questions that might help the reader to reflect on some salient points:

- What do your people do? Do they know how to *get people to do*? What's standing in their way?
- What problem-analysis methodologies do your people have? Are they learning to solve problems?
- And you, how do you focus your management responsibilities? What problems do you solve?
- How do you see training? Is its purpose to increase productivity?
- How do you achieve the sharing of informal knowledge?
- What is the content of your company's common sense? What actions are you taking to develop this?

VII
The Operational Dream and a Five-Star Service

We'll delve now into trying to understand how a service is conceived, and how Operational systems are designed in order to provide that service. To develop efficiency in Operations, one requires a thorough understanding of these activities. In our case, we're trying to see how the Teatro Real came up with them, and what structure they take. We will verify that conceiving an Operational Dream comes before making it a reality. What is an Operational Dream? It's the realisation, in broad strokes, of the features that an Operational system must have as a function of the service that it's going to provide. That is to say, you can have the idea of the service you want to provide, but at some point you have to look at the bigger picture of how that service must be constructed. The Operational Dream is, as the name implies, a dream. A dream of how you're going to construct a service. It's the intermediate step between the dream and the Operational reality. Very few companies have Operational Dreams and, if they do have them, very few have the opportunity of putting them into practice. In the Teatro Real they did have them, and they did put them into practice. They were able to do all that they hadn't been able to do previously. It's like leaving behind a world of frustration and finally being able to make the dream come true.

Another critical matter in the design of a service that we tackle in the next two chapters is that of resources and their provenance. Specifically, we're talking about the pros and cons of using your own resources, or third parties. Operations books say that the differentiating aspects should always be internal, part of the company. But here we'll see a different view. The differentiators or core competencies actually don't need to belong to the business. They can be internal or external. Perhaps an opera theatre doesn't need its own orchestra? Indeed, in the Teatro Real the orchestra is subcontracted. The key is to behave as if it were your own resource. By adequately managing the three levels of the Golden Triad, your contribution to the competitiveness of the company is assured.

We will see, in the next two chapters, how a service is conceived, and what effect it can have on the implementation of a different Operational method.

The subject of this chapter is to explore the idea of the Operational Dream. For this, we will try to understand in general terms how the Teatro Real was conceived as an opera theatre, who are the clients of the theatre and what are the resources they use to be able to provide the necessary service.

Daniel, how did the Teatro Real, as it is today, come about? What was your dream?

In 1987, José Luis Tamayo was named Operations Director of the Teatro Real. The idea was to convert an old theatre into a new and modern opera theatre. José Luis called me immediately. I was the first person to start work in the Teatro Real. And then they started the building work... I hate bricks, I don't care whether the wall is here or there. Anyway, he continued on the technical management side, and I took charge of organising the human side. We were a fantastic team, with a great understanding between us.

Tamayo had a very clear vision of what he wanted to achieve with the Teatro Real. The first day of work, he said to me 'Look, here we're going to do what we've always wanted to do, in all the theatres we've ever worked in. All the things we've every moaned about, not enough signage, the emergency doors not working properly, poor access for the trucks, the seamstress not here on time, the coffee machine's on the blink... everything, Daniel, everything.'

We had the chance to do everything exactly the way we wanted. At various stages we were gleaning information from the experts, from here and there. We put it all together in a cocktail shaker, and out came the Teatro Real. It was making the impossible possible: making this theatre the theatre we'd always wanted but never had.

And do you both still have that dream?

Yes! In fact, very few of the people have changed. Well, one person left, but that was to become the Technical Director of the Español theatre. Those who've remained have continued growing. For example, Carlos started as Stage Manager, and now he's Assistant to the management. The core of the group is the same as when we started, and all the people that have joined since have joined with the same ideology, if I can put it like that.

How did you make the dream a reality?

There are two worlds here. One world is the production: making the set. But then there's another world; giving the artist what the artist wants. This world, the world of service, must be like a five-star hotel. Availability, professionalism, thinking in advance about things, all of this is a part of it. The mission of the Teatro Real is to be an artistic flagship, a world reference. For this, everything has to be five-star. When you go to a five-star hotel, you expect every last detail to be taken care of. The tiniest detail must be managed with care and elegance. Well, here it's the same. All the details must contribute to the artistic product, to the work of art that we're creating. To achieve this, an important function is to locate and channel all the talent towards the end result. I'm talking about understanding my artists. And I'm not only referring to the set and costume designers. I'm surrounded by talent! The props people, the hairdressers, wardrobe...they're all valuable artisans. All of this talent needs to come together, and be apparent in the end result, the product. If not, we're wasting time and money, and we'd be better off buying everything in from the outside.

Our guideline is a five-star hotel. Things have to be clean, the service level has to be very high and things have to be done well. An example – Oscar, the Stage Manager, has to prepare a preliminary set design. We want, as a policy of the theatre, that this 'pre-design' is as close as possible to the final set that it's the best pre-design in the world. We talked about this once, years ago, and have never mentioned it since. He's achieved this on his own since then. In fact, sometimes you have to say to him 'Whoa, take it easy, don't put every last detail!' But as he's always there at all the rehearsals in the rehearsal room, he knows as well as anyone that the better the pre-design is, the better life is for everyone – life will be calmer, because you won't have the Stage Manager saying 'and what happens here then?' or 'where are the stairs supposed to go?' No, Oscar will put the stairs in the pre-design, and everything will be clear. There are some things that you need to say only once, then never again, full stop.

Another example. If a soprano has been singing for 20 minutes straight, and she goes into the wings before her next cue, what should you do? Well, the 'done thing' is to move over towards her and ask 'would you like some water?' And always have someone from wardrobe to help her or to fix her hair. This is the kind of attention from a five-star hotel. Of course, it's much easier if you've got the resources. But it's also about good manners. You don't need to be rich, you should still behave like that. I've seen theatres that perhaps don't have so much money, but still they love their work so much they still pay attention to these kinds of details. In a five-star theatre, when a singer comes off, there's always a Stage Manager, someone from wardrobe, someone waiting with a glass of water and someone else to dab away the sweat. In the majority of theatres, the singer is looked after by their husband, wife, partner, or whoever, who waits in the wings. And sometimes they have to go to the dressing room to have some water, but at least they get some.

I have to foresee that problems will occur. If a Stage Director comes up to me and says 'get rid of that Stage Manager; he doesn't understand me', I have a problem. This is another detail of those five stars...if I provide an excellent Stage Manager, who gives a good service, then the Stage Director will be happy.

So, in fact, your customers are not the audience members?

Absolutely right. If I worry about the public and not about my internal customer, I'd decorate the seats with braid and individual air-conditioning, anything it took to make them comfortable. But if the product you sell is bad, then all of that would count for nothing. This is the fundamental problem of theatre directors – they think more about the externals than they do about what they have in their own 'house'. For me, the most important is to make a good product, and see that it's delivered well to the client.

Let's say that the client is the Stage Director. He talks, good and bad, with the Stage Manager. He asks him for things and he moans about other things. And if our Stage Manager doesn't sort things out, then the Stage Director will do what a hotel guest would do: 'No, no, I want to speak to the Hotel Manager', won't he? Here the equivalent would be 'Right, now I want to speak to the Operations Director'. And this must never, ever happen. We give our Stage Managers the time and the people to enable them to take the initiative and to give the right response at all times. This is his function; it's what he's supposed to do and what he has the authority to do. This is what Stage Managers do! And this is the service mentality that we want to have towards our clients.

Do you have other clients?

Well, here in Operations Management, no. But the theatre does, yes. Apart from the public, the most obvious, the theatre has other clients. For the theatre, the [Spanish] state is also a client. The state subsidises the theatre's activities to maintain a cultural launch-pad that can show the modern face of Spain to the world. The management interprets the wishes of the state, that it wants the Teatro Real to offer a wide spectrum of shows, and sometimes that includes swimming against the tide by programming works that are considered to have great potential but the paying public doesn't appreciate.

There are also many companies, particularly the sponsors, who reserve boxes here at the Teatro Real that they use to entertain guests or to close deals. The operas get an average attendance of 96.7 per cent, which is extremely high for the prestigious events we put on, and is way above the majority of the rest of the world's opera theatres. For concerts the attendance declines somewhat; something like 93 per cent. And for the musical evenings (such as recitals, oratories, concert versions of operas), the attendance is quite low – around 67 per cent. The speed of ticket sales also depends on the type of event. Italian opera has a huge demand and tickets sell out quickly. By contrast, Wagner[1] sells much more slowly.

---

[1] Richard Wagner, nineteenth century German composer. A late Romantic, and excessive in all his activities, his operas are all extremely long, complicated, and difficult to sing. For Wagner, opera was a complete work of art and founded upon

A theatre's reputation in the international press and media is really a word-of-mouth thing. News of the success, and especially the failure, of a production spreads like wild fire among the cognoscenti and reaches the music world through specialist press and trade publications. Music lovers around the world tend to be avid readers of the music press. That's why it's important that the media, whether specialist or not, has good things to say about the Teatro Real.

Therefore, it's not an easy world to navigate in. The Artistic Director, who has the task of planning the season, bases all of that planning on his own personal perceptions. And those perceptions come from his numerous contacts as well as the permanent relationship he maintains with the most important opera theatres of the world.

What external resources do you use to reach your objectives? What type of people do you work with?

The funny thing is that we often work with people who aren't theatre people, because that way you can save money... in theory. But in practice, they know almost immediately that they're working for the theatre. That happens because you start to change their lives. Making windows is one thing, because in the end you always cut the frames the same, but when it's for the theatre, things really kick off: this bit's eighty, that bit's eighty-one, another bit's eighty-one and a half, and another one is seventy-nine, and on top of that they call you to open up on Saturday because something's happened and, then, not surprisingly, the guy starts to realise who the client is and the next time he'll try to stick the price up.

Using resources in the Teatro Real

The majority of the world's theatres have their own fairly stable companies, typically made up of the orchestra, the chorus, the corps de ballet and support staff for the shows (ushers, ticket sellers and so on). In the Teatro Real, all of those

---

almost all the other arts. In his operas, he tried to create a brand type of German mythology, with gods, knights, valkyries and other more or less colourful beings that defy logic in pursuit of their superhuman afflictions. Wagner was the creator and greatest exponent of a new musical language, characterised by the avoidance of expected chords, which results in endless musical phrases that roll on and on, seemingly without end. He was also responsible for introducing the *leitmotiv* or *leitmotif,* literally meaning 'leading motif', in which each character has a recurring piece of music that is associated with them, and the action is reflected in the music just as the music is reflected in the action. Wagner tends not to leave anyone indifferent – people either hate him or love him, with many of the latter group treating his annual festival in Bayreuth as a sort of pilgrimage. The father of one of the current authors used to say 'I like Wagner's music. When it's played softly, I go to sleep. The worst bit is that I'm very quickly woken up again by them banging on the drums like they want to deafen me'.

mentioned are subcontracted, and some of the world's other leading theatres do something similar. The most famous case is the Vienna opera, whose orchestra is the Viennese Philharmonic. The Teatro Real contracts the Orquesta Sinfónica de Madrid *for a set number of hours and instrumentalists per year. The names of the musicians are not specified, so the orchestra's own management decides who will play and when. The chorus is also from the choir of the* Orquesta Sinfónica de Madrid, *who are also contracted for a set number of hours per year with the Teatro Real. The orchestra and choir also have activities, such as concerts, rehearsals and so on outside of their commitments to the Teatro Real.*

In this next part of the conversation, we are joined by Marta Maier, the head of the Stage Managers and the senior person in charge of stage management in the Teatro Real. Marta's an energetic woman in her mid-forties and originally from Germany. She smiles very little, but when she does it's infectious. She expresses herself with great clarity and precision. Her comments below are prefixed by 'MM.' to distinguish them from Daniel's, marked 'DB.'.

Is it complicated managing so many subcontractors?

DB.   You have to co-ordinate the timetables. I don't do that; it's done by the Artistic Management of the Teatro Real – they co-ordinate all the artists. It needs to be programmed carefully, because there are days when the chorus is there, and days when they can't be due to their trade agreements. The technicians and the orchestra also have their own trade agreements, and that makes it really important to co-ordinate these three groups ... they have three completely separate and distinct trade agreements! The most comprehensive is the technicians' one. We have people here from eight in the morning until twelve at night. But the chorus also has its problems, its particular arrangements and agreements. If they have a wardrobe check, if they have a music class, if they're performing elsewhere ... all of this counts towards their maximum working hours and you have to watch out for that.

The basic idea is these groups contribute to the prestige of the theatre. It's well known in the trade that the average artistic quality of a show depends essentially on the orchestra. Therefore the relationship with the orchestra is a very close one and requires tight communication, because it's an intrinsic part of our operations and our service. MM. The communication with the orchestra is always through their Director. There's a camera that's always focused on the maestro while he's conducting, so that the singers can see him on the screens.

On the Director's music stand there's a red light and a green one. The maestro arrives, greets the public, turns to the orchestra and when the green light goes on, then he can start. If you want him to stop, you have to put on the red light. We tell them all 'if the red light goes on, even in the middle of an opera, stop immediately.' It's the only way to communicate with the orchestra during a performance, putting that red light on, but sometimes the maestro is so engrossed in conducting that he doesn't see it – even if we've all noticed that the singer is choking, he might also have to see it before the spell releases him!

But if nobody says anything, the maestro continues...?

MM.   Of course, if you don't say anything... but our only means of telling him to stop is by switching on that red light. He also has a telephone but, really, we're not going to call it – can you imagine him picking up the phone?! That phone was used once by Maestro García Navarro,[2] who'd get really worked up if you stopped him. He had to stop one time during I don't know which opera, and immediately he started getting agitated, and snatched up the phone. 'WHAT? WHAT'S GOING ON?' Well, we explained to him what the problem was and in the end he just said 'ok, ok.'

DB.   The singers are the least important. A performance with good singers and a bad orchestra is much worse than one with mediocre singers and a good orchestra. The orchestra, by framing and driving the voices, brings out the best in them and improves the quality of the less talented singers.

MM.   The chorus doesn't have such an important role, and nor does the corps de ballet but, nevertheless, in both cases it's essential to maintain quality at the highest level possible. The chorus has been working with us for four years now; it's got to the stage where we all know each others' names.

What other things do you subcontract or hire?

DB.   One example is the wardrobe. For example, we hire costumes from a costumier company called *Sastrería Cornejo*. For *Don Giovanni* we needed to hire military dress from the Spanish civil war, but no problem – this costumier has maybe more than a million garments! They've been going for over a century, and they have warehouses and warehouses full of costumes.

The ushers are from an external provider, who is contracted by the management of the Teatro Real. It tends to be the same company year after year, but they still have to submit to the same rigorous principles of public contracting. The ticket sellers are also from an external company, although each year they tend to be the same people. Learning the characteristics of the Teatro Real's shows and ticket systems is not an easy task; so it is made simpler if there's some continuity of staff.

MM.   The treatment of the corps de ballet is somewhat different. When we need to prepare a dance piece for a particular opera, we hire dancers specifically for the purpose. Then we put together the corps, who will participate in the production, and later that corps is disbanded. DB. The Teatro Real doesn't have any singers at all on staff. All the singers, from the leads on down, are brought in 'from the market' for each production.

---

[2] Born Valencia, 1941. A fine Director of Spanish orchestras, he was the Artistic Director of the Teatro Real in its early days.

VIII
Achieving a Five-Star Service

In the preceding chapter, we saw how the Teatro Real became, for our protagonists, the realisation of a dream. We've also seen that they describe their service as 'a five-star service' and discovered who the customer of Operations Management really is – sorry, but it's not you. You're far off in the distance, perhaps reclining at the back of the auditorium or in a VIP box. For you to experience this five-star service, you'd need to fade away and materialise in the body of someone close to Operations.

We've also seen that many of the people with whom the audience comes into contact are actually not part of the Teatro Real, but are subcontracted. How is it possible that many of these resources, critical for providing good service, are not in-house? What value does this bring? We'll look at this, and offer our impressions and thoughts, in the next few pages.

The significance that the Teatro Real has for our protagonists

We need to start analysing the concept of operational dream. The *operational dream* is what some would call the specifications list of an Operating system, and it's the intermediate step between the germ of an idea and its operational inception.

Clearly, the Teatro Real was an operational dream of people who, in their working lives, had come up against certain obstacles that were, while small in appearance, very irritating, and these people wanted to make those obstacles disappear. It's the typical dream of a person who is *close to Operations*, catches sight of some failure of shortcoming, and wants to make sure it never happens again...and this is the way to focus your energy on those elements most relevant to getting results. It's 'Ah, right, if we can get this out of the way...' or 'What if we went back to the beginning and...'

What is your operational dream?

What is interesting about the 'Tamayo-Bianco' focus is that they defined the dream, the specifications list, as *'things we mustn't do'*. It's a specification of the things they want to avoid. The moment of defining the dream is too soon in the creation process to say *what we should have* because we're still missing some basic elements, some basic knowledge. But with talented people, who have experience and knowledge of other situations, it is possible to enumerate the things that have bothered us before and that we don't wish to fall foul of again. For example, 'in the Teatro Real we don't want to communicate by a series of grimaces and frowns during a performance'. Or, 'there's no prompter and we need one', or 'the emergency doors didn't work properly at my last place' and so on. In fact, it is a useful focus of people experienced in the sector that they can point out cases (i.e. theatres) in which can be found evidence of those very things that should be avoided.

And you, dear reader, do you have an operational dream for your company, and for each area of responsibility? What is it that you shouldn't have? Have you ever thought of sitting down with your people and listing all those things that impede the delivery of good service and that, if you could start again with a blank slate, they'd avoid?

A friend of ours says that in every company there should be a Director of Destruction, in charge of eliminating, destroying and generally getting rid of anything that does not serve the greater good, or that has become a hindrance. We're not sure whether there really should be such a post, but wouldn't it be advisable to take an occasional moment to reflect on these things. And, if you prefer to put it in a more positive light, *'All those things that we've always wanted to have but were afraid to ask for'.*

A five-star service

The image of five-star service conveys the idea of attention to detail, looking after the operation, and getting results. And, above all, achieving the desired result of the client. The image of these 'five stars' is a way of formulating the dream that can be shared and enthused about by all the people involved. We know intuitively what a five-star hotel is, or at least we think we do. And we know that to enjoy one is increasingly difficult and expensive. It is an interesting metaphor, particularly as a method of communication, but it is no more than that – a metaphor. And there's no room for these in Operations; when we want to get down to the details, it's an inadequate tool.

Luckily, our protagonists intuitively understand what a five-star service means, and they translate it into *care for detail* and

| What is the *'spirit'* emanating from your company? |

anticipating the needs of their internal clients. Daniel and his team are in a highly developed Operational Culture, and that's why this five-star concept has been adopted and conveyed in such a natural manner.

Logically, to implant these ideas there have to be processes and procedures. At the Teatro Real, we see they have more than just these, however; they have a *spirit*, a work philosophy. 'Here you have to do things well', says

Daniel. This is not achieved by saying, but by doing. Daniel and his team have learnt this, intuitively. Really, they've never stopped to consider the implications of their actions. For them, there are no hours, no obstacles, just an obsession – to do things well. And this is translated into their style of management, which we'll look at more closely in Chapter XXII.

And now we turn to you, the reader, and ask, what is the spirit that exists in your company? Because it does exist, even if you haven't established it. There are some companies that want only to earn money, and others that want to change and innovate. Others simply want to survive, while some call for decentralisation and initiative. Nevertheless, in these latter companies the verb most often used is 'control'. Are you consistent or are you, like these, a bit contradictory?

Who the client really is, and how to make them happy

> **What are the five critical Moments of Truth of your service provision?**

There is not even the shadow of a doubt about who the Teatro Real technical management's client is: he or she is the Stage Director. Yes, 'he or she' – even though Daniel hasn't mentioned it, there are some very illustrious female names in the business, such as Núria Espert, whose portrait hangs on the wall of Daniel's office. The Stage Directors are the people who receive the service.

Daniel knows his client, knows what they need, and helps to turn their dream into reality. These are the interactions with the client that we call MTs, Moments of Truth,[1] and these delimit the service relationship. There are many moments of truth, but it is essential to identify those that are critical, in which you're 'playing for keeps'. How to do this is easy: there is an intuitive method. Get together with your closest colleagues and get each person to list their five critical MTs. Then, put all the MTs in a list and vote for them, maintaining a discussion of why (if) each one is critical. From there you can distil the five critical MTs of your service provision.

Identifying the MTs is necessary, but it's not the end of the story. Daniel says 'I have to *foresee* that problems will occur'. You have to foresee possible problems and act before they happen, not afterwards. To foresee problems is to understand the current and future needs of the client. Years ago, it was fashionable to talk of 'surprising the client', but don't worry, this isn't it. The message is something different, but very clear. *Listen to your client* and try to catch sight of problems before they appear. Get to know your clients in such a way that you don't need futile surveys that serve no purpose. Ask yourself, what do I really use these surveys for? Do they really give me any accurate

---

[1] MTs are the interactions between a company's Operations and the client.

information about the reality of my service? Or do I use them only to quiet my manager's conscience?

Don't trust *statistics*. Statistics only provide summaries, by definition, in terms of the most representative clients, the most *normal* and, therefore, contain barely any useful information. The interesting client is one who has something to say, not one who is just normal. Some companies are beginning to discount surveys and going back to directly asking not just the client, but also the people providing the service to that client. And when they do ask a question, it's often centred on the aspects of service that the client ends up praising. This is how to understand your differential, that which some people call your differential competencies, or *core competencies*. And, once you understand what your client wants and what you can give to the client, go that stage further if you can. Be prepared to *give more* that the client asked for. Of course, being prepared to give doesn't mean actually giving; it simply means being able to do so if necessary.

> **Do you know who your crusader clients or your lead users are?**

Clients don't just value service; they also praise it and recommend it, and these are called *crusader clients*, as they are a source of recommendation whereby your business can attract new clients. Another type of client is the *lead users*,[2] so called because they are the most innovative clients, and can be used as idea providers, by trying out new services on them, evaluating a new service or testing out new ideas. Go for these individual clients, and forget the 'normal' and average ones!

> **Do you impose or propose? solutions?**

Getting to know your client and what they want is the first step, but the second step is solving their problems and offering them solutions. In the Teatro Real, they negotiate, listen, sympathise, understand and propose. They don't impose; they formulate technical solutions that are viable. They look after the details and they suggest ideas to solve problems.

In your company, what do you do? Do you impose solutions? It's a disgrace, but the current trend is to do just that, leaving the client helpless. But perhaps this will drastically change in the future. Movements of rebellion are just beginning among certain switched-on clients, sick of the abusive actions of closed cartels. Are we seeing the beginning of a client revolution? Are they learning to use the power they possess, to demonstrate their dissatisfaction with what they see as unreasonable terms? This seems to be beginning in France, a country where the idea of the voice and power of the people is deep-seated.

---

[2] Term used by Eric Von Hippel.

Do you have to be a resource millionaire in order to deliver a five-star service?

Specialised literature in this field suggests that all the critical areas of a company should belong to the company, and should not be outsourced. In the Teatro Real, the orchestra, the chorus, the corps de ballet and the singers are all subcontracted. Does this mean that maybe these functions are not critical to the Teatro Real? Well, clearly nobody can afford to have Plácido Domingo on the permanent payroll. That'd be like, for example, if a company needed a marine expert from time to time and hired Jacques Cousteau as a permanent staff member. In a company like the Teatro Real where, as Daniel says, 'you need the support of a lot of talented people to produce a work of art', all of this would lead you to retain a whole host of resources, *just in case* you need them. But the orchestra, the chorus, the ticket vendors and the ushers?!

> **Do you need to own all the critical service activities?**

Let's start with these last-mentioned, the ushers. The ushers at the Teatro Real are probably the only ushers in the world who don't expect any tip. It's easy to see that they're very happy with their work; they're friendly and always ready to help the public. Their MTs are positive and the customers appreciate this. What is their secret? Simply a good selection process and, on their part, placing an extremely high value on the work they're doing. The ushers at the Teatro Real are typically people who are studying theatre, who love the theatre and who really appreciate the opportunity to work in one of the leading theatres of the world.

First consideration: Can I give rules to my subcontractors so that they achieve the goals that I desire? Can I manage, by supporting their efforts, to achieve a mutually beneficial situation, a *win-win* situation? The operators of the AVE, Spain's high-speed train, think of it that way. The staff on board, at least those who are customer-facing, are subcontracted...but the company that manages the AVE has set some very clear rules in the staff selection and training processes that assure the desired level of quality. For example, they train their people on mock-ups of the trains. Their training is real, serving food and attending to the public (not *public* public, but people nonetheless).

Let's continue now with the orchestra. That the orchestra is subcontracted is even stranger, given that this body of people is absolutely critical for the end result, the delivery to the public. A good orchestra can help to cover up other weaknesses, we were told earlier. Any lack of cohesion and integration can spell disaster. So, wouldn't you feel inclined to totally control them, to make them your own, precisely *because* they're so important? If not, let's look at something else that Marta Maier, the Head of the Stage Managers, told us: 'In the Monte Carlo ballet

> **Should you rethink your policy on subcontracting?**

once, one of the musicians hadn't turned up. They had to wait for him because he was one of the key members. They had to delay the performance and wait, with the audience in the theatre, for him to arrive. I don't know whether he was ill and they were trying to find someone else, or what, but finally they had to give up on the evening and empty the theatre. And you can imagine what that was like – the bad feeling, the disappointment...'

Second consideration: Is it really necessary to 'own' all the activities that are critical to your service? Or can we start to think in terms of an *extended company*, in which the service is divided between distributors, providers and even clients? We think it's really worth thinking about. At least it might help to come up with some new alternatives. But be careful – there is a trap. The orchestra is not free to come and go as they please. There is a rehearsal schedule, and every last detail is taken care of. Let's see, for example, something that Daniel told us: 'This year we've changed the music stands. The orchestra complain if they don't have strong enough lights in the music stands, but at the same time I need them to have less light, not more, because it affects the view of the stage. Knowing that there are rehearsals at 1600, I go down to the auditorium and have a look. I'm there every time, just showing my face... and that actually provides me with a fairly exhaustive quality control'.

Are you achieving co-ordinated solutions with your subcontractors?

At the start of the Teatro Real's latest incarnation, they were faced with the difficult choice of whether to have all these activities in-house or subcontracted out. They took this decision in a rational manner, taking into account certain classic criteria that they admit were, and still are, in the light of more recent experience, questionable. Criteria associated with the working environment and the availability of service around. The result has been a situation, now fairly consolidated, that works very well, perhaps because of unexpected reasons that have nothing to do with the original thoughts that led to the decisions. Some aspects that have made the decision to subcontract turn out well include the way they can deal with problems with subcontractors, mutual learning and the integration of subcontractors into the company. In concrete, they are managing the *Efficiency, Attractiveness and Unity* of the company in tandem with the subcontractors. The way they manage these three dimensions, and not the narrow criteria originally suggested, has led to the current excellent results.

Should you rethink your policy on subcontracting?

Third and last consideration: How can your company get the problems and knowledge to flow between parties, and thus add value to the service? How can you manage the Golden Triad with your subcontractors?

It could be said that the Teatro Real has had a lot of *luck*. Without knowing it, they manage their subcontractors in exactly the right way to obtain the best results. But it could easily have been the other way round, and have resulted in a spectacular failure. Upon analysis, it turns out that the success of the subcontracting actually has very little to with classic criteria, and much to do with management style. Hallelujah!

Conclusions

In this chapter, we've seen how, in the first place, each company must define its operational dream. The *operational dream* is the definition, in broad strokes, of how a system of Operations should work in order to deliver the desired service. We then analysed the need to identify who are your *real clients*, not just the end customer. And this implies the need to understand those clients and stay one step ahead of their needs. Finally, we've seen that it actually *matters very little* whether a *competency* is *core* or not for the company to get the maximum benefit from subcontracting. The important thing is to manage the subcontractors according to the Golden Triad; that is by supporting their Efficiency, Attractiveness and Unity.

We'll finish this chapter with a few questions to help the reader reflect on a few relevant points:

- Have you ever sat down with your collaborators to define your operational dream?
- Should you provide a five-star service?
- Who really is the customer of your service? Do you know who your *crusader clients* are, and do you know what to do to get those who are almost *crusader clients* to become complete 'crusaders'?
- Have you evaluated what core activities you should own, and which you can subcontract?
- How can you manage the 'Golden Triad' with your subcontractors, to ensure the excellence of your service?

IX
Operations

Operational efficiency, after the Operational Dream, is a function of designing its structure in adequate detail. Unfortunately, in Operations every last detail needs to be specified. It is not enough to discuss or make grandiloquent promises. How many HP should this engine have, and where should it be mounted in the car? How should it start and stop? And after that comes a long list of etceteras. In this task, with so many decisions, one runs the risk of losing focus; that the presence of so many trees will obscure one's view of the woods. José Luis Tamayo was entrusted with two main tasks – define the dream, and then make it happen. In this chapter, we're going to look at the second of these tasks.

Designing the Operational structure of the Teatro Real was a long journey involving a lot of problem-solving and implementation of those solutions. But, strangely, it was achieved without excessive constraints on either time or resources.

We'll see how Tamayo essentially discovered a methodology based on six variables. This methodology allows problems in the Operational system to be solved in the most applicable manner. The use of already-existing knowledge helped him to come up with the Operational structure in a systematic way, thus reducing the need for research and investigation to a minimum.

The next two chapters take a closer look at these concepts.

José Luis Tamayo is a young man of some 50 summers, tall and thin. He dresses casually and, when he speaks, he expresses himself in a very reasoned way. It's obvious that here is a man who knows what he's talking about, and that he loves explaining things to interested amateurs. In addition, he demonstrates a deep knowledge of technology; something fairly rare in a 'man of letters'. In this interview, José Luis was very relaxed while remembering, with obvious pleasure, his time as the Operations Director of the Teatro Real.

Now, you *are* a man of the theatre ...

Yes, when you live in a powerful family environment dominated by my uncle,[1] who was in his day a star of the theatre, you become imbued with it. I lived in Granada, which is where I was born. My uncle was born in Granada, and my family lived in Granada. In those days he was the famous relative and he used to take me, when I was three or four, to see rehearsals, set building, wardrobe ... I studied in the Ramiro de Maeztu Institute[2] and I remember one time when we had extra holidays, because the other schools held their exams too. My mother gave me 5 pesetas[3] a week back then, and that wasn't enough for anything during these holidays. Then the second week, I asked her for another 5 pesetas, and my mother said 'Work'. So I did – my uncle stuck me in one of his companies that was touring locally, and that's how I started to work, as a technician, every summer. Later, when I was studying Humanities, my uncle had an Assistant Manager who'd been with him all his life, and who managed the entire company. They had some kind of problem and found themselves in the middle of the tour without an assistant. He asked me to help out with their predicament by stepping in and taking over. Whether I liked it or not, there I was, bang! Twenty-two years old and all of a sudden pretty much directing the company of 60 players, plus orchestra, plus I don't know who else ...

From there he properly made me the Assistant Manager. I worked with my uncle until it dawned on me that I couldn't continue on that road because he would become an insufferable millstone around my neck, so I left and started to look for work ... and Marsillach,[4] who was at the time directing the Centro Dramático Nacional (National Drama Centre) called me. But my stint with him lasted only a year, because the following year Núria Espert,[5]

---

[1] José Luis's uncle was José Tamayo, one of the most famous post-war Stage Directors. He inaugurated the Theatre of the Zarzuela and brought the amazing voice of Alfredo Kraus to the world. He also dared to stage several major shows that, in their day, were very novel in Spanish theatre. For example, in the *Sagrada Familia*, Barcelona's iconic cathedral, he staged a Eucharistic play by *Calderon de la Barca*, with set designs on a truly grand scale.

[2] A prestigious school in the heart of Madrid.

[3] About 2p (just under €0.03c).

[4] Adolfo Marsillach (Barcelona, 1928–2002). A multi-talented artist, actor, writer, Director of theatre, cinema and television. One of the most important people of the Spanish post-war scene, he frequently ran up against pro-Franco aesthetics, censorship and ideology. After *La Transición*, the period following Franco's death when Spain passed from dictatorship to democracy, he was one of the leaders of the Spanish cultural renaissance, and founder of the National Drama Centre. His memoirs, titled *So Close and Yet So Far,* make essential reading for anyone wanting to learn about Spanish post-war society and the history of the Spanish theatre during his lifetime, a history in which he was often the protagonist.

[5] Born in Hospitalet (Barcelona) 1935. She was a great dramatic actress on stage and screen who later became a Stage Director. In 1984, she won the National Theatre

José Luis Gómez[6] and my father came on the scene; my father as Director of Administration. Also, with Núria Espert came, for the first time, *el Lliure,*[7] the company directed by Lluís Pasqual. They came simply as a guest company, invited to do a small season, and that's where I met them. I had a great rapport with them, and I got to know Lluís Pasqual. Eventually, José Luis Gómez left, because they offered him the Teatro Español. So then they called me and named me Technical Director.

Here in Spain there had never been Technical Directors; that position just didn't exist. I remember that my uncle always had two Assistant Directors; one was very smart, cultured, and he knew a lot about the theatre. The other was a bit scruffy and spent all his time on stage doing technical stuff. I think that's where the profession of 'Technical Management' was founded. Later Lluís Pasqual joined the management of the María Guerrero, and he called me to go and be his Technical Director. Back then there were no references one could use for setting up a technical office, as it was a new concept, but there was one thing I understood damned quickly. I thought 'What we need here is someone to work on the technical side, but who also understands the artistic side. I don't have that. For example, when we need to go and source a crown, which is my responsibility, I have no idea what's good and what's bad. I need people who know the artistic side, but who work in technical side. Technicians who know art – a Set Designer, who isn't a practising Set Designer, you know?' And I found one in Barcelona, but one day he came to me and said 'I'm off, I can't do this anymore. I've got to go back to Barcelona; I'm homesick'. And he did. At that time Gerardo Vera, the Set Designer who is now Director of the National Drama Centre, was contracted to design the set for us and, one day, he sent us one of his assistants, a young lad who did the sketches. This lad was Daniel Bianco. We were looking for someone and we said 'Wow, this guy is working in set design, but he also seems interested in working on the technical side'. So we hired him and he was with me for many years.

---

prize. She has done many productions for the Teatro Real and has worked with the majority of Spanish opera theatres.

[6] Born in Huelva, 1940. Initially a cinema actor, he later passed to the theatre. At 19, he went to study in Germany and lived as an exile there until the death of Franco in 1975. In that same year he won the Silver Palm for best actor at the Cannes Film Festival, and the Grand Prize the following year. He has acted in numerous productions and is also an excellent Stage Director. He was Co-Director of the National Drama Centre and the Teatro Español.

[7] The indirect influence of Barcelona's Theatre Lliure appears to have been of great importance in the genesis and structure of the present Teatro Real. The theatre's Technical Directors, specifically, had close connections with people at the Lliure, especially with Lluís Pasqual, one of its first Directors. Ever-present in the background of the Lliure is the figure of its founder, Fabià Puigserver, one of the key figures in the evolution of Spanish theatre during the 1970s and 1980s.

I later left the María Guerrero, when I felt we'd done just about all we'd set out to do. If I come to do a job, then once that job's done there's really nothing left to do. But Lluís Pasqual insisted 'Now we have to enter another phase'. He stayed for another year, with Daniel. There was a change of government and, here in Spain, when there's a change of government, a lot of the senior positions in public companies and institutions tend to change too – there are a lot of political appointments, directly or indirectly – and either they move people around or they throw them out. I, meanwhile, had started a company making machinery for the theatre.

I knew about the plan to reopen the Teatro Real – people were speaking about it all the time. I didn't know the place; I'd never been. Then one day I got a call from the Culture Minister, and he said 'Look, the Teatro Real is about to reopen; would you be interested?' My instinct was to say 'yes' immediately, but I said I'd think about it.

Well, of course, I started at the Teatro Real and quickly thought 'I'm never going to make it!' You see, to go from a theatre like the María Guerrero, which was the biggest I'd ever worked in, to suddenly finding yourself in the Teatro Real, it's like you've been making little transistor radios all your life and then somebody asks you to build a space station.

Why the María Guerrero; is it a traditional 'hemp house' theatre, as they say?

Ha, yes, at that time, when I went to work with Lluís Pasqual, it was a 'hemp house' – all movement of heavy loads, such as lighting and set, was literally operated by people pulling on ropes; it was all sweat and blisters. The great technological revolution we instigated was to introduce counter-weighted fly systems. These had been used throughout Europe since the nineteenth century, but they still hadn't arrived in Spain. At the María Guerrero it was purely a question of rope and muscle, so the counter-weights seemed like cutting-edge technology! Basically, you have a bar here, and a cradle there. You put the things you want to move here and the counter-weights over there, and suddenly it's easy to move scenery and lights.

When I arrived at the Teatro Real, I had an advantage: there was no doubt about exactly what we were going to be doing at the theatre. By that I mean that now, working in the theatre, we ask each other if we'll have to sort out the tennis finals, a Formula One championship, a golf tournament or something like that – it's a joke, but these days the theatres can be used for practically anything. These days most things need to be useful for everything, and not specifically for one purpose.

Well, in the Teatro Real it was always clear that this was a theatre for opera. But we couldn't work 'flat', which is what most modern operas do, where all the necessary elements are on a single horizontal plane, making changes very easy. Instead, we had to have what's called 'cruciform theatre'. This means that you take the visible stage, that which the audience sees, and you put another free area of the same dimensions behind it, a backstage area that we call the *chácena*, then a shoulder to the right and another to the left. It forms the shape of a cross, hence the name 'cruciform'. Everything on the visible stage can move up or down, backwards or forwards, left or right. It's the most traditional system, and it's very 'clean' for the audience.

To work 'flat' or horizontal is cheaper than in cruciform, but the Teatro Real didn't have space for that. We did study the possibility of doing it once, with the horizontal plane reaching all the way to the streets either side of the theatre, but it was just too much work and, additionally, it would have cut all the traffic in the theatre – anyone wanting to cross the theatre would have had to go up five flights of stairs on one side, then down another five on the other.

So, instead we had the idea of working the *depth* available to us. We built the visible stage, and behind it we put this backstage area, which we call the *chácena*. Beneath the auditorium, there used to be a couple of old rehearsal rooms, but these didn't meet any of the health and safety standards so, with just a few modifications, we were able to adapt them and incorporate them into the stage structure; we call it the *contrachácena*, a sort of below-stage area. And with this additional area we ended up with five spaces: two at the auditorium level and three below. When you're working with a 'flat' horizontal structure, then five spaces means four possibilities, but working in vertical, in cruciform, then five spaces means only three possibilities, because you have to leave a passageway free.

The most difficult thing was understanding the platform system. The upper part, the grid, is the most important part in all theatres. It's fundamental. There's always a grid, then something lifts it up and down, whether operated by ropes, counter-weights, motors or laser beams. At the lower end is always a bar, and from this bar you can hang stuff and raise or lower it. But there's never been a tradition of how to manage this lower part, whether with or without ropes, so there was no precedent.

One of the first big decisions we had to take was to motorise the fly system or not. This was a time of transition and any theatre person would tell you that a motorised fly system was not right for the theatre, it was too 'cold', and that it would never work in the theatre. I love fiddling with cars, my house is like scrap yard full of old car bits and pieces, and I ride a motorbike. So, I thought to myself 'I think we're in the process of evolving – we used to start motorbikes with the kick-starter. Then some came with an electric motor, but they were so unreliable they still needed to include the kick-starter. Finally the electric motor became sufficiently reliable that many bike manufacturers felt comfortable taking away the kick-starter'. So, what happens if the motor breaks down? Same as with a car – you either push or call a tow-truck.

But still they said I was mad for putting in motors. For example, Waagner-Brio, the company that did the preliminary plans for the machinery and a very experienced company in Europe, told us 'What you need to do is have at least three counter-weighted flying bars plus one motorised, for the heavy loads and as a backup'. We didn't understand. If I have a fault one hour before curtain-up, what do I do? Take all the scenery off the bar that doesn't work and stick it on one that does?! And what about the rest of the set-up? This was in no way a viable solution. Furthermore, in these big spaces, there will always come a time when the counter-weight system can't be used for one reason or another. Then what? I can't move five tons by hand, and even if I could use a winch to get it moving, once it was moving it'd be impossible to stop!

Counter-weights work well for loads below 500 or 600 kg. In small theatres, the bars are short and tend to be used for smaller loads. In big theatres, logically, one needs to manage a lot of weight. Set design is a booming business, and every day the sets weigh more and more.

In Europe, we saw some theatres that did have motors, and all of them said to me 'we always try to use the motorised bar; if only all of them were motorised...' So then, going somewhat against the rest of the world, I took the decision to go for a totally motorised system. It was a hard decision.

Without doing any tests?

I'd seen the development of variable speed motors. In the old days, the only type of motor with controllable speed was DC (direct current, as from a battery, which has very little working power); the AC motors (alternating current, as from the mains, and providing a lot of power) were much simpler, but much more difficult to control – they required variations in frequency, and then they made a horrible racket. But, in general, we saw that the whole system of speed control was improving greatly and, sure enough, today we can control the speeds with an incredible degree of finesse – we're talking about speeds of 1 mm per second, which is so slow and so quiet that you practically have to touch the bar to see if it's moving or not. With this new generation of motors, for example, you can contemplate effects such as 'This piece rises gradually throughout the entire first act', same as you can with the lights when you say 'sunrise lasts the whole of the first act'. The lights start at 0 and go up to 100 per cent. One problem with this generation of motors is that, at minimum speed and maximum load, they get incredibly hot, which limits their Operational time at these conditions to about 15 minutes. Either that or get refrigerated motors, which is possible inside a room but not in the theatre grid, because they make too much noise. So, the only solution is to install servomotors, or motors of a much higher rating that you need. This is feasible, but a servomotor costs ten times as much as a conventional motor of equivalent rating.

And all of this is controlled digitally, with computers?
Because 15 years ago that surely wasn't the case ...

They said to me 'Have you really thought about what you're doing?', and I had to say to them 'We're going to do a test; we're going to buy one counter-weighted fly and one motorised. And I challenge you to tell the difference'. Sure enough, when they saw it in action, they accepted it.

The philosophy of the theatre is that the flying system must always be variable speed. But, strangely, variable speeds are used relatively rarely. You have a large amount of money invested, just in case, but you don't typically use them. And, in proportion, it's even more expensive when you're on tour because then, if the theatre that you're going to doesn't have the infrastructure to move the bars either by counter-weight or by motor, then you need to take a lot of equipment with you to be able to do this on-site, and this takes a lot of time and money to do. Only when you have to adapt to something time-critical, some movement, a musical tempo, or an actor reciting some lines, do you need the bar to be programmable at variable speeds. Many systems have been invented for this, but all are still hugely expensive. Once they're cheap, nobody will argue. It'll be like lighting – at first it was all expensive, and we'd say 'ok, we need about 700 connection points, but I'm going to have a dimmer at every point because they're expensive; so we'll use a patch instead.' That is, we'd connect the dimmers to only those connections that required them in a given performance. It's a lot of work. But then came the day when the cost of dimmers had come down sufficiently that it was cheaper to have a dimmer at every connection than work with the patches, because patching is still a skilled, manual task. Anyway, the same will happen with motors. It hasn't yet, but it will ...

Did you have the authority to decide that
everything should be motorised?

Well, let me explain that a bit. There was a reasonable investment made in the Teatro Real, although it was very poorly publicised. I mean, in relation to the various other European theatres of similar specifications that were being restored at around the same time. How did they decide to restore the Teatro Real? Well, they retained the same firm of architects who had worked on the previous conversion to a concert hall. They prepared a budget and the bottom line was that 5,000 million pesetas[8] would do it. So when I arrived, I had that figure in my head, 5,000 million. But nobody had thought about the rest of the building; that the whole thing was going to become a theatre and not split into different functions as it had been until then, with a dance theatre in one bit, a musical theatre in another.... So one day we sat down and we started to come up with our own numbers, home-made, and

---

[8] Approximately €30 million. 166.386 pesetas = €1.

we came to a figure of 19,000 million.[9] Of course the reaction was 'This isn't possible, it can't be!' Then a famous architect, Fernández Alba, came along, had a look at our calculations and said 'More like 22,000 million'.

So, there had been this big political idea to renovate the Teatro Real, provide an auditorium for the National Orchestra, and move out all the other groups, such as the dance school and the school of dramatic arts that had been moved there because, as a concert hall, the building had been half-empty. Well, we need to find places for all these people to go, either short or long term, and only then could we get stuck into the work. This much was clear. So now someone had to decide precisely how far we were going to go in the renovation; someone had to make the bid decision. Nobody was making that decision...so I did! And nobody said yes or no.

But who were you dealing with?

Technically, nobody. I said 'I can't involve other people, because if I'm a genius, then I'll turn out as a genius, and if I'm stupid, then I'll end up looking stupid. There's no filter.' Which is not to deny that had there been a filter it might have turned out better.

There's an old joke – What is a camel? Answer – A camel is a horse designed by a committee of experts. You see, it's a load of good ideas gone wrong. When I arrived, there was a basic architectural project on the table, and in my opinion that project was inadequate. I remember that it was that project that got me caught in a trap – there was a meeting called to discuss the project, and I didn't know the architects were going to be there. And in front of those guys they asked me 'ok, what do you think of it?' On the one hand, I said 'I don't know if I should get involved' and on the other hand, I'm thinking 'well, this is what they're paying me for' and, of course, it was a disaster. The relationship with the architects was really hard for the next 18 months.

The day I arrived at the Teatro Real was the day they were opening the sealed bids for the machinery. It was all specified up-front, and companies were bidding against that specification, around 2,200 million pesetas. And I said to the Director 'This is all wrong.' And he said to me 'ok, but I can only let you go up 20 per cent on the refurbishment and 10 per cent on the settlement, which means you've got 30 per cent over this price to make whatever changes you think necessary.'

The contract for the lighting, which had been with Siemens of Germany, was eventually given to a Spanish company. We had a lot of problems in both countries, due to a lack of understanding, different mentalities and different legal implications that affected the lighting systems we were proposing. In fact, there were two basic systems. One possibility was to leave the lights fixed right from the moment of design, like they do in many

---

[9] About €113 million.

theatres. But of course, there's little or no flexibility there. So we decided to use a method borrowed from television – 'you point and I'll put a spotlight there'. And we did it! It cost a bit more, but it gave us huge flexibility.

No audiovisual system had yet been contracted, and we had to organise everything ourselves. We said to ourselves 'if we're here, then it means we're the co-ordinators and it's us who have to be able to contract everything and integrate it'. So we contracted the machinery from one place, the lighting from another, and the sound system somewhere else. The only thing we all had to do together was the cabling the different installations, because it seemed a mad idea to try to get all that done with various installation engineers all at the same time. We also held 33 different tenders to buy all the bits and pieces the theatre needed; the majority excluding installation. For example, the scaffolding, transport systems, clothes trolleys, lighting trolleys, washing baskets ... the list was endless.

First we made a list of all that we needed. Then we looked at what was already available on the market and what would need manufacturing. Later you have to do the specifications ... and I went through a period of extreme exhaustion. Not through work; in fact I'd never worked so little, but because of the mental strain; it was all so new, so different. I'd come from a theatre where there was very little time between the set design and opening night. There we'd had to have a team on-hand so that the idea could be made reality in just a few weeks. There was no time to evaluate whether the path you were going down was the best or most logical. It was the only path, because you were in a hurry. Pick up the phone, call someone, tell them, 'come on over, close the workshop, work exclusively for me, do me this, make a test, no, change that, do this instead, take that away ...'

Up until then, the longest process or delay that I'd ever suffered in my life was two months, from the time that someone had asked for something to when you could see the results. Your brain had only just got the idea of what it was supposed to be doing by the time it was already done. But at the Teatro Real, when we were facing a decision we were thinking, 'Ok, in 1989 I'm making a decision that I'm not even going to see until 1997. I just cannot imagine it'.

Until that time, the largest amount of money I'd ever spent on one production was 180,000 Euros, and now suddenly I was managing budgets of 35 million – it was a huge leap. I couldn't sleep, and not because I was working too hard – I was leaving work at six every day, something I'd never done before in my life – but because of so much responsibility. The opening seemed a long way off, and there were times when I thought of just walking away. But then I thought, 'Ok, two things can happen. First, I'm never going to know first-hand if everything I've done in the last eight years is good or not, and second, everything that doesn't go right from day one is going to be my fault anyway. So, I prefer to just get on and do things, and if what comes out isn't what was expected, then at least we can have that discussion later. You see what I mean?' And I stayed two years as Technical Director.

During those two years, were you fine-tuning everything?

The Teatro Real had an advantage, apart from the disaster that everybody was talking about and that was time – we had time to spare. We had a meeting with a minister, I don't remember who, but it was in 1991. It was a very serious meeting in his office, with the builders, the architects from the Ministerio De Obras Publicas Y Urbanismo (the Ministry in charge of Public Works) which was also putting in money, and the project architects. And the minister said 'and all of this is viable for 1992?' We were at the beginning of 1991, and they all said 'yes, yes, no problem' because, frankly, if tomorrow they can then come back with a million different excuses for not having reached the target then, really, what did they have to lose? Finally, someone said 'Look, we have here the senior technical boss, he should say something'. And I said 'Well, from my point of view, to achieve what you're talking about, two years is more than I need. Two months is more like it.'

'What do you mean, two months?' they asked me. And I said 'Yes, I can put on a show in the theatre down the road, a football pitch, or in the middle of the bloody road. The Teatro Real doesn't yet have a stage floor? Fine, we'll hire one. No lights? Hire them. No dressing rooms? Hire them. No technicians? Contract them; there are thousands of companies dedicated to that. For me, an opening is easy.' In fact, as an aside, this was demonstrated brilliantly at the Liceo en Barcelona when it burnt down, and they staged a recital in the ruins.

'Getting to that point is no problem for me,' I said, 'Now, minister, please ask these gentlemen if they can organise the seating, the bathrooms, the insurance and so on, so that everybody can come to the theatre and find all the necessary health and safety requirements in place.' The minister looked at everybody and said 'All that's possible, yes?' and these guys started to get all co-operative, saying 'yes, yes, no problem, of course, since you put it like that…' Anyway, we decided to forget the opening date in 1992, which had been the only milestone we'd set and, not having any other milestone in place, time was suddenly in our favour. Additionally, once we'd practically finished the Teatro Real in 1995 or 1996, thereabouts, there were general elections and the opposition party got in. Of course, no new government takes the reins immediately and, with the Teatro Real not being top of the new government's list of priorities, the opening was postponed another season.

What happened during that time? I don't know about in other countries but here it was exactly what you'd expect. You draw up the technical specifications of something, and then you say 'I want 40 of those'. Nobody really tends to look at the details, so then what you ordered appears, but it's got the wrong fittings, or it's the wrong colour, or it's not the material you asked for ... so then you come along, you're in a terrible hurry, and you say 'That's not what we ordered!'

'What do you mean, not what you ordered?'

'Read the order.'

'Wow, you're right. Ok, we'll send it back.'

There were people who, seriously, took two years to bring us the right things. They were going mad because they'd bring the wrong thing again and again, and we'd reject it again and again. We weren't in the usual rush, and this allowed us time to do our homework, hire in the right people by means of proper tests, hold training courses ... by the time we opened we were more than ready. Of course, there's always something crops up when you're doing the ultimate test – doing it for real. Like in any production, no matter how much you rehearse, no matter how long you take to get it in front of an audience, even if it takes 500 rehearsals, it's always going to be touch and go. But at least we had the luxury of finishing the project well – out of all the theatres in Europe, I think ours is the only one to have opened during that decade and remained open. The rest have all had to shut again for one reason or another.

Really? Do many open and then close again?

Oh yes, just look at the Palacio de las Artes in Valencia – they did a concert, believing that everything was all fine, then they've closed again and aren't due to open until next year. In the theatre we've always thought of ourselves as complete botchers and bluffers, all capable of standing on our soapbox and delivering a most important lecture, while the only really serious professionals were the builders, the industrial types. Well, I remember one time a Director of the Lliure just let rip, because he was a man of the theatre, and he blew his top at the suppliers: 'You people are disgraceful, shoddy, amateurs! We thought we were bad, but you can come here to an opera theatre and ask today – today in 2007! – you can ask what we're going to do in 2008 and they'll tell you, well, on 14th of March at 8 p.m. we're premiering Aida. A premiere with all the trimmings, everything in place. Not like you people – we open a door and find it's not finished, or there's a leak in the ceiling or that passage is only temporary but somebody's built a plasterboard wall and now it's going to have to be torn down ... When you see the performance of Aida, the music is complete, the costumes are complete, the lighting is complete and the sets are complete. Why? Because the next day you cannot go back and do anything. It's over.'

To me the theatre has always appeared to be a vulgar medium. You stick yourself wherever and do whatever. And it's well known that there just aren't the resources, we just don't have anything, and so the actors end up in some really dingy dressing rooms. I suppose it comes from the time of the travelling player who, like the fairground workers, always had to stay on the outskirts of a city. I saw Woody Allen in an interview the other day, and he said that there were hotels in New York that refused to have comedians staying. I suppose it's the same long tradition of a perceived lack of respectability, even though when you go to London, for example, you see that it's one of the major theatre cities. In fact, theatre is the third biggest industry in London, in terms of turnover. But when you arrive in Madrid you notice that there is a big difference.

My obsession was how to get rid of this air of vulgarity from the theatre, even though Lluís Pasqual always thought I was wasting my time, trying to achieve the impossible. I wanted to do this by giving the Teatro Real an air of being well-finished, of every object being the right thing in the right place; an air of quality, rather than rushed jobs and gaffer tape and dangling wires and ropes – you know the type of thing, like when you go to an outpatients or a doctor's waiting room and the walls are covered in photocopied posters held up by sticky tape. It just feels wrong; it's just not quality.

Nobody was putting obstacles in my way, so I just continued on forwards, submitting quotes and budgets, and they just kept getting approved.

And do you think that this perfectionism, or just wanting to do things well, has led to a different operating method?

I was talking about this with a friend I worked with in the María Guerrero when Pasqual was the Director. She said to me 'I'm going to leave, because this isn't what it used to be, it's become something impossible, everything's a problem with official agreements, everything's about health and safety laws; the Technical Directors have become mere administrators looking after timetables, teams, labour laws…they've never been down to the stage in their lives, and they have no idea what's going on.'. And I said to her 'look, when we arrived at the María Guerrero we were just 30; we had no plan that we were going to be doing this stuff. It's a generational thing – we found ourselves with a bunch of things that were an assault on our previously held ideas. But we didn't have a plan of attack.' It's like when a kid argues with a parent. Am I going to change the ideas of my father? No, I'm simply going to refuse and instead argue for something else.

Well, that's what happened to us. We arrived and, sure enough, there was a series of customs and habits that went against our way of thinking. For example, when we needed an electrician to come the following day, the whole team would come…and I don't mean the whole team of electricians, but the whole technical team! And so we started to break with tradition and change things, from the uniform to the tools. The first time we went on tour we were like a bunch of gypsies, if you'll pardon the expression. Everything was in cardboard boxes, tied up with rags…impossible. I managed to get a budget for touring gear, with metal boxes – it was the first time we'd used flight cases in the theatre, as they had been considered too special but, in the end, we changed that.

But I realised, with sadness, that it was like pulling a spring. AS long as you've got the strength and you pull the spring, it'll stay this long... but the moment you let it go, BOING! It snaps back into its original form.

Since I left the Teatro Real, I've only been back once, and that was because Daniel called me. I saw all the things they'd done since I'd left. They'd followed the style that I'd initiated, and that seems logical to me.

But we didn't only have to develop the mechanical part. We also had to create the Technical department, draw up the labour agreements, make a list of all the functions, the number of people required for each and then hire the staff. We wanted to get rid of many of the bad habits that had existed previously. We looked at previous labour agreements, thinking about what worked and what didn't, and why. And later we looked at all the procedures. An order for buying nails... how does that work? And what uniforms should the technicians wear?

It's a world in itself that later gives rise to a system. For example, we had to define the role of the Stage Managers. In the theatre, the Stage Manager is pretty much in charge of the performance, but they don't tend to know much about music. This is quite a deficiency in the case of an opera theatre, because if they don't know about music then it's more difficult for them to follow the timing, the tempo and know exactly when to give the command for something that's supposed to happen. One alternative is to get a stop-watch and time it all, but that's not very musical. Theatres have had to overcome this problem somehow and, in the majority, the in-house or staff maestro (which is a very important figure in the opera world) ends up taking on the role of Stage Manager, at least in certain respects. The lighting master takes the score and marks on it all the cues for lighting effects, which means it's not the Stage Manager giving the lighting cues, but the lighting master. This seems wrong to me – it's not the job of a lighting master to give cues; it's the job of a Stage Manager. So we think 'We should oblige Stage Managers, as a condition of their employment, to be able to read music perfectly. We don't need a musical maestro to cue the chorus's entrance onto the stage – why would he ever do that? Just because the Stage Manager can't read music?' And then we think 'ok, the in-house experts should stay doing what they do best, whether directing musicians or singers or whatever. An in-house maestro is going to continue to direct what they should direct, but the Stage Manager will continue to be the Stage Manager.'

Another important point, and they'll kill me for this: How do you give orders in stage management? Suppose I'm an operator and a Stage Manager comes to me and says 'get ready to lower the curtain'. First of all, that's long-winded. Second problem is when I say 'ok, curtain going down'. But when? How will I know? How will they signal to me? Because there has to be complete silence, and the Teatro Real's stage is massive. So we had to start thinking about this and realised it's a bit like the communication used between pilots. They don't say 'I think I can see some hills in the distance...' The language has to be clear and categorical 'affirmative, negative, left, right' and based on key words. Additionally, we thought it should be onomato-poeic, to have an impact, a point, tick, tock, whatever. I'd heard about *top* in France, which means nothing in French or Spanish, it's just an impact sound, like the cinema clapperboard – '*clack!*' So I decided on that and told them all 'all we're going to say in this theatre is 'ready 8... and top!' and each person has to know if cue number 8 is theirs or not. I'll give you all a list of your 'tops' and if, for example, the props guy doesn't have cue 8 on his list, then he knows he doesn't need to do anything. But if someone has number 8 on their list and it's 'smoke machine' then when he hears 'top!' he has to operate the smoke right then, full stop. It has to work.'

Well, they were sceptical. They said it'd never work, nobody would know their cues, it's never been done like that before, it'd be a disaster and so on ... And for a while, in the beginning, they were right. We just didn't have time to get all the tops updated. Suppose there's a lighting rehearsal in the morning, and loads of tops are defined. Then at four in the afternoon there's another rehearsal, for the guy who's operating the lights. And then you've got to finish the afternoon with all the effects ready and all the tops numbered. The tops from the morning rehearsal should now be incorpo-rated into the afternoon rehearsal, which must then all be consolidated into one list! Well, to achieve this we finally decided to use a computer so now, when the Stage Manager finishes the afternoon rehearsals, he incorporates the changes, clicks a button and only those teams affected by the new changes get the new tops list.

The key question is whether a system like this, which is clear and defined, will become a straitjacket for people because they become locked-into it. If for example Daniel finds a system that is better or more powerful, then changing to that will be difficult because, good or bad, the previous system has created a series of relationships between people and those relationships are implicit in the system. You create a system and if that system works, then everything that comes later is simply following what went previously.

So in fact, you and your team created what is today the entire functioning system of the theatre, from the tops to the technical know-how ...

The Teatro Real was pretty much created from zero, yes. We had no experi-ence at this level. Our philosophy was like having a coffee in Belgium, where they bring you a jar of coffee and another of milk, and you do what you like with them; you can mix it with a lot of milk, a little milk, no milk ...

We thought that, in a seasonal theatre such as this, the worst that could happen was to get stuck in a rut and stop developing. There is a maxim that says that elements with many possibilities tend only to be used in one way, and we wanted to avoid that.

This was the philosophy we worked by, and within this philosophy, we also created the working model. To achieve this I worked with a team of three people. Daniel left the theatre after a while; he's not a very technical person and said to me 'To discuss the colour of a socket and whether it's 10 amp or 20 ... I don't know, and I'm not interested.' And off he went to another theatre.

The time had come when we weren't discussing anything, because we'd already discussed everything. We'd had to specify and standardise everything, and for this we'd used a lot of people from engineering disciplines, but the functionality was always our thing. In the mechanical design and implementation, especially for the platforms, it was very useful to have the knowledge and experience of Waagner-Brio and the technical support of the installation guys. But I think we reached a very high level of understanding, despite the fact that, for us, it was very difficult to talk about technology because none of us had much experience in movement systems.

But you've greatly determined the way the theatre functions ...

Yes, I'd say we have, to a large extent. But we also had to design the way we worked. For example, we had a lot of discussion about personnel issues. In Spain we work with shifts and overtime. And I started to hire people, not on the basis of labour agreements, but on responsibilities. 'You don't have a timetable. If you can do your job in one hour, then fantastic, if you need 40 hours, then tough, but I'm hiring your responsibility, and it has to work'. We also had to create a system for passing on information, so that if someone had done something in the morning, someone else could repeat it in the afternoon rehearsal without the first person having to be there too.

But there are many exceptions. I remember something that happened with Lluís Pasqual at the Palais Garnier, which is now the Paris Bastille opera. Lluís was directing and I was helping with the lighting. It was a type of musical, a modern opera. In the second act there was a scene with a concentration camp, and about 200 people playing the prisoners walking around in Auschwitz. The three follow spots were moving around like searchlights. Suddenly, the lights had to go, in time with the music, to the face of the actor who was about to sing. Then, when he'd finished, the lights had to go to another actor for their part, and then back to the first guy; back and forth a few times. The team that had rehearsed this was the morning shift but, as it was the end of the month, they'd swapped shifts and now the morning shift was on afternoons, and vice versa. Problem. There is absolutely no way that, on the night, even using headphones, you can tell an operator where to focus the light. 'Get ready to focus on that bloke just left of centre ... the one with the hair ...' And all in time with the music! So, in the end Pasqual's assistant and I had to operate the follow spots. So, you see, there is always someone in an opera to whom you have to say 'no, forget shifts, YOU are going to be at all the rehearsals and all the performances too – whether that coincides with your day off or not.'

But these effects, aren't they programmed or controlled by computer?

Not all of them, no; it depends. For example, smoke effects depend a lot on the heat of the day, how the singers are, whether it's a full house or not... When you open the tap, out comes the smoke, but it can drift this way or that. Whoever's been rehearsing with it will have acquired a knack, and that's not something you can pass on to anybody else.

And are the people well disposed to stay and work?

Up to a certain point, yes, some of the teams are. For example, the red-shirts.[10] They have a different labour agreement – they can work up to 14 hours, and they're compensated by breaks and time off. This is so that they can cover two shift and that way, if, for example, they had to change something unexpectedly in the morning, then in the afternoon nobody can say 'oh but nobody told me'. If it's the same person on both shifts then this is never a problem. Even though we created a fairly elaborate system for passing information, there is a very easy way to pass on basic info, things that aren't so artistic – 'We're only using 17 spears, not 18, because the last one comes out of box number four on the right.'

But the person, or the people, who have created a system must always be there when the system starts running. There's an unwritten rule in theatre – 'If you build a set and it all works perfectly the first time, then take it down and investigate.' You have to adjust here, tweak there, and then the thing that was giving you nightmares at the beginning, will end up running like clockwork.

---

[10] The name given to one of the work teams; some of them wear red shirts as a kind of uniform.

X
The Nature and Structure of Operations

The conversation with José Luis Tamayo documents the process of designing and setting up the Teatro Real's Operational system. It is rare to find an Operations Director who was able to 'set up shop' from scratch, without being subordinate to previous structures or norms. This is why the interview with him was a unique chance to vicariously experience the creation of a sophisticated system of Operations from the ground up, and straight from the mouth of the principal protagonist.

As with the majority of our protagonists in this book, José Luis learned the theatre by working in the theatre. Also in common with the majority, he comes from a family with close ties to the theatre. He had to acquire his knowledge through the purest form of learning: learning by doing. José Luis, a student of Humanities, found himself in a theatre job with no previous experience, and from that day on he just had to get on with it.

What José Luis was given was not a theatre in need of rebuilding, but a project in need of designing. What was needed was not architecture, which was at least drafted and budgeted, but a system of Operations; the way in which the various components of this machine, the theatre, need to work together in order to deliver the service that the client has been promised.

We know that designing the Operational system of a company is an arduous and fairly technical task. José Luis said, 'I'm never going to make it!, when he saw the complexity. It's easy to get into a mess when a system has so many variables, and whose values need to be taken into account. But this, as our friends in Operations know, is typical when designing a new Operational installation. And to avoid getting into this sort of mess, the Operations experts have designed methodologies that help alleviate the problem, that at least help us to sleep better at night, knowing that we haven't missed anything vital and that everything has been taken into account. Engineers are experts at proposing technological solutions, but as we heard in Tamayo's account, they perhaps don't have the same precise sense of 'finish'. In the case of the Teatro Real,

> **Do you have a consistent Operational design?**

the engineers didn't have a sense of theatre. In addition, they don't tend to have the adequate methodology to design a system of operations; the way in which everything works together to fulfil the projected service. And less still, they don't tend to know how to incorporate the role of the system operators; a role which should also include the development of a corporate culture.

Our man, like many engineers, was not an expert in Operations, but he was a man of the theatre. Theatre people don't like the word 'impossible', and invent methods to solve their problems. And, as we saw from the interview, they often aren't even aware of it.

But a note of caution: theatre people cannot work miracles, and miracles have nothing to do with Operational systems. What Tamayo did was *rediscover* and apply various basic problem-solving principles and techniques in different situations of *incomplete knowledge*.

To be able to better understand the extent of his work, we must examine in detail what the design variables of an Operational system are, and the way in which our man managed to reach those variables when starting from the rather vague project beginnings that he was handed.

The two key themes of this chapter are as follows:

1. The different methods of solving problems with incomplete knowledge.
2. The structure of the variables of an Operational system.

The conjunction between the definition of service and the Operational structure

To begin with, we need to know: What are we building? What type of theatre do we want?

In Chapter III, we've seen that, without a clear definition of service, it's impossible to design deliverable operations. The designer has to interpret, from their often-biased point of view, the wishes of the management, and thus, if the designer doesn't have the purpose of the operations clearly defined, then he'll end up with no clear direction in which to head. Not a good way to start! When José Luis took the task of designing the Teatro Real, nobody told him what the *mission* of the theatre was. Nobody had proposed it, because it wasn't part of the political decision to refurbish the building.

So, in this situation, Tamayo himself defined the parameters necessary to be able to progress. In the first place, and luckily for him, an opera theatre already has a fairly obvious mission from the word go – it sounds blindingly obvious, but an opera theatre 'must present opera'. And this musical genre requires several fairly clear basic service components which are implicit in the theatrical common sense.

An implicit mission sounds a bit vague. How does it affect the design? Very simple. With this in mind, the only alternative is to consider a set of possibilities or missions, and then to specify a system that is sufficiently *flexible* to be able to handle them all. As we don't know what we're being asked for, we design something that can fit all possibilities. Tamayo had no option but to opt for a theatre with a flexible structure.

In business, this is often the case. Where there is no clear definition, the mission is automatically defined by including 'highly flexible'. The system is designed to cope with all the possibilities under consideration. If, as we said in Chapter III, flexibility and cost are antagonistic, then the result will be increased cost. Or, as our protagonist said, we'll have motors 'just in case' – we'll use them infrequently, perhaps rarely, but they're there if somebody needs to move something at variable speed. In general, this tends to be the reason for higher costs; it's the investment in capacity that goes unused for much of the time, but is there when you need it. Of course, if flexibility is a competitive attribute of our company, that's fine – we've spent more money, but our flexibility is greater.

When it goes horribly wrong, however, is when *flexibility* is not necessary for competing – we have a flexible installation that we don't need and cost us more, and thus we've burdened ourselves with a competitive *disadvantage*.

In a certain sense, the former is the case with the Teatro Real. This flexibility gives it a competitive advantage in the service it provides to the Stage Director, obtaining the best products and complementing the strategic objectives of the institution. But let's take ourselves back in time … José Luis still doesn't know that, which means he is running a big risk. He is aware of this, too – he told us that he wasn't actually working much day-to-day, but still he was really suffering: '… so much responsibility', he told us.

What does Tamayo really do? We can answer that, on the face of it: he's designing a theatre. Ok, fine. But since he doesn't have a design methodology to hand, what he's really doing is developing that *methodology*. And the way he does that is by deconstructing the initial problem 'to design an opera theatre' into sub-problems, and then by resolving them one by one. He makes a *catalogue* of problems, addresses them in order of priority, and later puts all the results together, hoping it all fits. Of course he's used reasoning *a priori* to conclude that everything *must work* – clearly our protagonist is a very smart man, but you never know. There could be things you've overlooked and find out later to your cost.

It is clear that the first problem he encounters is fairly obvious, because it's easy to describe, diagnose and enunciate. This is the problem of how to move heavy loads vertically on-stage. All modern theatres use the flying gallery system, where the set pieces are stored in the large space above the stage, and can be lowered when needed. These set changes, which our protagonists talk of so frequently, can be done in front of the audience or behind the curtain. Essentially, there are two alternatives – move them by muscle power or by motor. The first alternative has two varieties – pure muscle or counter-weighted. A basic knowledge of physics tells us that the system needs a small amount of force to get the load moving, but once we double the moving mass (the load plus the counter-weight), we introduce all sorts of problems when trying to stop it moving. We can fairly easily push a car that weighs 1,200 kg, but once it's moving it's a really bad idea to try to stop it using anything other than the brakes. Deceleration requires force to be applied over a long time. Petrol tankers need to be put into reverse a long time before you might think. So, for this simple matter of physics, Tamayo knows that the counter-weight system is good, but only for relatively light loads.

José Luis has a good knowledge of manual systems thanks to his many years of experience in traditional theatres. Even in the María Guerrero he introduced the innovation of counter-weights. But this is not the case with motorised systems. Not only didn't our man know this type of system, it would also appear that nobody in the world at that time had a clear idea of how to make motorised systems work reliably, silently and accurately in that required context. There is a (huge) lack of knowledge about one of the possible design alternatives. If José Luis had complete knowledge of all the options, and given sufficient analytical capacity, the solution process would be relatively easy. He would only have to apply existing knowledge and combine it in such a way as to come up with the solution. This is what almost any engineer would do, but at the moment of confronting the problem, Tamayo doesn't have all the knowledge.

In companies, something similar often happens. There is a lack of complete knowledge about the characteristics of a problem, and therefore there's no clear way to deploy a systematic procedure[1] which takes you, step by step, to the desired result. So, how can we resolve problems like this?

> **There are two basic problem-solving processes: applied and exploratory.**

Problem-solving methodologies

There are two basic ways to solve a problem, that we'll call *Applied* and *Exploratory*. The first is simple – you just apply the knowledge you have. If Magellan had only wanted to sail as far as the Antilles, then he could simply have used Columbus's map and instructions; that pre-existing knowledge, rapid and precise, would have been sufficient. Of course, that's always supposing that we know everything (necessary) about the problem, or to put it another way, we have adequate knowledge.

---

[1] What the (grandiloquent) experts call an 'algorithm'. Note from one of the authors: the 'grandiloquent' opinion was inserted by the other author, in a display of pure spite for which they should apologise but probably won't.

The second method is what, to use Magellan again, he used once he'd reached the Antilles and wanted to continue. Trial and error. *Explore* solutions and possibilities until you come up with the adequate solution.

Exploration, *trial and error*, doesn't have to be attempted on the final solution. For example, there's no reason to construct a huge stage before you realise that it won't fit in the theatre. There is also no reason to construct an under-stage 'depth system' with five spaces, to discover that it doesn't work, because there are only three possibilities and not four. No, the process description that Tamayo recounts clearly shows that, bit by bit, incrementally, our protagonists suggest ideas, they discuss them and discount what they *anticipate* will give unsatisfactory results, or what they think won't work. And this task is done bit by bit, path-finding, and not abandoning an attractive idea until it's proved unviable.

When we reach a dead end in our exploration, either real or virtual, we typically undo a part of the construct in order to return to the situation prior to the decision that *probably* led us into error.

If someone says, 'It was difficult for us to understand the way it worked', we get the idea that there has been a long process of exploration, mainly mental, until they reached the conclusion that the design was adequate and it could be implemented.

José Luis explores, whether mentally or physically, different possibilities. Mostly mentally, because he's not actually going to end up building many of them. He is alone in his abstract analysis, but it's often sufficient to see where the proposed solution is adequate or not. As a methodology it is perhaps a bit slow and quite expensive, but, and this is the crucial point, Tamayo can do it because nobody imposed *conditions* of time or cost. He always has more time, and the budget keeps going up. 'I just continued on forwards, submitting quotes and budgets, and they just kept getting approved'.

Exploration is highly inefficient, but nevertheless it contains great potential for learning and creativity. Effectively, you learn by exploring; all the successes as well as all the failures.

It is very difficult to find the *best* solution to a problem when you explore. You have to list them all until you find the best, which means that if you find a solution, you then have to go back to the beginning to see whether you can find a better one. 'But that's a terrible waste of time and money!' Ah, but in practice there rarely are 'better decisions'. The majority of problems are problems of *feasibility* not *optimisation*. There is almost never a choice between two solutions to a problem. One of our colleagues, Rafael Termes, who was an illustrious figure in Spanish banking, used to say 'I don't want best. I want things to be good.' Of course, he said that in Catalan, and perhaps we're losing something in the translation, but the idea is still clear. In the world in which we live, with managers facing ever-more complex demands, the most important priority is to find a solution; just one, but one that is feasible, acceptable. A solution that takes us in a reasonable manner to the desired result is not necessarily the best.

One advantage of the exploratory method is that people learn and will often be more creative, because exploration necessarily brings new situations into consideration; situations that those people have never experienced before. And if the exploration is sufficiently successful, then in all probability they'll be situations that *nobody* has ever experienced before. It is clear that there are some people who are better at exploration than others, but there are also people who are lucky and immediately stumble upon solutions. They used to be called inventors. Beyond pure knowledge of the problem, what is important in exploration is the personal characteristics and methodological knowledge that the people have.

Conclusion. When you ask your people to go down innovative routes, that they're not familiar with or that they have only incomplete knowledge of, then your people will have to explore. But remember what we said. You cannot ask for rapid solutions to a problem that requires exploration. You, esteemed professional, must know what type of problem you're setting your colleague or subordinate. If it can be resolved by an applied process, then the result can be rapid and efficient. But if it's resolved through a process of exploration, then the solution will arrive only slowly, although this could also open up possible new directions for your company, which is something that you can and must ask of your colleagues and collaborators. More time and increased cost in exchange for *learning* and *creativity*. If, on the other hand, you have limited time and resources, then it's better to anticipate how you can help to reduce the scope of explorations. If not, then you won't meet the objective within the deadline and on budget.

Note that the answer José Luis gave the minister in that meeting could be interpreted as: 'I can easily resolve the problem of putting on a performance. But if you're asking me for a structure, within which we're capable of staging any opera that occurs to any artist, then the problem is much more complicated, because I have to explore many more possibilities. I have to imagine situations and assure myself that the system covers them all. Nevertheless, I agree to provide that structure, and later I'll fine-tune it'.

Unforeseen exploration is often the cause of important delays in projects. The authors have seen first-hand a project that ended up with a month's delay after only one month! Our reaction was 'What happened? Hasn't anybody worked during this month?' On the face of it, our reaction might seem justified, but it was wrong. In a nutshell, we had estimated the average exploration time needed in that phase. And there's the problem – the average is the average. Half of the time it's a pessimistic estimate, and half of the time it's an optimistic estimate. We were just unlucky.

The fundamental reasons why exploration produced such effective and creative solutions in the Teatro Real were the long amount of time available, ample resources and the creative and methodological abilities of the responsible team. They invested time, resources and brainpower to come up with a design that, at the time, was pioneering and probably unique in the genre.

We very much doubt that the reader will have found him- or herself in that sort of enviable position with such favourable conditions. Unlimited time and resources are, not surprisingly, rare in companies. There are always restrictions and pressures limiting both. And if there aren't such restrictions, then it's the job of a good administrator to impose them. This probably happens in personal projects, such as building a boat or a piano (yes, we have friends who do this sort of thing), but not in company projects. So, then, what can we do? Because it's very rare to have complete knowledge that allows us to realise an applied process. Should we renounce the advantages of learning and creativity that exploration brings? The answer is 'not necessarily'. Some alternatives that may be employed are as follows:

Hire knowledge. Analysts and consultants are sources of knowledge that, if well managed, can help to reduce the extent of exploration. But we don't want advice from them; we want participation in the project...so be careful with consultants!

Manage a priori *the time and the budget,* defining limitations that are calculated to allow a moderate degree of exploration. The higher those limits, the better the solution that can be obtained. When there's more time and more budget, then we can test and explore more. But unlimited time and money will only fall foul of the human weaknesses in the participants; they will relax, lose motivation, get bored or even become frustrated because they cannot say 'that's it, we've fixed it'. Let us agree, but remain conscious that the solution will only be the 'best possible' within the established limits.

Help to ensure that the exploration methodology is efficient, if not the solution, then at least the application of our exploration. For example, let's try to generate adequate *heuristics* to be able to recognise when certain avenues of exploration are going to prove pointless. How did Magellan know that that flowing current was not the pass that he'd been looking for to get to the other side but was instead just a river? Probably heuristics – the water was fresh, and continued to be a little further upstream. So, that exploration could be abandoned and they could return to what they now thought of as the river mouth, having a reasonable supposition (but not absolute certainty) that they had not just eliminated a good solution. The nature of heuristics is precisely that; rules that allow us to monitor the exploration, with a degree of reasonable certainty that, when we do discard something, we're not throwing away anything advantageous. *Organisational procedures,* in the same way, should be used to ensure that people learn and share the knowledge obtained by all participants in the effort. To expand further on these concepts is, unfortunately, beyond the scope of this book.[2]

The central problem: creating an Operational system

The choices that José Luis made were risky and brave. His decision was to do something new that had never been done before. The reaction of those around him was 'you're going to destroy our lives!' Every *innovator* is a *creator of problems* for other people. It is too easy to get by in a company that doesn't innovate; you just follow procedures that rarely change. But to innovate is to cause problems that the people involved had to solve. The result, given the ability to create the necessary management style, can be improvement and learning or, in the absence of that ability, resentment and frustration. In Chapter XXI we'll deal with the management style necessary to withstand the current of problems generated by innovation.

With his exploratory methods, José Luis is going to discover not just one solution, but rather a systematic way to resolve the next problem at the same time. Oh, the advantages of exploration! Let's look at six key themes, that we call '*key variables*' in the design of an Operational system.

The first is the most obvious: *the process*. What technologies support the Operating process? How should the internal procedures of the Teatro Real's Operations be? How do we make 'You point and I'll focus the light' Operational? Procedures cover everything from how to manage the additional spaces by the stage, to how to buy nuts and bolts. All at a sufficiently high level of aggregation to avoid becoming bogged down in the details. Afterwards, when we've finished the design, there will be time to fine-tune the processes, but for the moment it is unnecessary. For example, when the activities are particularly numerous or *unpredictable* it is impossible, and unnecessary, to specify with detail. It is enough to give some key reference ideas and leave the rest to the initiative of the people directly involved. All the processes should be subject to specification, with a variable degree of detail according to the required flexibility of the system.

At the same time, José Luis must decide on the Operational *flows* within the system – in each case, what should be the logical order of Operations. Should he work on various productions simultaneously, all in different stages of development? How are they going to use the various spaces available beneath and behind the stage? Some of these decisions are closely linked to certain processes, but they are not only confined to them. They have much more to do with the relationship between the processes, the way in which the various *processes interact* with each other. For clarity, we separate the decisions about the structure of the process, the technology and the resources, from the decisions about the way of using them together; that is,

---

[2] But you can find all the details in our previous book *Problem Driven Management*.

decisions about the way the processes flow and interact over time. These correspond to a variable that, for want of a better name, we'll call *'flow'* or the *'structure of Operational flows'*.

If José Luis goes for the motorised fly system – and that's the decision he explores first, because he doesn't know about it and yet it appeals to him – then he needs motors capable of variable speed. We have already talked about the factors that determine flexibility. The most important is the need to have extra capacity, *just in case*. There is an additional cost incurred with this and, since flexibility is expensive, it is important to design this capacity and determine what the reasonable values in each of the different areas are. This means we need to dimension the system, calculating the capacity required to meet the demands. The variable *capacity* considers all these questions, to finally determine how many hours of each resource we must have available for use at a given moment.

This is the third variable that José Luis stumbled upon. Having designed the process and its relative, the flow, then comes the time to dimension the whole scheme, to *determine the capacity*. This, however, should not be done before previously determining the two aforementioned variables. The process is often undertaken erroneously, determining the capacity before describing the processes. Of course, when we're dealing with problems of capacity, there is no option but to predict the most *probable* use of the system. And there will always appear *random* elements, associated with the uncertainties of demand or the specifications of the supporting technology, that make the estimation of capacity a problem of deciding in uncertain conditions, with all the resulting difficulties. José Luis resolved the situation in the usual manner, by creating a capacity *buffer*, which would allow him to absorb these random eventualities.

> There are six variables needed to design a system of Operations: processes, flows, capacities, information system, the rules system and human resources.

There are two additional design variables that were also clearly described in the conversation with Tamayo. These are the *information system* and the *rules system*. The information system is the mechanism for collecting and conveying information to co-ordinate actions. A great invention of our protagonists was the *real-time information* system used to co-ordinate during performances. This sounds like such a fantastic invention, it should have a fancy name such as RETIMINS ... but it turns out that it is known by the much humbler, but snappier name of *Tops*. The entire *tops* system is this: a system of co-ordinating the action of all the people involved in the operation. It is an original and very well-thought-out design. The conversation detailed very clearly the problem of communication with precision in a silent environment, then set out the method of implementations and finished by listing the changes in the processes (and even in peoples' jobs – remember the shift workers) that this system produced, due to the necessity of it being complete and consistent at all times. And, by the way, the *tops* system is not really an Information Technology system, even though it uses technology to support it. What this clearly demonstrates is the confusion possible between the system and its support platform, which is, in the majority of cases, IT.

If the reader stops to think for a moment, he or she will see that the purpose of an Operations information system is always to co-ordinate the actions of the participants. Isn't it like, for example, the accounting information systems that summarise the historical financial information about a company, usually presenting it when nobody needs it? Why do I need to know my costs for the past month? The past has passed! What I want to know is how my costs are changing as a result of what I'm currently doing. And previous months' costs only serve as a benchmark if *céteris paribus,* everything else remains the same, which is almost never. We always say that the typical information systems used in accounting are systems for regretting decisions, rather than for helping take the decisions in the first place. They help you regret something you did rather than help you to plan what you must do. This is an empty exercise, regretting an action without taking steps to fix it. Information systems used in Operations must respond just at the time that operations are happening. In Operations, it is of no value whatsoever to have an information system that only summarises what went wrong in our sorry pasts.

And now, the *rules system*. What's this? Well, it's what José Luis knows as the 'way of working'. It is in the rules that we find the Operational Culture defined! When the reader reaches Chapter XXII, and we sincerely hope and pray that you will, you'll find there a list of rules that must be in force in the Operational Culture that we propose. And, guess what – the rules that we propose are very similar to the ones we found in action at the Teatro Real.

Until we reach that chapter, however, we must be content to give only a couple of pointers about how to implement a rules system in an organisation. In a similar way to the Teatro Real, we must first establish a *formal organisation*; the way in which the work is shared between the different participants. One Stage Manager is in charge of the stage when the curtain's closed, and another, similar to a television Floor Manager, during the performance. Ok. The Stage Manager is a part of the opera from the beginning, and attends all the rehearsals. There are operators who must be present for the whole opera. And so on, successively.

But a formal organisation is not enough. A large number of interactions are produced in the *informal system*; a parallel system which contains the majority of the unwritten rules that govern the interaction between the *people* that make up the Operation. The managers are responsible for the creation and evolution of an adequate informal system. To see how, the reader must remain patient and wait for later chapters. In the meantime, please do continue reading.

Finally, the last of the design variables appears: *human resources*. This covers the type of *people* and the type of *knowledge* required, and the *relationship* between those people. Remember the responsibility contract described by José Luis. On the one hand, there are rules covering action 'You have to be there on the day of the premiere', for example. However the principal condition of human resources is the knowledge profile required for the company to achieve the desired service results. And our friendly designer, José Luis Tamayo, had this very clear, as could be seen when he related the way in which he hired people.

Now the list of our six variables is complete: *capacity, flow, processes, human resources, information system and rules system*. The problem of design is solved when we've determined the configuration of these six variables. Easy!

One last comment. Tamayo's focus gives rise to a very simple yet effective rule: *keep it simple, because it'll complicate itself.* It's a variety of Murphy's Law, which is well-known but still wisdom for all that. For example, the lighting – the traditional solution (fixed lighting) – requires that the position of the light is fixed at the moment of design. It's clear that this position cannot be the perfect position for all the productions, with the consequence that the lighting people for each production must adapt to this solution that was fixed, maybe many years earlier, by the designer. Clearly the solution of 'you point and I'll focus' is much simpler. Similarly, the *tops* system is a model of effective simplicity. But coming up with both of these systems was nothing trivial. The best creative solutions are often characterised by the fact that they appear, afterwards, to be simply a matter of common sense: 'why didn't we think of that before?' Making things simple implies digging deep and exploring those solutions that appear intuitively, because intuitive solutions are not always good ones – all the preconceived ideas and biases of the person can get in the way. The *tops* system is obvious, *a posteriori*, but it took a lot of time and much discussion to become what it is today, a 'common sense' system. A simple system can also adapt more readily, because everybody understands it. By his actions, José Luis provided the solution to his own concern: 'I don't want my successors to be locked-in'.

But making something simple is not simple. It requires, first of all, a *sound methodology* and, second, a *high degree of exploration* in the solving a problem process.

Conclusions

The conversation with José Luis Tamayo illustrates the six design variables of an Operational system. Without knowing it, without conceptualising it, our protagonist discovered (by trial and error) the six variables in question. But he suffered a lot in the effort, even though we suspect he had a great time, too.

We have looked at the problem-solving process from its two aspects, exploration and application, and understood their respective pros and cons. In the next chapter we will examine how José Luis Tamayo's work configures the operation of the theatre. In the meantime, a few points to reflect upon:

- Does my Operational Culture include problem-solving as an essential value?
- What are our basic problem-solving methodologies? Do we exploit existing knowledge, or do we reinvent the wheel every time?
- How do I help my people to solve problems? What do I do so that they can do this better every day?
- How do I manage my time and resources in exploratory cases?
- Do my people have the necessary knowledge to tackle problems in an applied way, instead of requiring exploration?
- Do I have an adequate operational structure to deliver my service commitment? How are my six variables today and how must they be in the future if I want that service to be optimal?
- Do we have, in our Operational Culture, a tendency to complicate our lives with too many teams and meetings?

XI
Operations Management and Translation

In the next two chapters, we will describe the internal workings of the technical area of the Teatro Real. One important idea that surfaces is the concept of Operations as a form of translation. The Promise must be translated into facts, operating realities, and this is a useful way of seeing Operations. We will also see that the translation of Operations is seen as a waterfall effect which must always continue flowing.

We analyse why the Operations Director can and must remain with his feet firmly on the ground, and how the operators must not question the strategy, but instead help to implement it. Ok, we'll allow five minutes of questioning per day, to call attention to things that perhaps haven't been fully thought out. But the fundamental function and purpose of an Operations Director is to find solutions that contribute to the company's mission, managing the problem-solving process of everybody involved.

In this chapter, we're talking with Daniel Bianco and his assistant, Carlos. The central theme is the process of translation that the Technical Management does between the Stage Director's proposal and the realisation of the production. Daniel conceptualises this process as a translation between two languages.

How does a production begin?

DB. The process of an opera always begins with the theatre's Artistic Director appointing a Stage Director. This happens some years before the production begins. Some months before the premiere, we get in touch with the Stage Director and his artistic team, so that we can begin our work. The Stage Director is the one who thinks, who creates the production. He's an artist, a man who creates a dream. And to communicate this dream he must encapsulate it in an understandable form, a mock-up, of sketches and plans.

The Stage Director arrives here and presents his project. It's like someone trying to sell you a new kitchen; they have to prepare the project and then they have to sell it to you.

He sells it to you?

More particularly to the Artistic Director. What happens is that, in my contract with the Teatro Real it says that I have to confirm the viability of all the activities that the Artistic Director wants to undertake. So, nobody has to sell to me whether the stage is going to have a revolving platform here or there, but the kind of thing I have to watch out for is that there's no piece of set that is too big for the stage, which is something that does happen.

And they come with those sorts of details, a revolving platform over here...?

They come to present the project with many things decided. In the presentation of a project we have to rapidly evaluate it all and know if it's viable or not. Often, when studying a project, we notice that in the performance we're not going to be able to move as many things as the project design calls for, perhaps because we don't have sufficient resources or time.

But right from the start you have to see, from a bird's eye view, rapidly, if the project is viable and economically feasible to start working on. We don't negotiate much, but we do have to evaluate whether it's a million-euro job or 200,000, if it's viable with our people, and whether we're going to have to run it in parallel with another opera or concert and if it can be put on quickly or not.

We don't see all of this quickly in one conversation. You can't get bogged down in lists of problems. If we say to an artist, 'Look, this has a lot of problems', perhaps because it weighs a lot or whatever, the artist always replies 'Well, that's just a technical issue'. We always have to propose solutions. 'Ok, we could take out half of this, or do it some other way...'

Now the relationship starts to build between us and the project begins to boil. The artist starts to change things and begins to see that maybe we have different visions, but maybe they're complementary. The artist has his initial vision, and we go along developing that with him. In *La Dolores*,[1] for

---

[1] Opera by Tomás Bretón (1850–1923). One of the works by which Bretón attempted to create 'Spanish opera'. In fact it was the only success that Bretón had in the wider genre. The author is much better known for his *zarzuelas*, especially the *obra maestra* of the *chico* or small genre, called *La Verbena de la Paloma*, 'The Dance of the Dove'. *La Dolores* is a costume tragedy, set in Catalayud. This gives Bretón the chance to insert the most famous piece in the opera, the well-known (in Spain, at least) *Jota de Dolores*, now practically an obligatory inclusion in the old fiestas of some Spanish towns. 'If you go to Calatayud, ask for Dolores...' goes the chorus, which even today bothers the inhabitants of this tough village in the province of Aragon. The plot is fairly childish: a serving lad, Patricio (who also features in the song) is in love with Dolores, but she's promised to another. To cut a long story short, Dolores gets stabbed and everything ends up in chaos. This opera is rarely performed and remains in the popular memory only due to the aforementioned song, which is a model of rhythmic happiness with a popular flavour.

example, the artist had the vision that the whole set would be projections of photographs that start off real and evolve into abstract paintings when the death is announced. But we had the vision that the projections begin to move, because in some of the scenes, the set was on the first plane and in the next scene it had to start separating and opening up...

The translation

This'll help you understand the role of the translator [continues Daniel]. I'll give you another example of *La Dolores*. We suggested to José Carlos Plaza, the Stage Director, to put a net over the front of the stage, because if he wanted to work with projections and give it a dream-like ambience, then this net would diffuse the stage appearance. You'd see the singer perfectly, but you wouldn't see exactly where each projection began and ended. So then he liked the idea and developed it. 'Ok, then we can project onto a net...' and this led to us putting the projector at the end of the auditorium, for which we had to remove some seats.

In that phase the project wasn't yet finalised; it was alive. Of course, this has limits. As we say in Spain, there comes a time when you have to kill the chicken to be able to eat it – otherwise months pass and you'll never eat the chicken, close the project...

How long do these negotiations last?

Hmm, long enough to do all the administrative work, and for the set to have been built by the day of the first rehearsal. In the Teatro Real, on the day after the premiere of one opera, we bring in the set for the next one and, while one opera is performing, the next one is being built below it. And so it continues, in a cycle. Before we go on holiday, we leave the next opera set in the theatre, but not yet built. You just don't have the time! If we don't start bringing in *Macbeth* the day after the premiere of *La Dolores* then we simply won't be able to do everything in time. Contracts with set providers are always signed with penalties, but I never reach the real limit date – I always put it a few days before, to give us a cushion. It's like with forecasted budgets, you have to allow for the unexpected, those 'unforeseens' we mentioned earlier.

The whole project is a project that relies greatly on the relationship, the trust and the understanding between us and the Stage Director. There are people with whom you have a greater understanding, and those with whom you have less, but over the years you learn that you have to be professional, that your obligation is to try to understand and translate the wishes of the artist. Even if it sometimes seems impossible to do!

So it's shoulder to the wheel, side by side with the Stage Director?

Yes, although 'with the Stage Director' is actually more metaphorical – it's not so clear-cut. Sometimes it's just with the Set Designer, sometimes just with the Stage Director, sometimes both. It's also a question of power and politics; there are some Stage Directors who are very, very powerful, and the Set Designer will only do what he orders, whereas sometimes it's the other way round, because the Set Designer is the powerful one. Of course, then there are also times when both people are equally powerful, and times when the two roles are performed by the same person ...

Of course, we don't just spend all day 'translating' – there is another aspect to our role that is just as important. I'll give you an example. Yesterday we went to Italy, with the Set Designer of *The Barber of Seville*[2] and Carlos, to order the set for it. We visited the workshop that's going to build it, and we met Luciano there – he's the painter, the artist and he's the one who'll really be painting this set. HE said something that made me think of you two and this book you're writing. It was perfect. We gave him all the plans and photocopies, books, documentation, the works; everything he could possibly need. He looked at it all and said 'yep, fine, but the end result ... *how does it smell?*'

---

[2] *The Barber of Seville,* an opera by Gioachino Rossini, is based on the novel by Beaumarchais. It tells the story of the relationship between the Count of Almaviva, a Sevillian nobleman, and Rosina, an orphan of a good family, who lives with her tutor, Don Bartolo. At the centre of the action is Figaro, the eponymous barber, who, as he says in his celebrated aria, is 'the factotum of the city'; he lets blood, cuts hair, trims beards, and gossips. Figaro is a facilitator (a euphemism) who will ensure that the relationship between the protagonists turns out well. The count, who is a flirt, passes himself off as a poor student by the name of Lindoro and, in this guise, falls in love with Rosina who, for her part, wants to be in love in order to free herself from her old tutor, who wants to marry her. Everything develops from this basic plot into a lively bit of vaudeville. The count tries to see Rosina alone, and in one scene he disguises himself as a curate, takes the place of the music teacher and gives Rosina singing lessons, in the presence of Don Bartolo who is being shaved by Figaro. In another scene he poses as an official of the King's regiment who has just arrived in Seville, and turns up drunk at Don Bartolo's house wanting to stay there. Between gossip, waffle and the most delightful music, the opera concludes with the two protagonists becoming engaged. The Barber of Seville is one of the pinnacles of opera, and not only because of the quality of the music, but also because it achieves something quite rare in the genre; it is amusing, it really makes people laugh and, amazingly, there isn't a single dead body! There are no dramas here, just glorious music that extols the joys of life. Almost all the musical numbers are famous, but highlights, for us, include Figaro's aria 'Largo al factotum de la città' (which almost every man has sung at least once while shaving), Rosina's aria 'Una voce poco fa' in which she tells us that she's 'docile and obedient but ... she can be a viper if provoked'. Also, there is the wonderful scene of Lindoro's serenade with the two arias 'Eco ridente' and 'Io son Lindoro' in which the tenor does some complicated vocal juggling that has given rise to the prototypical style of the 'Rossini tenor'. And, last but not least, we'd also pick out the aria of Don Basilio, 'La calumnia' in which the music teacher spouts some cheap philosophy about the effects of slander, comparing it with 'a breeze that grows until it becomes a hurricane'. If you see only one opera in your life, we urge you to consider this one. Go on, see it and have fun.

You see, to do the job properly he wanted to know how it 'smells'. What should the set be? Is it a realistic structure, fantasy, should it look aged? He needs to know these things in order to really get into it. We have the same thing, too. When someone brings us, for example, *La Dolores*, we have to understand what it is and where we want to go with it. The artist is the one who's leading the way, but I have to understand where we're going because I have to accompany him on that journey and it's my job to make it easier.

Of course, putting it like that, somebody might think that this guy's mad or a bit stupid. No, you can't spend the whole day talking about philosophy that's not the point, but you do have to understand the fundamental vision.

Gerardo Vera is currently doing the set design for *Macbeth*, and he's got the plans, drawings, everything, all mathematically perfect. But then Gerardo starts talking about a feeling, he's talking about ice, cold... When he started, the proposed set had a floor covered in snow. Of course, that's practically impossible, so now the idea is for it to be wood, with just a bit of snow around the edges. But he's constantly talking about cold, about fear, about what has to inspire. It sounds weird, but it's really important – when you go down to props and they ask 'excuse me, but Macbeth's throne – exactly what's it like?' then you know how to answer. You know that the throne needs to be of a suitable material to represent something cold, frozen, severe, aggressive... it must instil fear.

Once we see if this is more or less viable, then we have to propose the budget. For example, in the case of *Tosca*, we knew we were going over budget. Same with *Macbeth*. In general, you always start off by going over budget, and they you have to find solutions to get the costs back down again. Sometimes that solution is not just changing something metal for something that only looks like metal.

There's a trick that many artists use: just start by vomiting everything up. Get it all out, and then start cleaning up. Artists always clean up afterwards; they always come up with more things and later take them away. You remove material, remove scenes, change one thing into another... sometimes you change the way you're working, going from building something to just painting a representation of it. Other times you start with something painted, but that doesn't work and you have to actually make it of metal...

Once the budget is resolved, we hold a meeting with all the bosses of Technical Management, and we present the project. There we tell them about the cold, the ice, you know, the metaphysical stuff – they're sensations that we have to convey. From there the project starts to subdivide. The props people talk directly to the Set Designer, who in turn talks with the workshop. Each one now has his work. But I think the secret of how we all work so well together is that we always, always keep ourselves at the centre of the production.

I continue holding meetings now and then with my managers, for example the guy who has to work with the Set Designer, because there's a very clear point here. If I'm the Set Designer, and I try to talk to you, the Props Manager, about a problem with the props, and you don't take any notice, then I'm going straight to the Operations Director, to see if I can get him to sort it out. We always try to avoid this, of course, and we do this by constantly following the solution of problems. The Props Manager will ask Raquel, his sculpture specialist, directly if he wants her to make the Christ for *Tosca*. But we'll know. The entire process is like a *waterfall*, with the water flowing down over everybody. The only secret is that *the water must continue to flow*, always. If the water's not flowing, then you've got no waterfall!

Something else we have to do is ensure that our work is compatible with the other theatres, the ones we're co-producing with. And I don't just mean the Set Designer or the Stage Director, but us too. Yes, the Set Designer will get involved, but there are many other things that need considering. Steps, for example. Sometimes, to save money, you don't make new steps because you've already got some general purpose steps in stock, property of the theatre. Like in your dining room at home, maybe you can sit eight people, but if you're having four extra to dinner then you might bring in the little table from the kitchen ... well, this is the same, really. The problem is that, when you lend the set out, you can't lend those steps because then you're left with none.

Keeping your feet firmly on the ground

So you believe that you have to understand all the problems that come up?

Absolutely. Imagine that I'm a maintenance guy and I get sent to fix the air conditioning at a hospital. Imagine that I don't know something, for example, that the surgeon has to work at 22°C. What happens? Maybe I arrive and ask someone who's been working there all their life, and they say 'careful, the surgeon has to work at precisely 22°C'. And let's suppose that keeping the operating theatre at 22°C costs a fortune. What do I do? Do I put it at 22°C? I don't know, because I know nothing about the life of a surgeon.

I understand that managing finances can be the same in one company as it is in another, but setting up the Operations of a company is a different matter. What shocks me is when people tell me that it's the same thing to manage a shoe shop or a factory. I can't believe it's the same. I do believe that the basic functions should all be there, like accounting, and you can't do without them, but ... Sometimes I see, among people I know who manage companies, that they have strange ways of managing. What do they manage? Paper? What do they talk about? Resources? Resources of I don't know what, expenses of I don't know how much...but they don't seem to know what the hell goes on in the *service*.

I've asked Stage Directors and they've told me that in some theatres they've never even met the Operations Director, because he was always upstairs in some important meeting or other. There isn't a single Stage Director who could say the same about the Teatro Real. When I'm in a meeting with a bunch of managers, I like to say to them 'Look, let's stop messing about, our job is to get on and work!'

Anyway, I'm well involved in all that happens. I don't believe in these Operations Directors who don't know what's going on day to day. I'll tell you an anecdote. The other day Renée Fleming[3] was here to sing, and I went down for the rehearsals and sat in various reserved seats. From some of them you couldn't see her very well, because the conductor was in the way. So I tried to see her on the big screens, but I noticed that none of the cameras did close-ups. A singing concert can get very boring if you can't see the singer's face, so the next day we had a meeting with her people and I said 'I think we need to either get close-ups, or move the singer...' So we did, and that improved things hugely. All because I sat down like an audience member at a concert. It simply cannot be that you don't know what's going on; you have to, and not through the grapevine, but by being actually involved. If nobody goes down there, and nobody sees and nobody says anything, then maybe nobody knows. They're on the stage, and there are things that they don't notice, because you simply can't see them from the stage. So somebody has to watch it like the audience does. If nobody up there notices that you can hear the noise of a motor during a quiet piece of music, then somebody, observing as a spectator has to say something.

I think in some companies the bosses have it too easy. Sometimes they just don't know what's going on, they only have a connection with their secretary or others at the same level as them, and they invent a bunch of projects that really don't matter if they succeed or not. And I say that based on the experience of friends around me who are sick of being involved in projects that end up nowhere, either they're cancelled or the boss changes the idea or something, and the project dies. Sometimes I notice that nobody has really got the idea or made the connection, that the motivation is zero. And instead what seems to matter is a *civilised way of fighting for power*, the

---

[3] American soprano, born in Pennsylvania in 1957, mainly sings opera and *lieder*. She received her first award in 1988when she sang the role of the Countess in *The Marriage of Figaro* at the Houston Opera. From there she debuted in New York at the Royal Opera House (1989) and the Metropolitan (1991) and then Paris's Bastille Opera (in 1997 playing Manon). Her voice and expression have an extraordinary intensity, which makes her unsurpassable for certain repertoires. One of the current authors remembers with quite some emotion Fleming's interpretation of the 'Last Four Songs' by Richard Strauss, in which she manage some matchless levels of expression.

bigger office, an extra window... That's what happens in some companies, doesn't it? The bloke with the corner office is the senior boss, the guy down the hall with only one small window clearly ranks lower. And the objective has probably been lost.

This can't happen in the theatre. If something doesn't work, then the whole world knows, starting with the Stage Director, who isn't even one of our own guys – he's contracted in. If we do a good job, he'll be more successful, and if we do a bad one he'll lose reputation. We make this man's dream become a reality. Imagine what he'd say if things went wrong... so, no, we can't be locked away in here away from the reality. This is the big difference. *As boss and the person responsible for the stage, I have to touch the product.*

How to you manage the production process, from an administrative point of view?

The set building, if it's done externally, must be put out to tender. This is an obligation under state contract law, because the Teatro Real is a public company. We invite bids from seven or eight companies throughout Europe and we give them a copy of the formal project.

The bids come in and we decide who wins the contract. But it's not just a financial decision; they also have to outline the artistic value. Some of the projects are so huge they need to be subdivided, and this means a lot more work. In the *Barber of Seville* we did the metalwork in Toledo, the floor and painting were both done here in Madrid and the sculptures and frames were done in Rome, because they're the specialists in that. Of course, I've save a lot of money by subdividing, but it's a lot more work.

Once we've got all the bids, I start comparing the costs, and when I've got a more or less clear understanding of the offers from each company, I then start talking it over with the Set Designer. We have to be sure that the company we're choosing has the capacity to do the job properly. We've learnt over the years that while one hour of time away from the stage might cost €60, that same hour of work, if carried out on stage, could be worth, say, €5,000, because if you stop something on stage you have to stop maybe 70 people. That's why we consult the artists, we go over it all with them and we get their opinions.

Of course, there's always the possibility that the artist will say to us 'no way', or insist on some other alternatives. That happened to us in *Tosca*. For the sculpture of the *Pietà* the artist told us he wanted a specific workshop to do it; he thought it was the best one for the job, but it was more expensive – €2,400 more, but they did it and, well, the sculpture turned out perfect!

Once we have a winner for the tender, the Production department does the contract. We put in some clauses, guarantees, penalties, delivery dates, certificate requirements for things such as fire-resistance and so on. We also insist that every hanging element, or anything that's going to be above where people might be, has to be certified by the official engineering authority, which guarantees the capacity of the material to support the load ... see the kind of stuff we have to get into?

How do you begin work on a production?

The first thing we do is call a meeting between the company that won the tender and the artist, so that he or she can explain the whole vision, absolutely everything. The company can then propose things, 'Look, I don't think an 18 by 20 profile exists in the market, but how about 20 by 20?' 'Perfect, do it with 20 by 20, that's fine by me'. Or 'I'd like to do this in sheet metal, but I don't know what type', 'no worries, I'll bring you a selection of samples'. In one case we'd proposed making a sheet of foam covered in latex, but when the Set Designer explained the end result that he wanted, the atmosphere and everything, the guy from the company said he had a better idea, and would show us an example. He took us to the workshop and said, while showing us the samples, 'What you want to achieve is going to be better with this material than with the other' and, yes, he was right, and the Set Designer was happy.

Now we start to work on various things at the same time. One is the technical part, the nuts and bolts. I don't get involved in that; that's Carlos's side. We've been working together for 20 years, and he's a fundamental part of my life. You see? This is a team! The only thing I'm proud of is having the energy to get everyone else working; they know how to do the clever stuff.

We also at this stage continue to verify that everything we sketched in the plans is being realised correctly. We do this by job visits, which concentrate on the structural details, by overview and by observation. We also do artistic visits, with the Set Designer. He's there to check on the artistic side, and I'm there to make sure that it's feasible and it can happen, and therefore he can be happy. And if he's not, then I want to know why and what can be done about it. It might cost more money and I have to approve that, but otherwise it could all turn out wrong.

One of the great things about this job is that you get involved in all other sectors and industries. Suddenly you might say 'ah yes, I reckon we could get this done by a T-shirt stamping company ...' For example, a company in Toledo is doing the metalwork for the *Barber of Seville*. The guys in that company have no idea what a theatre is nor have any experience of a stage; they're metalworkers, you know, blacksmiths! But we've been able to guide them along a path that they're now finding really interesting.

And, then, finally, the processes come together and everything arrives on stage! Once it has arrived, you start to build it, and once it's built, you start to use it. Sometimes difficulties arise, but it's very rare, because we work well in advance and allow a large buffer for unexpected things to happen. Normally we insist that the set has been built before it's delivered to us, which means most of the problems have already been detected and ironed out.

We have a saying that all our guys love to repeat: 'don't worry; just deal with it'. The difference between worry and action is the key. If I'm getting on with things, then things happen; but if I'm worrying about things then nothing happens except the creation of a collective hysteria among people when they see things not happening.

This is the principal secret of the theatre. If you have time and space, you can achieve anything. But what we absolutely can't have happen is that a set arrives two days before curtain-up, and we find it's got problems, there's a bit missing here, or that ring for the supporting cable is in the wrong place... No, that kind of thing must not happen.

So you give the contractors a free hand to create things, to invent?

No, no, being creative is strictly limited to the work that's done with the Stage Director. Once all that's done, however, you still have to get down to the last details. Nobody can say that, 'oh, in item number two of the screws have to be countersunk'. So you deliver everything finished, artistic finishes included, even though someone will add an afterthought, a postscript along the lines of 'the finish should always be in line with the wishes of the artist', because the artist could come along tomorrow and tell you that this needs to be red, or that needs to be blue, and then you just have to do it.

You have to disassemble the entire set, because if you don't then you might miss some important detail – like if someone uses a piece of wood that's more than two metres forty, and then you find out it won't go through the door... you can't have that kind of thing coming at you by surprise.

(At this point Carlos joins the meeting)

Carlos.   Yes, for example, in the *Barber of Seville*, they've made all these flats, or pieces of scenery. The set is made up of 25 flats, each one on a trolley,[4] so that's 25 trolleys besides the one trolley we made as a prototype.

DB.   Yeah, exactly, but this is a really artistic issue, it's a theatrical thing, not a mechanical one. If Carlos hadn't been there with the draftsmen, these guys would have had no idea what they were doing, at least in a theatrical sense. They draw, but it's Carlos who knows what type of wheels to use, because this set need to be moved by the extras, not the stagehands, and how the floor should be... Again, we're the guys who translate. If we had let the draftsmen do the set, they would have done the job, quick as a flash. But we're the guys who 'translate things into *theatre*', and we can say to them 'be careful here, this has to go over this part, or back here, and you're in danger of wrinkling the cloth...

Carlos.   We made a prototype trolley in the Teatro Real's workshop, to be able to design the real thing, which was approved by the Set Director and the Stage Director. Now we have clear what we're going to do. For example, all the trolleys are hooked to each other, and in this way we've learnt how we want the hooks to be so that building the set can be as quick as possible. The

---

[4] In this case the trolley is a flat, wheeled platform that carries a set or a part of a set. As it's on wheels, it can move about and appear or disappear as required.

prototype trolley could be mounted in 20 minutes. But using this linking-hook system that we designed, once all the material is here then we can have two people mount all 22 trolleys that make up the set in just 15 minutes.

These trolleys, are they more or less the same for each piece of set?

DB.   No, they have different formats for different purposes and, what happens is you get to know a lot about how to do them. I'll tell you a silly anecdote. One time we had to get two armchairs on stage by themselves. The guys couldn't see how to make this happen without making a noise. They tried trolleys, wheels... Finally, someone put a piece of carpet underneath the armchairs and pushed. It worked perfectly. When you're 20, you work in the theatre, and you see something like that and it stays with you. The next time you come across a similar problem, you can say 'hold on guys, I know how to do this. Give me a piece of carpet...'

Who has designed this way of working?

I can't take the credit –this type of opera theatre is the brainchild of José Luis Tamayo. But the entire working world needs blueprints. It's then up to each person to improve upon them, make them prettier, more informative, more explanatory. The specific method here is ours, but it's just a work style. The complete system of procedures comes from no one person; it's the culmination of many things from many people. When you see that people are asking a lot of questions then you realise that they haven't understood what you want. And if they haven't understood, then it's because I haven't explained it well. And if the people don't want this method of working, then why are we doing it? I'd have to find another system to get us to the desired result. But, yes, there are times when I say 'Carlos, I don't want more details', because too many details can be scary.

Italians, for example, are scared of too many details. 'This looks expensive!' they say, but it's not true. They only say it because that level of precision scares them, and they decide that the best thing to do is say it's too expensive. It terrorises them when you say 'and these screws here should be number tens'. Of course, sometimes such precision isn't helpful. As I said, I believe everybody's objective is to keep the water flowing, that it passes over everybody, and everybody is then 'in the loop'. *Responsibility and capacity to understand.*

All of this is a part of the translation. In the end you've got a good result with the artist, and you feel good if the set is well done, if you've met the financial requirements, if you've managed to put it all together quickly, and if the artist has got the set he wanted. Two worlds co-exist here. One is the production: make the set. The other is creating the world that the artist wants. In this last goal, the service is all about availability, professionalism and thinking of things before he does.

XII
Characteristics of Operations Management

One of the critical functions of a manager is to translate. Translate the mission, the purpose of the company, into material elements (machines, processes, products, information, etc.) that provide the service. This translating function became very clear in our conversation with Daniel. To achieve this properly, the Director must *keep his feet firmly on the ground*. You've got to go down and listen to the client and understand his problem in detail. We'll look at these key points in this chapter.

Translator

Operations is a process of translation

The first point is to conceptualise Operations Management as a translator. In a high-tech opera theatre, two traditionally opposed worlds co-exist. On one side are the artists, and on the other is the operational system. The Technical Management team says, 'Our obligation is to make possible the idea of the artist'. For an Operations Director, the translation of this sentence is 'My obligation is to make possible the ideas of the strategy'. This has two implications.

Strategies are not for discussion, they're for fulfilling.

First. The strategic objectives are not up for discussion. If *Macbeth* has to be scary, or cold, this is not incumbent upon the Technical Management or the team. It is impossible to dismiss a strategic objective out of hand; it can't be dismissed until it has been demonstrated that it's impossible to achieve. And take careful note here. We said impossible. How do you know if something's impossible? Well, you don't. It's impossible to know what's impossible. We know this. It might sounds like a play on words, but at heart it is simple. You can't know that something's impossible until (a) it's been logically demonstrated from certain premises, or (b) all the possible alternative actions have been listed and all have been discounted.

Perpetual motion. Do you believe in the second law of thermodynamics? If so, then perpetual motion is impossible, because it contradicts a premise that you accept, that you believe to be true. But if you don't believe, then you'll have to try it. You need to prove it. Non-believers have been trying for centuries, sometimes with highly creative efforts that are not at all obvious. Maybe somebody somewhere will find a solution, a proof, in which case the second 'law' will have been proven false and all the people who believed in it will have been wrong... and we'll have to come up with a new theory. But this could take a long time to happen. Therefore, supposing that we're not disposed to wait for centuries, until all the possibilities have been exhausted, it will not be possible to prove the operational impossibility of perpetual motion.

From a more practical point of view, for example, staff should not argue with sales targets. We're dealing with strategy, and strategies are not for discussion, they're for fulfilling. Or at least, efforts should be made to try to fulfil them, or to understand why they can't be fulfilled. Sometimes strategists can change their ideas by being confronted with the consequences of those ideas. Consider the work of our protagonists. They have a budget and some physical limitations, but they must put on the production. Now the question is how to achieve that production within those limits. If it's necessary then things can be changed, but it's no bad thing to change an idea that could be made operative by a more imaginative process. This is a fault unworthy of a good worker. Can you imagine that the telephone wouldn't have been invented if nobody had known about copper wire? It's inconceivable. As Daniel says, 'I can't let silly things make me fail'. And if somebody can't accept the strategy of a company then the solution is very simple... but please ask them to close the door behind them. You cannot remain part of a group whose goals and values you don't share. That is not a cohesive group; there's a lack of unity and it's doomed to failure every time.

Second. Maybe we've been a bit too hasty. What if we realise that our strategy has a weak point? Not that it's wrong; that's not demonstrable, but just that it has a weak point. In the end, all the preliminary work done by Daniel and Carlos consists of conscientiously analysing all the weak points of all the ideas – the strategies – of the artist. One weak point is a 'what would happen if..?' For example, 'if we did it like this it'd be very expensive', 'it'd take too long', 'it'll need three motors' or 'we can't put it together in the time available'. At the end of the day, you have to be able to question strategies, but only until we agree on which ones can be implemented. As our protagonists do. 'Until I'm convinced', says Daniel. In many companies, it's a corporate hobby to question strategy. 'No, if they don't know what they want' and 'where are we going with this?' or 'where are we heading' are questions frequently heard

You can be a strategist for only five minutes a day.

in bars near the office, asked by people aspiring to be the Managing Director.

Enough of this wasted and wasteful effort, please! We must avoid this constant question that disorientates and demoralises. You can only be Managing Director from 08.00 am to 08.05 am. In those five minutes we can question anything and everything. But once the time's up, you have to make it possible. Put all the ideas in a list and stick it on the main entrance door to the office, and see how many discussions it'll save.

There is another aspect that it's worth mentioning. Probably without knowing it, in this concept of *translator*, Daniel has summarised a (hefty and academic) theory of Operations, and this concept of translator simplifies it and makes it more digestible.

So, in the end, in Operations you need to operate; things need to be done. And to achieve this in an adequate way you need to have the necessary knowledge. Both the current authors 'know' how to make a Spanish omelette. But our knowledge is different. In one case it turns out as a pretty reasonable tortilla. In the other it turns out as a messy pile of egg and potato.

Less trivial. Lighting a scene requires a series of operations, lighting the spots, selecting the gel or filter...later this will be recorded on a computer sequencer that can replay the order of the functions during a performance. All of this works as though the different elements were giving orders to each other, in a language that both the order-giver and the order-receiver can understand clearly and without ambiguity.

The orders given should become more precise in proportion to the 'stupidity' of the last operator in the chain. If the last operator is a lighting expert, then it's probably sufficient to say 'keep the spot on the singer during the whole aria'. And that's that. But not if the final operator is a computer. In that case the commands need to be translated into a form that the sequencing software can understand, perhaps something like 'MOV SP, AX; ADD AY;...' and other such poetry. For this sort of cryptic language you need a translator, someone who 'speaks' both 'languages', that of the lighting expert and that of the sequencing application.

A large proportion of the problems encountered in Operations revolve around the creation of procedures to enable various 'processors' to collaborate in doing whatever necessary to achieve the desired result. And these processors generally speak a different, specialist language, to which the final result needs to be translated and expressed in another language. This is the function of translation; to reach a specification, from a general starting description, of the detail of required operations, and specified in such a way that all the processors can understand.

In light of these comments, the reader is advised to reread the previous chapter, in order to understand up to what point the presented scheme is in accordance with the process described. We think you'll be convinced that the preparation of an operation of any type is a Process of Translation, and that this is the central role of the translator.

Plans and translation

Translation in the theatre is not only done between two languages. There is a whole hierarchy of intermediate languages that cover all aspects of the theatre. From the set to the way the orchestra should play, whose final translation is the job of the Musical Director, but for the moment let's stick with the set.

The set painter asked Daniel what the set 'smells' like. The Stage Director specifies how things must move and evolve. Daniel and Carlos (men of the theatre, and therefore people who understand the language of the artists) transform everything into instructions for the Technical department. This is a language of trolleys, wheels, times and movements. And the Technical department goes away and puts that in terms of profiles, weights, hooks and flats; a language far removed from that of the artist. The excuse is the contract process. But it is a good excuse, because it signifies a commitment to document, in an unambiguous manner, everything that has been discussed and agreed. We know, henceforth, that we know exactly what we want. Here are some plans! The height of specification.

Of course, the set is an important part, but still only a part, of the final service; the opera. At this point we have it almost translated to the final language that'll allow us to put it all together. This is an old process in the industry. Plans are our daily bread – no plan, no nothing. Everybody makes plans...but not so easily in services. As the language of service can be ambiguous and elusive, it's difficult to make a plan the way it should be made. Imagine the plan of a good meal in a nouvelle cuisine restaurant. Yes, yes, we know about recipes. But the difference between a recipe and a constructive plan is enormous. The processor who interprets a recipe needs a lot more prior knowledge than the processor who follows a plan!

So is it that our protagonists can't award themselves medals for having discovered something that the industry has known for ever. Maybe they deserve medals for having introduced it in the world of services, something that might have been thought impossible. What is important though is that that had arrived at this knowledge by the growing need to document and specify, with precision, a service.

Keeping your feet firmly on the ground

Allowing for all the subtleties of the case, Daniel is absolutely right when he says that managers in some companies are totally obsessed by power.

The reader will have noticed that in recent years, particularly in big companies, they started to think that the client – each client – is simply a small extension of the company. And there are so many of these individual clients that one more or less doesn't matter much. Try to get some satisfaction from them when something goes wrong, and you'll see the result. The present authors collect examples of bad service and lack of attention. Lately we've had to buy a bigger folder to keep them all in because they're coming in faster and faster. Especially prevalent are examples of bad service received from the customer service telephone lines.

It's been years since the senior management of big companies have dealt with a client. The big bosses of the banks have no idea about the real people who are their customers. They're too busy wielding their *power*; buying, selling and sometimes swapping companies. The power associated with their positions is enormous; it is very, very difficult to resist the temptation of using that power, and that spirit is easily propagated throughout the entire organisation. We've known many companies where power is the central focus of the company. Oh yes, and some of those companies also have those things ... what were they called? Oh yes, 'clients'.

A company exists to provide *service* to the *customer*. This should be the most rigorously followed objective of all the management team.[1] To achieve this, Operations must work without failures. Didn't the so-called Quality Movement say something similar?

The Operations Manager must keep his feet firmly on the ground

The only way to be sure of all these things is to be on top of them, stuck to them. You have to follow the Operations in great detail. *An Operations Manager must have his feet firmly on the ground.* A restaurant owner should eat at least once in his own restaurant (disguised, of course, so nobody recognises him, otherwise the test is invalid). The president of Iberia should fly – incognito – on one of his own planes as just another passenger ... and in tourist class.

Our protagonists have this very clear. They see what happens at rehearsals, they observe the difficulties, and they get to know their providers personally. In this last case, they don't only select the providers, but also carefully follow the entire subsequent creation process. 'We can't find out later that it makes a noise ...', 'We can't find that it doesn't fit through the door ...' Every day they examine the evolution of each element in the

---

[1] A good illustrative case is that of Coca-Cola. A few years ago the company experienced significant drops in its share price, which led to the substitution of its chairman. The new president announced, upon his arrival, that he'd come to improve the customer service and to restore the competitive capacity of the company ... and that this was far more important than restoring the share price or earning money for the shareholders. The price of the shares plummeted within days, but the company has reversed this trend and is recovering its competitiveness. Now, its shares are considered, by the experts, as offering some of the best investment prospects on the market.

production, without getting in the way of the initiative that each person needs to have and to use, but still keeping the entire process in mind and the purpose of it all.

'The entire process is like a *waterfall*, with the water flowing down over everybody. The only secret is that *the water must continue to flow*, always. If the water's not flowing, then you've got no waterfall!' says Daniel.

A recent study of successful European companies confirmed that the condition of 'keeping feet firmly on the ground' is present in (almost) all. In successful companies, the Operations Managers are very involved in the detail of the service provided. No ifs or buts. And this means they open their doors and they go to have a look at things where they're happening; on the ground. Without getting in the way, and perhaps incognito, but they don't stay in their offices like gods on Mount Olympus.

If you don't get down to 'the trenches' you'll lose contact with the real world. You might gain power, but you'll lose reality.

Conclusions

In this chapter, we've seen how one of the basic functions of Operations Management is translation. Operations is a process of translation and the Operations Management must turn what the strategy dictates into reality. This goes hand in hand with two other aspects: one is to not constantly question the *strategy* of a company. Five minutes a day is more than enough to alert senior management about the potential risks of a strategy. The second aspect is the necessity to remain with your *feet firmly on the ground*. An Operations Manager must 'live' the service. It's indispensable to understand what the client's realities are. *Translation, not questioning the strategy*, and *keeping your feet firmly on the ground* are the three basic points in the role of an Operations Manager.

Finally, we propose some questions for you to reflect upon:

- How do you focus the function of translation?
- In your company, do people constantly discuss the strategy?
- When was the last time you saw a real, live client?
- Are you a client of your own service?

Part II
Attractiveness

As we have already analysed Operations from the point of view of Efficiency, we'll now take a look at the second component of the Golden Triad: Attractiveness. This could be defined as 'getting brain power to learn', and this learning should revert to both the individual and the company; to the former because it increases an individual's stock of knowledge and to the latter because it helps to solve service problems. How to achieve this is the focus of the next six chapters.

In previous chapters, we've seen that the source of knowledge acquisition is problem-solving. This is what leads the individual to learn, and thus is the basis of Attractiveness.

The biggest creator of movement in a company is innovation. We define innovation as 'doing things, new or old, in a different way'. Innovation is, then, a great generator of problems. Given that learning is achieved by problem-solving, we can conclude that there is no learning without innovation and nor, therefore, is there Attractiveness without innovation. This is why it is essential to understand what it means 'to innovate', how it is done and how it is channelled.

The Teatro Real appears to be an innovative company, given that they introduce various new products every year. On further investigation, we will see that the process of innovation at the Teatro Real is always the same, given that the source of this innovation is, essentially, the creative process of the Stage Director. Operations are structured to help the translation process flow from the desire of the innovator to the reality of the production. The process is always the same, but gives freedom to each agent to be able to make changes. Innovation is not synonymous with chaos. The Teatro Real provides us with a perfect example of a company in constant innovative movement, but with perfectly structured processes in place to achieve this.

The New Operational Culture needs to integrate the process of innovation, and people at every level of the organisation play a part in that. A company cannot be Attractive if it doesn't innovate. But that's not all; a company that innovates too much is not an attractive company either – it becomes a mess, and the huge quantity of problems generated as a result creates too big a challenge for people.

In addition, nobody has brilliant ideas every day. Or at least, if they do, they probably belong in a museum, not in a company.

In Operations, it is not necessary to constantly chase fantastic ideas. If we do this, we'll overlook hundreds of smaller ideas that might have great potential to become big ideas. There must be room for innovations that propose modest changes to the already existing. Our slogan must always be: 'We don't want one improvement worth a million Euros; we want a thousand improvements worth a thousand Euros each!' With this vision, every person in the company feels invited to implement his or her thousand-Euro innovation; not just the few geniuses thinking of big changes. This massive-scale innovation has to be achieved in the New Operational Culture.

XIII
The Innovation Process

In this chapter, we'll be talking again with Daniel Bianco about the change process that each opera introduces in the Teatro Real.

How does artistic management choose a Stage Director?

We search in the market. France – well, Spain too, but especially France – is desperately trying to convince Almodóvar[1] to do an opera. I have no idea if he actually wants to do an opera, but it'd be a great bit of marketing, having Almodóvar doing one ... I've also heard that Spielberg[2] is going to do Wagner's Ring cycle, though, so I don't know ... Lately it seems that they're trying to get many people from prose theatre and cinema to do opera. I think it's a different business. Nevertheless, there have been some good results: Herzog[3] is a great film-maker and he's done opera in two of the great opera theatres of the world. Visconti was also a great Stage Director at La Scala. And

---

[1] Pedro Almodóvar (Ciudad Real, 1951) is arguably the most successful and certainly the best-known Spanish film director. Winner of numerous awards, including Oscar wins for best screenplay (*Hable Con Ella, Talk to Her*) and best foreign film (*Todo Sobre Mi Madre, All about My Mother*) and almost-countless nominations, Almodóvar has probably done more for Spanish cinematography than anyone since Luis Buñuel.

[2] Steven Spielberg (Cincinnati, 1946). Cinema producer and director, with more than 100 films to his name. A multimillionaire, he has amassed a fortune and a first-rate reputation in the film industry with his vision and passion. He has had some incomparable successes such as *ET, Close Encounters of the Third Kind* and the Indiana Jones trilogy, known throughout the world. His incursions into graphic animation through his company SKG DreamWorks (the initials of Spielberg, Katz, Geffen) have also placed him in the vanguard of this genre, alongside Pixar.

[3] Werner Herzog (real name Werner Stipetić, born Munich 1942). He grew up in a remote Bavarian village and, as a child, he didn't see television, let alone a film. He has produced or directed over 40 films, published various books and directed more than a dozen operas. One of his best well-known films is *Aguirre, The Wrath of God* (1972) in which he tells the story of Lope de Aguirre, the *conquistador* who first navigated the Amazon river in search of El Dorado, and featured an incredible performance by the great Klaus Kinski in the lead role.

Zeffirelli, of course ... There are many people who can do many interesting things. But in reality more or less everything's on the market. Even a Stage Director always tries to invent something different, something unique. Maybe it works, maybe it doesn't, but you always try to be creative.

And do people specialise?

People expect a certain type of result from a certain type of person. In the same way that if you wanted to buy an abstract painting for your living room you wouldn't get an Antonio López, because he is a hyper-realist painter; well, here it's the same, although perhaps not so exaggerated. There are some people who you see better suited for comedy or tragedy. Some people manage groups well, others are better at dealing with individual characters but not groups and then there are people who are more skilled at visual stuff. If you call Bob Wilson to do an opera, then you know the kind of result you'll get; you know his 'language'. He has a way of dealing with the cast where the characters practically become another part of the set. So, there are operas that he can do and others he can't.

You said earlier that one should always be 'five minutes early' ... ?

Well, sort of – in the theatre you should always be *five minutes ahead*. In fact, I have to work on projects a year in advance, but the daily reality is five minutes ahead. In the theatre, there's a job that's been lost, the prompter. Well, not completely lost yet in opera, but in prose theatre it has completely disappeared. To be a prompter is a difficult thing, one of the most difficult jobs in the theatre. Can you imagine how difficult it is to intuit when the actor is going to lose his or her way in the script? If you give the prompt early, when the actor's still talking, it's pointless. You have to anticipate that they're going to get lost, that they're going to 'dry up', as we say. Well, that's like our job here – we have to anticipate when something or somebody is going to get lost.

Another example: a guy working for Volkswagen spends various years designing a car, making models, spending millions. But once that car gets past prototype, they make six million of them. We are always building prototypes, *even though the steps we take are always the same*. The way of building a prototype is always the same; we always have to contract a singer and a Set Designer, we always need a model of the set, we always need to prepare a plan, we always have to build it, we always have to rehearse ...

Still you have to try to anticipate everything that can happen: logical or illogical, but possible. And this task is only helped by the experience you gain in the theatre; exposure to things that shouldn't work, but do.

I'll tell you another daft anecdote from years ago. Marta Maier was working as a costume assistant and Set Designer in the Zarzuela theatre. She came to help me on an opera as an unpaid trainee. Anyway, she'd just arrived and still had no idea as to how to get hold of weird things. On one particular day we were handing out the shoes – it's an appalling job, everybody hates it. I ask you what size you take, you say 40, I bring you a 41, and they're always too small and they hurt something chronic; always. So anyway, we were handing out the shoes. There was one singer who took a size 37, and we'd had some shoes made to measure and lined with the same material as her costume. The singer tried the shoes and said no, they were too small and there was absolutely no way she could wear them. Marta came to see me, tearing her hair out, thinking that we'd have to send them back, get some more made, line them again ... 'Daniel, Daniel, Daniel, the shoes don't fit, the shoes don't fit!' 'Calm down, it's ok.' 'It's not! We have to get the shoes made again and everything!' So I said to her 'don't worry, let's go and talk to the singer'. So we did, and the singer said 'it's impossible, the shoes are too small'. So I said 'No problem, we'll have it sorted by tomorrow.' Well, the next day we went back with the same shoes, unchanged, for her to try on. 'Ooh, they fit perfectly!'

It doesn't always happen like that, of course, because sometimes it's true and the shoe's too small. But I had tried that approach before, and when they'd tried on the shoe I realised immediately that it was just pre-show nerves, the hysteria of the day before opening-night. Marta always tells that anecdote as a demonstration of the kind of illogical problems we sometimes have to solve.

There's a rehearsal called *ante piano* which is a full rehearsal, with set and costume, but only with piano accompaniment. This is the day when everything goes haywire; their petticoats are bothering them, they can't sing because the wig's too tight, they can't bend because I-don't-know-what will happen with the hat ... normally, it's all just pre-show nerves; the 'hysteria of the day before'. But you have to remember that they might have a point, and you have to give them time to adapt. Beatriz, imagine that I now put you in a hoop-skirt ...

You can't bend down ...

Exactly, so what do we do to anticipate these situations? We start in the rehearsal rooms, using outfits that are similar, in volume and *drop* characteristics, to the ones they'll be using in the show. You already know on the first day that, in Tosca for example, everything's going to bother them: the set, the props, the costumes ... everything. That day is always a day of conflict. Over time, you learn to distinguish between a singer who's ill, for real, and when there's some other problem and health is just an excuse. There are many related psychological issues.

Why does this happen? *Because we're working with humans who are trying to create something new.* It's very hard for them. I've lived through it and I know. I know what it's like to be doing a set design and you go to bed at night without knowing what to do, how to do it. It's like a ... a pinch in the stomach ... maybe you've said to yourself ah, fantastic, I'm going to do it this way, but how the hell do you do it that way? And this sensitive side, the human side, is the one you work with.

You always have to go *five minutes ahead* of what's happening. If you can predict things, then they can't catch you by surprise. For example, if you're with the artist, much of the time you know what they're going to ask you for. If you see the artist is stuck on a scene with the extras, it's just not working out; you know that at some point he's going to ask you to call an extra rehearsal with the extras. If you see that he's blocked, you have to try to solve it. This is going five minutes ahead.

You can never play catch-up. The artist cannot say to you what's going to happen; you have to be ready, and when the artist says 'I'll need a few more rehearsals because something's missing' then at that moment you have to be able to say 'of course, we can schedule them for such-and-such a day at such-and-such a time.'

Does everybody agree with that philosophy?

I have to ask it of all the section heads, but even the technician who's working the lights should anticipate it. Everyone, in his or her own area, has to anticipate – if a technician has climbed 11 m up the scaffolding and is working on spot number 28, and he has it in mind that the next spot he's going to be asked for is the one next to him, then he's prepared for when the request comes 'please, give me...' and bang, he's done it before they've finished the sentence. But what we can't ask him to do is think of those lights from an artistic point of view, because he'll rightly say 'look, mate, that's your job'.

However, it is the same type of philosophy, yes. We notice this kind of anticipation a lot in props. The folks there get under the skin of the Stage Director, and you'll hear things like 'he asked me for six chairs, but I've got eight because I'm sure he's going to ask for two more'.

All the people in charge here, in particular, need to be five minutes ahead. If you know there is what we call an 'Italian' rehearsal,[4] if you know you'll need two extra chairs, if you know you'll need lights for the score ... of course, if you're doing an open-air show you can't predict so far in advance that it'll rain on that day, but it's fundamental to always have the answer ready for the day-to-day stuff. A theatre works well when it's working in advance, ahead of schedule.

How does this affect the senior Stage Manager?

He's the Technical Director of the opera, the boss of everything that happens while setting up. But once the rehearsal or show has begun, it's the Stage

---

[4] The 'Italian' is a rehearsal with no set or stage activity – the chorus, singers and orchestra go through the entire opera 'musically'.

Manager who becomes the boss. For example, if the fire curtain is supposed to drop to do a set change, then that's the decision of the senior Stage Manager, but once the curtain's up the action is directed by the Stage Manager.

The senior Stage Manager hands the performance over to the Stage Manager. In fact, if you listen through the headphones when there's a rehearsal at, say, 1700, then at 1630 you'll hear the senior Stage Manager address the head of the Stage Managers and say 'all ready, handing over'. And from that point, it's the Stage Managers who have control of everything. But if something happens during a break or a change, then it's back to the senior Stage Manager.

The appointment of these Stage Managers is crucial. I give it a lot of thought; I don't know if they know that but I do, because I think that some of them are better at certain things than others. I don't mean professionally, though, because in that aspect I think they're all top-class, but I do mean at the level of translation.

And the Stage Managers?

As you know, Marta Maier is the boss of the senior Stage Managers. Marta was a script-girl in film. Her brother-in-law is Ruggero Raimondi, so she already knew something of opera...but Marta had no idea, absolutely none, of what a theatre was about. She always says that she learnt everything that goes on backstage from me. I'm like her big brother; I'm the only person who can tell her off.

Beneath her are two senior Stage Managers. Each of them is in charge of an opera, and each one of these senior Stage Managers has a group of 'normal' Stage Managers, four or five depending on the opera, who run all the performances of that opera. I try to keep those groups together; the group that did this opera should do that one, then have a rest and do another. It's Marta's job to keep the adrenaline flowing. The senior Stage Manager is, during the performances, the most senior person on stage.

Marta assigns a senior Stage Manager to each opera, generally according to the type of opera – between a German opera and one by Verdi there's a huge difference in the profile required. You have to like the opera you're managing![5]

The other Stage Managers are physically on the stage, in the wings. They're the ones who call the entrances, exits, props, arrivals... a lot of things happen around the stage! Choirboys, chorus... you need to take them down, bring them back up, get the smoke going, stop the smoke... loads of things.

During the performance, the Stage Manager controls things, and there are many things to control! His orders are short and sweet – he'll look at the

---

[5] Author's note: German operas tend to be quite long; sometimes you can 'happily' spend half an hour listening to one person singing.

singer who's about to go on, and when he says 'enter' they go on. No questions. With the extras, who don't know music, it's more complicated because they often have to enter in time with the music 'Extras: and 1, 2, 3, 4, 5 6...' Imagine if there are three different entrances with 30, 30 and 20 people! The Stage Managers give them all a number and call all their entrances as they go...

The Stage Manager who sits at the central control desk, as well as calling the *tops*, also does the PA announcements for the whole theatre. He starts with '30 minutes to go', then calls 15, 5 and the final call to start the performance. Later he starts cuing the artists, in various languages and in a personalised way. For example, 'Mrs Whoever, please go to the stage'.

The senior Stage Manager is the one who takes decisions when something happens. He also carries a report book, where he notes second by second what has happened, what time it started, when it finished... he notes everything down as it happens.

(Enter Marta Maier)

DB.   Marta, could you give us an idea of how you work?

MM.   All the Stage Managers know music, and our work revolves around the score. What I have here is the score of *Macbeth* [she shows us the score, which she frequently refers to during this conversation]. It's the reduced version for piano and voice that exists for almost all operas. On the back of each page, which is usually left blank, we note down everything that happens. Stage Managers always use pencils, so you can rub things out... the money we spend on erasers is incredible!

For example, this note here shows Felipe, at entrance 3 (box 3), where a wagon comes in with a group of the chorus. Here are the names of the chorus members who go on, plus six dancers. We put their names down because many of them forget where they have to go on. They never know so it's always 'oops, where am I supposed to go on?' 'Let's see María, you go on there...'

I'm present at all the operas, but only supervising. I don't watch to see whether María or Alicia have gone on or not. Later the senior Stage Manager will tell me. 'María and Alicia didn't turn up so they didn't go on.' But of course I can see certain things that they can't, and I'll tell them later.

What procedures does a Stage Manager follow?

MM.   The idea of the *tops*, as you know, is not mine; it was created by Tamayo. But the work system that we use in the Teatro Real is mine. What should be written, where, and how it's organised, not just the artistic side, the stage management, but also the technical. In the *top* schedule of a rented production, for example *L'Upupa*,[6] we already know how the opera should be

---

[6] Opera by Hans Werner Henze (1926–), the full title is *L'Upupa und der Triumph der Sohnesliebe*. It's a modern opera with an oriental setting. The Grand Vizier of Manda has lost his hoopoe – yes that sounds like nonsense, but bear with us; a hoopoe is a

and what it looks like, so for every change that should happen we stick here [she shows the back of a page] a colour photo of the set and a small plan. But *Macbeth* is a new production, and as it keep changing there are no photos yet. In every case though, we mark the score with a different colour for each singer. Pink is Lady Macbeth, yellow is Banquo, and this one here should be Malcolm ... And this here is the chorus [she shows the reduced score]. For example, here, these three start singing and these don't. At the rehearsals, you're often dashing about on the stage and this is a very quick and easy way to see when things are happening, you know?

We also have a scene index, with descriptions and the people who appear in each. This is because when you start the rehearsals, suddenly they'll say 'ok, let's go to scene 9' and you, as Stage Manager, have to call all the people in that scene, so you look in the book you say ahh, well in this scene this person, and this person, and this person, and this person, are in it and you call them, and that's it.

Before a rehearsal or performance, the Stage Manager telephones all the extras, dancers and singers who are involved. He or she calls them at home, to remind them of the dates and times they've committed to. It's a courtesy we like to employ; not all the theatres do it.

The place where we've seen people working most like us is Holland. I picked up many tricks there. In Holland, just a few girls manage to do everything, absolutely everything.

And if something goes wrong, what do you do?

MM.   The worst problem is when you have to take out the Emergency Book. Imagine this: this is an example that actually happened to us, in *Madame Butterfly*.[7] We're about to start, we've given the 5 minutes to curtain,

---

beautiful bird – and it was apparently his pride and joy. He lost it because, while trying to capture it in his hands, it flew away, injured. His three sons set out to find the bird, but only the third son, Al Kasim, really applies himself to the task, while the other two indulge in alcohol and gambling. Along the way, Al Kasim, with the help of his demon, finds the love of a beautiful woman and a magic box, and overcomes a series of tests that end up going on beyond the end of the opera itself.

[7] Opera by Giacomo Puccini. Set in Japan, as Puccini liked exotic environments, it tells the story of Cio Cio San (Madame Butterfly in Japanese). An unscrupulous American, Lieutenant Pinkerton of the frigate Abraham Lincoln decides he doesn't want to sleep alone and, through a 'matchmaker' who charges for the service, he finds a wife in the person of Butterfly, a geisha. He marries her, on a short-term contract, although she believes it is binding. When her uncle, a monk, finds out he hurries to the wedding and curses her. Cio Cio is sufficiently daft to fall head over heels in love, and gets pregnant. Pinkerton returns to America to marry, in his words, 'a real American wife', but promises that he'll return and Cio Cio believes him. She continues dreaming of her sailor, waiting for the 'beautiful day when we'll see him sailing back into port', as she sings in the well-known aria 'Un bel di vedremo'. Finally, the American cynic returns to Japan, married to an American woman, and

we've dimmed the lights in the auditorium, the maestro hasn't entered yet... and the singer says she can't go on, she can't sing.

DB.   In these situations you cannot improvise. So we have this book, where all eventualities are listed, and the procedure to follow. Of course, not to the level of detail like tonsillitis or appendicitis, but certainly what to do in general in the case of a medical emergency or whatever. You read what it says you should do and then, well, you go ahead and do it.

MM.   The Emergency Book was originally written by José Luis Tamayo, and we've revised and changed it as we've gone along. It also contains operating rules. For example, if there's a three minute delay, then you can safely leave the audience sitting in the theatre, but if it's more than five minutes you must put the house lights up so that people have the chance to leave. If it's more than half an hour, you have to give the public the offer of a refund. If they've left the theatre, then you have to either wait for them to come back another time or to call you.

DB.   You know why this book exists? This problem must occur in all the professions. But in the theatre, and in Spain particularly, when there's a problem, everyone has an *opinion*. Twenty-eight people giving opinions and there is no-one, *no-one who is solving anything*. The book is the code that must be followed. For example, in Macbeth, there's a set wall and we had problems with the motor for it. We had problems during two rehearsals, but never during the performances. We called a small meeting with the section heads, the Stage Managers, the set managers, the machinery managers, and we came up with a plan of action. If it fails at the start of the performance, we have to do this, if it fails half way, then we do that, and if it fails at the end, then that, and nobody has to be in two minds. Fine. So we go to the performances, and it fails in the last one. All the sections reacted perfectly, everybody knew how to react. That's why we have the book. It's an amazing situation, to have to turn on the microphone and have to give the warning, because you don't know if what you're doing is good or bad, and you need somebody to help...

MM.   The Stage Managers also check if everyone's present. It's supposed that you don't raise the curtain until everybody's present and correct,

---

well satisfied with his exploits. Butterfly feels that, under the circumstances, she can't continue living and she calmly commits *sepukku*, the ritual suicide commonly known as *hara kiri*. The opera contains a very famous love duet, at the end of the first act, which Butterfly and Pinkerton sing when alone after their wedding. It is, in the opinion of some, one of the most powerfully erotic moments in the history of opera, only comparable with the duet in Wagner's *Tristan und Isolde*. The simplicity and naivety of Cio Cio is juxtaposed with the crudeness of Pinkerton, who tries to seduce her almost purely for the sex; the music conveying this much better than can be managed here in writing. Puccini gives us here some sublimely beautiful music with incredible, amorous overtones.

because that's extremely risky. Even if a person's cue isn't until an hour into the performance, we still tell them they have to be at the theatre at least quarter of an hour before curtain-up.

Do they have to sign in?

DB. The extras do, but I've no idea about the chorus – they're subcontracted, so they're independent.

MM. No idea; the chorus inspector will come and say 'we're missing seven today' and he's fine with that. And I can't do anything about it. In the case of the soloists, who all have their dressing rooms on the same floor, the Stage Managers go to each one to check who has arrived and who has not; in a performance they come down to the stage an hour early and check that everything is in the right place; the props, the makeup... everything they call the final check-up. The other day in *Rita,*[8] we couldn't start on time because this young extra hadn't arrived, he was in a traffic jam, and we had to start seven minutes late. He was a very important extra; if he had been one of the masses we could have started, but he had a bit of action just at the start of the opera. You can't say we're going to start and just hope he turns up, can you?

DB. But the Stage Managers do much more than this. When we inaugurated the theatre with *La Vida Breve,*[9] we had this donkey that had to cross the stage, and the donkey started peeing and defecating on stage... we had to call the cleaners in! What was it called, that donkey?

MM. Not sure... Vanesa? Yes, Vanesa.

---

[8] Rita is a little-known opera by Gaetano Donizetti (Bergamo, 1797). One of the most representative composers of *Bel Canto*, Donizetti is wonderful for singers, as he treats their voices with the greatest care; allowing the necessary space for a voice to shine. Despite being considered a trivial composer, he has composed some masterpieces such as *Lucia de Lammermoor, La Favorita, L'Elisir d'amore* and *Don Pasquale*, among others. All of them contain some moments of pure joy for the singers. For example, one of his works, *La fille du Regiment*, contains an aria for tenor, known as the Mount Everest for tenors, or the nine-C aria, in which the tenor must be high C nine times fairly early on in the piece, leaving not much time to warm up to it. Obviously, this kind of aria is only within the reach of small number of singers such as Alfredo Kraus and Luciano Pavarotti.

[9] A short opera in two acts by Manuel de Falla. An opera with a gypsy setting, set in Granada in the Albaicín. An Andalusian gentleman, Paco, is going to marry the rich Carmela nevertheless he woos and wins the gypsy Salud without her knowing of his commitment to Carmela. Paco ends up marrying the heiress, to the desperation of Salud who must be lacking something because she manages to die when faced with the scoundrel, and thus ends *La Vida Breve*, the 'short life' of the title. The plot of this opera is almost just an excuse to present an Andalusian folkloric scene, with all the (stereo-)typical clapping, singing and dancing, all set to Flamenco music in Falla's particular style.

DB.   'Announcement to Cleaning team, please, Cleaning – can you come to clean Vanesa please, because she's just...' And, sure enough, they did!

What about the orchestra?

MM.   They're also independent. When they are called to go to the pit one of the Stage Managers goes down with them, and then he reports back 'everybody's here, we can now start'. At that point we dim the lights and they start tuning up. But the orchestra is like the chorus, independent, they do what they want. Another Stage Manager goes with the maestro to the pit because there's always something that happens at the last minute. 'The maestro's entering the pit... oops, where's the baton?' And then he's got to go back to the dressing-room for the baton or the glasses or whatever it is this time. It's happened loads of times. That's why we don't dim the lights completely until we have the maestro in position and ready to go, otherwise it would be just too scary...

DB.   Yes, because sitting there waiting for 10 seconds in the dark is like 20 minutes in the light, you get the sensation that something bad is going to happen, the audience gets restless, and that's a really bad way to start the opera.

Do you have people waiting in the dressing rooms?

MM.   Everybody's in their dressing room, everybody has one, and we call them as and when we need them. Then they come down to the stage and wait in the wings at the position where they're going to come on. Each one waits in that position until we reach the point in the music when the Stage Manager says 'now, enter!' The Stage Manager's right there, close to them, and gives them a push... sometimes literally, because otherwise, sometimes they don't move and you have to say to them 'Go! Go! Go!'

Is this due to stage-fright?

MM.   For the extras and the chorus, no, but for the singers, yes. Sometimes you say to them 'go go go!' and they get stage fright. This only happens to the young or inexperienced, though, it doesn't happen to the older ones.

DB.   Well, it does happen to the older ones as well, but they just keep it a secret.

Case: Setting up Lluís Pasqual's in-house production of *Don Giovanni*

Now that we know the complete process involved in the production, we include here a section about the opera Don Giovanni, *as at May 2005, so that we can appreciate, in a more concrete form, what Daniel has been telling us in general.*

The Set Designer has delivered the model and the designs. We are now in the process of making adjustments. We've studied the model, which has been extensively discussed with the Set Designer, the Stage Director and the

Technical management; mostly to ensure that it can be set up and taken down easily, to make it compatible with any other activity in the theatre and also to make sure that it fits within budget.

We've finished the bid competition and we have been trying to call the companies that seem most suitable for this type of show. Don Giovanni is set in Spain in the 1940s, just after the war, and takes place in a street. There's a fair with a carousel, and it's colourful, but the colour only comes from the carousel; the rest is grey.

It's a show that requires a very high artistic standard and must be very realistic. We've sent everything to the company that won the competition, an Italian company that seems to be really excellent.

In props, they're making two cars, two Rolls-Royces. They measure 5 m by 2 m, and one has an electric motor – you step on the accelerator and it works. This is because these cars have to move on stage. I prefer to do it here instead of sending them outside because the props workshop here is excellent. They're moulded from fibreglass, and later they'll be painted. They've made the wheels, chrome... all the details.

At one point in the performance, the stage completely rotates, and when it closes again seven dodgem cars are placed on the set that is now facing away from the audience. These are proper dodgems, which the props workshop is also building.

Now we come to the break, and we take down all the set decoration, leaving only the structure. What the audience can see are some fairground workers taking things down. While this scene is happening, they're taking down the fair, leaving everything empty. This is done by the extras: another reason why everything has to be easy to put up and take down.

There are moments in which you can see one part of the set and moments in which you see another. In the cemetery, you see the back part of the wall and you don't see the columns. Also there is one of the two cars, filled with floral crowns.

For the end, where Don Giovanni gets taken down to hell, the back wall opens, and a crane comes out with a 15 m-long boom, carrying a horse with the Comendatore riding it. It seems to fly. Don Giovanni gets on the horse with the Comendatore, they go galloping back and the wall closes.

The crane was designed by Carlos with the head of machinery and the metalwork people. It's completely painted black and covered in black velvet so that nobody can see it; you can only see the horse and those two. Don Giovanni is on the stage, gets on to a platform, and from there mounts the horse and they gallop off. At the end all the singers get up onto the platform as though it were a stage, and we project some fascist images from newsreels, mixed with live images of the singers. – The Comendatore sings from backstage with a microphone; he almost always uses a microphone to give his voice a supernatural sort of sound.

We have the set design shared between three workshops. There's a workshop in Italy doing the horse, and another in Italy doing a wall and one in Valencia doing the carousel and a curved granite wall. We have to travel to the workshops with the Set Designer so that he can check the work. We also have to travel with the Stage Director because we want him to see how to take down a piece of the carousel and therefore he can imagine how it has to be done on stage. At this point, we have to be a little patient and just monitor the workshops; you see we can't do anything more than just waiting to see what they decide.

Now we're with the Stage Director on the telephone. Last Friday he came and made the selection of extras. We also had a meeting with the lighting people, because the Carousel has more than 5000 light bulbs. Lluís Pasqual has everything more or less sorted; he's cast the extras, the dancers and the singers.

The next thing to do is to get all the technical details. The chorus is quite small, only 22 people. We need to know who is who, get all their measurements from the computer and send them to the costume people so they can start work.

Then there's also the costume designer, who today has returned to Italy. I've had her here for three days in the shop, Sastrería Cornejo, preparing the costumes. As we've already done the auditions of the extras and the dancers, we already know the measurements of everybody. We're negotiating the budget for costumes because, of course, it's one thing to see it in design, and another to see them in reality, and we're negotiating the cost.

And all the time attending to the Stage Director, setting up an interview for next week or whatever. Now everything is 'Can I do this? Can I do that? I thought of something else...', for example, the curtains of the carousel: he had thought, that as everything was going to be done by remote control, he wanted them to be separate. Originally he told us that he wanted them working in groups of two; but no, now he wants them separate. This is give-and-take. It is clear that individual curtains would give a lot more possibilities, because the spaces become distinct, where people can hide. Don Giovanni is an opera with a lot of dialogue, there are a lot of asides, so clearly it is much more spectacular, it's more like a comedy.

Here is where we can easily see our five-star service in action. When the Stage Director delivered the project, he said the curtains went in pairs, and we sent them off to be made. Later he called us on the phone and told us something different. We have various options: One is not to listen to him, because he said what he wanted and that's that. Another option, if they've already been made but we think it's important enough, we'll go back and redo them. Finally, we can try to see if there's a way of changing them simply. But in every case, except the first, which is not listening to him, the other options form part of what, for me, is a five-star service, total dedication.

Well, in this case it was very easy. We called the company that was making the curtains, and they told us that it was still possible to change so, that's it, we've changed them. If it was going to cost us money, we would probably have waited until he had developed the idea further or until we realised that there was no other way. Then we would have done everything possible to find the money.

And something that did cost us money, and we changed because it was within the budget, is the wall that goes up and down. Initially it was 5m above the stage, but Lluís Pasqual had a conflict with it and the stage. The problem is that the text says that Donna Ana descends; therefore, she was above, and he had no idea how to get her above. Talking with him, we came up with the idea of lowering the wall completely. If we lower the wall, we make a hole, and behind we put some steps, then she'll be in a window. But by lowering the wall we exposed a zone above of about 4 m. So we ordered a very simple set, continuing the wall these 4 m. This cost us more money, it was necessary. We didn't hesitate, we don't hesitate, when something is necessary.

The final delivery date has to be before we go on holiday. We want to enjoy our holidays, and the only way to do that is by knowing that everything for *Don Giovanni* is safely stored in containers in the Siete Iglesias warehouse. When we come back we unload *Don Giovanni* on the 29th of August, and we build it in one of the spaces below stage. Then we go straight to the opera *From the House of the Dead*.[10] Meanwhile we start rehearsals on *Don Giovanni*, then it's ballet, ballet, ballet, setting up *Don Giovanni* down there. Then we go to the first stage rehearsal, then rehearsal, rehearsal, rehearsal, Italian, full ensemble, full ensemble, ante piano, pre-general, general, general, general, and finally the first-night performance of *Don Giovanni*.

---

[10] *From the House of the Dead*, the last opera by Leŏs Janaćek, based on the novel of the same name by Fyodor Dostoyevsky. The work has an expressionist language, while at the same time is full of hope, and is a song to freedom. It deals with a period of Dostoevsky's life, when he spent four years in a prison camp in Siberia. The plot begins with the arrival at the camp of the political prisoner Alexander Petrowitsch and ends with his freedom. It is 'a daring and very modern opera'.

XIV
Implementing Innovation

Innovation

Would you say that the Teatro Real is an innovative company? Each year they put on no fewer than five new productions, each one of them with the complex characteristics that we've seen in previous chapters. Additionally, the work done is subject to inevitable changes imposed by a service company; singers become ill or hysterical, extras who don't turn up, sets that make noises... all these things have an important effect on the result. At first glance then, it does appear that the Teatro Real is indeed a very *innovative* company.

However, a first glance is not enough. At first glance, many things appear to be something they're not. So let's see if we can shed some light by using something a little more systematic.

First, what is all this talk of innovation, anyway? It's just another abstract concept so beloved of the specialised press. 'Spanish companies have a very low level of innovation', they say. But what does this actually mean? We have to confess that we don't actually know. Innovation, technology... in abstract, these are very difficult concepts to pin down, let alone understand. We know what *an innovation* is, but do not know innovation as a concept. We'll leave that kind of high-level conceptualisation to philosophy students and journalists. We'll limit ourselves here to the more mundane. So, what is *an* innovation? An innovation is something, new or old, that is done in a new or different way.

So, let's rephrase the question. Does the Teatro Real introduce many innovations? Well, that depends. The protagonists of this book, especially Daniel, insist that 'everything is always the same: theatrical common sense'. But it is obvious that there is a large volume of new things happening too. Maybe the distinction we need to make here is that they do a lot of new things, but the way in which they do them is always very similar. In technical jargon, we can say that the Teatro Real is a company that innovates a lot in products, but much less in processes, or at least in *metaprocesses* (a word which the spellchecker doesn't like, but we do), which are the aggregated operational processes that each contain further processes. As we saw in the last chapter, the creation of a set always follows the same steps, as does the artistic implementation of the production. Indeed, the rehearsals, for example, are highly ritualised and the scheme doesn't change from one opera to another, no matter how different the result is.

Having said that, the product and some of its ingredients do undergo some drastic changes: the singers, Musical Director, Stage Director, Lighting Designer and so on, they all change every time... and all these changes generate a different product for each production. It is clearly not the same to stage *Tosca* as it is to stage *The Barber of Seville*. Perhaps refining a little further, we could say that the Teatro Real introduces many new product innovations per year, but relatively few process innovations. In fact, at the beginning of the Teatro Real, the situation was exactly the reverse. With Tamayo at the helm, closely followed by Daniel, Marta and the rest of the technical team, they created highly innovative processes, but ones that have remained the same during the subsequent seven or eight years. So, this is not an innovative company, at least not in terms of processes.

Let's move on to the next point. Who generates these innovations? We're going to give them a name and, in a flash of imaginative brilliance, we're going to call them... wait for it... *innovators*. They're the people who bring together the right conditions to be able in introduce innovations. Following on from what we said earlier, we must look on the side of the product (service), which in this case is the artistic component.

Who are the people who give our team headaches? In the first place, it's the artistic management. They put together a season that they want to be different from more traditional opera theatres, and that satisfies their clients. And without relying on anyone else, just carried along by their knowledge and objectives, they create the season by specifying the events that will take place. They don't even budget for it in advance. Their intuition tells them what is feasible and, usually, it is. The details will follow. We're dealing here with a mid-term innovator, over two or three years. That gives our team time to prepare.

In the second place, it's the stage management. This is a short-term innovator, six months at best, and is the primary source of product innovations. But a word of caution here – the innovators do not usually implement. Usually this is delegated to the operational people, and so we can call them, in this context, the *innomanagers*. Well, why not?

It's odd how, in the theatre, it's the technical management that has become, in recent years, the principal source of innovation. This doesn't mean that, as Daniel says, they don't sometimes come out with a load of rubbish. But they do innovate. And do you know why? Well, the answer is not an easy one; nobody has been able to answer that for us. But if we apply some of the basic ideas of this book we can work it out. Opera theatres compete in a global market, and to do this they have to be different or better in some respect. Ask yourself in what way the Teatro Real is different to other opera theatres. Or, if you prefer, include Milan's La Scala in that exercise; in what way does the Teatro Real differentiate itself from La Scala? It can't be the singers, of course, because they're sub-contracted from the market, and thus within reach of anyone with sufficient money to hire them. It may be that some singers prefer to sing in one place to another, but they can still be considered a common resource. And what about the orchestra? Or the chorus? Maybe, but we're talking about a marginal advantage, and one that will rarely be mentioned when talking about the theatre. If the reader keeps on like this, eliminating various things, then it'll become clear that the principal way of differentiating between theatres is the staging. This factor causes people to speak well or ill of a theatre. At the same time, the Stage Directors operate in a global market, and it is in their interest to differentiate themselves through their work, through their staging. Conclusion: every Stage Director who wants to draw attention to his art will be seen to approach a production in a different way to the others; to stage 'original' productions. And with so much opera theatre being staged around the world, this means a production has to be *very original* to get noticed.

Perhaps that helps to explain why at the Liceo in Barcelona, in a production of *Un Ballo in Maschera*,[1] all the actors began the performance onstage, sitting on toilets and simulating defecation. The need to strive for differentiation and drawing attention can drive dubious taste to absurd levels, but it works. It does draw attention, in such a way that the very act of contracting a Stage Director becomes the seed of the product innovation that the theatre will realise.

---

[1] *Un Ballo in Maschera* is an opera by Giuseppe Verdi. It is unusual because it can be set in Boston or Sweden, purely dependent upon the version that is staged. It was, in fact, originally set in Sweden, based on assassination of King Gustav III (although not historically accurate), but the Swedish royal family got involved and it was censured, whereupon the action was set in Boston. Renato, the secretary and best friend of the Governor Riccardo (or the King, depending on the version) is married to the beautiful Amelia, the soprano, whom he loves tenderly. But Riccardo is madly in love with Amelia. In a vehement love scene, in one of the most passionate duets in the entire operatic genre, Amelia confesses to Riccardo that she is also in love with him. But, but...Renato discovers this shenanigans, and he doesn't like it one bit, despite the fact that this love is purely platonic with no hint of carnality (remember that characters in opera are superhuman, and don't' succumb to such pedestrian ordinariness). Things get complicated with the appearance of a fortune-teller, who foretells the murder of Riccardo by the next man to shake his hand. And who does this 'next man' turn out to be? Renato, of course. Riccardo scoffs at the fortune-teller, saying that it's impossible, that it can never happen...but in the end, at a masked ball held at the palace, the presumed lover, the Governor Riccardo, dies at the hands of Renato, his best friend, who, driven by jealousy, skewers him with an almighty stab.

Gentle reader, don't be too shocked. After all, similar things happen in your company (although maybe not the simulation mentioned above). Remember, if you will, that in the preceding paragraphs we've presented a general scheme of competitive analysis that does not take into account, at all, the fact that we're talking about a theatre. Do the test yourself – your company has to differentiate itself. If not, it'll be just another company, and will not be competitive. To achieve this it has to do things in a different way – innovations. Think that innovation is the source of life. To stay alive is to change. The constant, the static, is, by definition, dead. We know that might sound a bit affected, but it is true.

> **Identify the innovators in your company.**

Now identify the innovators in your company. One of the most important, surely, is the senior management or board of directors, analogous to the Artistic management in the Teatro Real. Without involving anybody else, and sometimes with a staggering ignorance of the consequences of what they suggest, they propose innovations that affect everybody. A strategist is, by definition, an innovator, even if it's only because he doesn't worry about the how, only the what. There is a high probability that you yourself are an *innomanager*. They say to you 'we need to double sales in Townsville' and you go and do it. But it's all relative. Nobody is purely an innovator or an *innomanager* but rather a mixture of both.

The consequences

> **Every innovation creates problems.**

What are the consequences of innovation in the Teatro Real? In the first place, the implementation of an innovation is not only limited to *innomanagers*. In our case, the implementation was achieved by Marta, the heads of section, Stage Managers, machinists, chorus, orchestra ... everybody! Everybody was involved to a greater or lesser degree, depending on the area of innovation. Innovation begets *innosufferers* (*innoreceivers* would be the politically correct term) but, in any case, people who suffer the effects of innovation. What are those effects? Very simple. Every innovation that is introduced generates problems for everybody associated with that innovation. Problems, in the sense that innovation invalidates some of those 'things we've always done' and makes us do them in another way. But let's be careful. The majority of innovations do not require changes to macro-procedures. If the set of *Don Carlo* needs to be moved as if by magic, this does not alter the fact that the rehearsals continue, whether ensemble, dress, Italian, ante piano or whatever. But within the rehearsals, it will have to be seen if and how that movement affects the extras, if it bothers the singers, if the set machinery is in a suitable condition to do this smoothly and quietly. More motors, more elements, more effects: direct and indirect.

Of course, not all innovations produce the same effects. In fact, from the conversation in the previous chapter we can see that there are two key factors. One is the reach or 'globality' of the innovation. It is not the same for the Stage Director to say 'No, this singer should come on from Felipe's part of the stage, rather than Carlos's' as for him to say 'No, this whole scene is bad, we have to change it.' One of the innovations causes problems for the Stage Managers, but not much else, whereas the second could cause problems at all levels. Nor is it the same to say 'this motor is noisy' as it is for the Stage Director to say 'I can't continue; the Stage Manager doesn't understand me.' Daniel says that, in the latter case, he'd 'have a problem'. But the worst is that, in this case, he'd have a problem that is poorly structured and difficult to solve. By contrast, the motor noise is a structured problem and can be resolved by a technician.

> **Every problem presents a challenge.**

All innovations, then, create problems. At the Teatro Real, in a bank, hospital or university ... and in companies. And this is so because innovation affects the existing world, where things were going reasonably well, and turn it into a world (or area) where something (or many things) now doesn't (don't) work well. Then there is no alternative but to construct a new world. Of course, some of the problems could be historic; the shoes of the singer, for example. But they are still problems for somebody, nevertheless. To change the shoes created a problem for Marta Maier that needed solving. And if the problem isn't solved, then maybe the performance could be in jeopardy.

There are occasions when a person doesn't have sufficient knowledge and they resist change, to defend their incapacity to resolve the problem that has come up. This is usually called '*resistance to* change'. One of the current authors is a bit drastic and says that this concept is 'sublime stupidity!' We think that this resistance to change doesn't exist; at least not resistance to change for its own sake. Why would we not want to change, given that we're always changing? People experience a heightened sense of satisfaction precisely through changing. Hairstyle, clothes, holiday destination, car ... resistance to change? We don't think so.

What is really happening is that every problem presents a challenge to the person who has to solve it. Sometimes it's a personal problem. 'It's so complicated, I don't know if I'll be able to solve it ...' Remember the pinch in the stomach that Daniel mentioned, when he had to solve a problem of the set design and he had no idea as to how to go about it? Other times, it might be a social challenge, 'what will they say if I don't come up with a good solution?', or an organisational one, 'what will my boss say if I don't sort it out ... it could be my future career on the line ...' All of these challenges appear because I don't know enough to solve the problem in an applicative way. I lack the adequate knowledge to solve the problem. I'll have to explore and, as we've seen, this can bring about great uncertainty in the result and the time needed. If I had the knowledge, or if I almost had it, my attitude would probably be different: 'they're going to realise that I am capable'. It is not the change but the *challenge* that causes the problem in proportion to the knowledge that the *innosufferer* has (sorry, *innoreceiver!*).

> **You can't exploit your peoples' potential by making them follow rules.**

In that sense, the Emergency Book is a very interesting issue. What is it really for? Well, it clearly appears to serve as a handrail, a support. Nobody in the heat of a frantic panic is going to follow the book to the letter, simply because in a random environment it is impossible to catalogue all possible eventualities, even though Daniel says it does. But the point is, it doesn't need to. The book typifies certain standard behaviours that are adequate for dealing with typical events. It's a kind of courtesy agreement. If everybody followed the norms of courtesy, to the letter, then we'd be living in an unacceptably stuffy and la-di-dah world. But the very existence of these norms and protocols, 'don't put your hands in your pockets, don't shout while eating, don't put your elbows on the table...' typifies and illustrates a way of behaving, 'by example'. In the theatre, when a Stage Manager needs to confront an exceptional event, then, by managing to identify its type (and this is probably easy), he or she then has a behavioural guideline to follow from the book, and this gives them the security that they're not solving the problem in completely the wrong way. In other words, in the absence of that book, the Stage Manager might decide to refund the price of the ticket, but someone else might decide 'you're mad! It'll come out of your wages!' But with the book in place, they can be assured that this is not going to happen. So, yes, it's a handrail, a support.

Once more, the reader should consider his or her own case. Rules and guidelines for your employees? They are necessary, not for their own sake but rather for the typology of behaviours they describe. Once that behaviour is internalised, we could throw the book away and that would be that... Except that in a highly innovative environment, problems change every day, the typologies possibly require constant modification, and this can make it difficult to set them down in a book. In these cases, the 'by example' guidelines can have the same effect. We imitate the behaviours of the people we look up to, of whom the boss is one of the most important!

We make rules, but we think they're simple guides, handrails. But deep down, they are not for following (at least, not to the letter). We want to get the best out of our peoples' qualities, and this is not achieved by declaring more rules.

An important issue. Has the reader observed the number of times in the text we've used the words 'we've learnt that...'? This is not simply a manner of speech or a coincidence. We've said that one learns through solving problems. More than this, solving problems is almost the only way in which adults learn. And in a problem-solving process like that in the

> **Another way of controlling uncertainty is to achieve a rapid response time.**

Teatro Real, one learns a lot. Early maturity is not unusual in these people; the majority are still young, but they've had the opportunity, sometimes the necessity, to learn a great deal.

In an innovative environment that creates many problems, where the challenge is sufficient or the solution to problems is well supported, the level of learning achieved by all can be very high. Compared with a traditional theatre, the Teatro Real has an enviable stock of knowledge. And, since they know more, they are able to do things better. If the current group is looked after well, then the potential of a company such as the Teatro Real is extremely high. They are already capable of achieving almost anything, but in the future, it'll be so much better. The essential problem is how to give them a horizon to aim for, new and ever-more demanding challenges that bring out their talent; this talent that is maturing and being polished through learning. This is the greatest challenge for every company, and we will deal with it in future chapters.

How to tackle uncertainty

Another way to control uncertainty is not by trying to avoid it, but by trying to achieve a fast reaction time; fast enough that the occurrence of an exceptional event can be tackled immediately without other people noticing its existence. This cannot be improvised; it requires that the Operational system is designed appropriately. An operating system that is termed 'agile'. An agile system typically provides the platforms and tools necessary to be able to handle many operations quickly, without needing to worry about organising them into an efficient sequence. Then, if something needs to be manufactured, for example, the system locates and supplies all the operations and organises them into an *ad hoc* process. The production is then carried out and, upon completion, all the elements are quickly returned to storage, ready to be begun again. Thus we can say that *agile = flexible + rapid*.

A *manual* operating process is always the most *flexible*, because man is one of the most flexible machines imaginable. Given adequate knowledge, man can provide almost any service. But he is not agile, because he is not fast. Traditional theatre is very flexible, but it is not agile.

Is the Teatro Real an *agile factory*? Yes, in a good measure it is. It is clearly flexible. It needs to be, to accommodate the seasons they put together with many and varied operas. That demonstrates its capacity to programme successfully. And the details that our protagonists have given us show this very clearly. Look, as examples, at the lighting, organised as in a television studio; the rehearsal spaces of different sizes to be able to attend rapidly to any necessity; the existence of the three underground building zones adjacent to the stage; the individual movement of all elements, directed by computer programs and so on.

Nevertheless, is it rapid? It's not easy to check. Of course, it is *Just in Time* (JIT), having something just when you need it, not before or after, and it is one of the *necessary*, not just *sufficient*, conditions of being agile.

At the Teatro Real, things happen when they're supposed to happen, and nothing happens when it's not supposed to. Thus, the Teatro Real operates JIT in staging the production, but not necessarily during the production. It is faster on the stage. All the people involved in setting up an opera work at a great speed and quietly. They place great stress on the amount of time it takes to make set changes, trying to improve them at rehearsals. The *tops* system helps to achieve things swiftly. And the Stage Managers' methods ensure that the whole system works JIT. But really they have no option other than to function JIT! Unlike many service systems, they cannot allow even the tiniest delay or setback. It's as though, in a company, all operations had to be achieved without any kind of stock – if there were no *delays* (between production and delivery), there would be no need for *storage*. That is JIT. Could you do that?

A just-in-time service

Therefore, we've just identified an operation of JIT service in the Teatro Real. A lot has been written about JIT ideas, which originate in manufacturing, and their application to service. And many of the things that have been said are fairly irrelevant, based on superficial analogies. But, having identified a case, we can try to see its characteristics, and from them we can describe some of the conditions that any system must have to achieve JIT.

Are you ready for the surprise? The basic condition to be able to achieve JIT service is to *get there five minutes early*. Sounds familiar?

But hold on, when Daniel says that, he doesn't mean that things have to be *done* five minutes early. This would create stocks and delays. He says, and we emphasise the words, '*to be prepared*'. This is an attitude of vigilance that leads you to constantly ask yourself 'what can happen?', 'how can I solve this?', 'what will I need to be able to operate?' And, at the same time, preparing the channels that must get to work if needed.

> To apply JIT in services we have to anticipate problems and have problem-solving methodologies.

But there is more. Five minutes early, for what? To solve problems. You have to be ready to resolve problems that might appear. And that implies *anticipating* the *problems* that can arise, and having *methodologies* prepared for their *solution*. *Five minutes early* and *problem-solving methodologies*; these are the two basic conditions for *JIT in services*.

The greatest difficulty, from the organisational point of view, is to get all the people in the organisation complying with these two conditions in their own areas. What happens at the Teatro Real? Remember what we asked

Daniel at the beginning of the last chapter – 'Does everybody agree with that philosophy?' and he said 'yes', 'Everyone, in their own area.'

With this vigilant attitude, we won't eliminate the unforeseens. *Chance*, by definition, is *not controllable*. One can mitigate probability, but it's impossible to eliminate entirely. One has to accept that there are always unforeseeable things that, well, cannot be foreseen. But we can try to anticipate certain things arising so that, if and when they do arise, we know what to do.

To resume, innovation generates uncertainty. Uncertainty is tackled by being *agile*, and a necessary condition for becoming agile is to achieve JIT in services. How is this achieved? By applying the two basic conditions: *anticipating problems* and *having problem-solving methodologies*.

How to meet the two conditions necessary to achieve JIT services

How do we achieve these two conditions? The reader must read again the previous chapter, and attempt to identify how this was achieved in the Teatro Real. Ready? We've also done it, and we have found the following organisational activities:

1. *Create an operating culture of highlighting problems. There are no guilty parties; there are only problems.*
2. *Non-parallel specialisation, segmenting problem areas.*
3. *Create generic procedures.*
4. *Always support the actions of a subordinate, even if they're erroneous.*

That's probably not an exhaustive list, but it does give us a clear direction on how to proceed.

1. *Create an operating culture of highlighting problems. There are no guilty parties; there are only problems.* This spirit permeates the Teatro Real; everybody 'buys in'. Everybody flags up problems to the others, and it's so deep-rooted in the culture that nobody takes offence. On the contrary, they appreciate the help. This culture is created by management example; management trains its people to be like that. See if that happens in your company. More in the next chapters.

2. *Non-parallel specialisation, segmenting problem areas.* In the majority of companies, there are specialist centres. If you have a restaurant, the kitchen and dining room are peopled with specialists. The chefs don't know how to wait table, the waiters don't know how to cook (or at least they don't want to know to the same level). To apply JIT in services we have to segment the problem areas and make the people multi-skilled within each area; being partially multi-skilled helps them to be more agile and thus better able to

respond to problems that arise, without them needing to abandon their particular specialisation.

3. *Create generic procedures.* It is always necessary to have a guide. The Teatro Real's 'Emergency Book' is the technical department's way to define how to react to certain, limited situations. It is a point of reference from which to be able to act.

4. *Always support the actions of a subordinate, even if they're erroneous.* To be vigilant and to be able to provide help and feedback if they've committed an error. There are no guilty parties, just conflicting situations that need resolving. One learns much more from an error that subsequently gives good results. An error is potentially the best source of learning for the organisation, and that is why it requires comment and communication. There are now companies that maintain databases of errors with the aim of helping people to learn better. But, for this to happen, a culture of *no guilty parties* is indispensable.

Conclusions

In this chapter, we've seen what *innovation* really is, and how it's managed. The Teatro Real is an innovative company in a certain sense, and here we've analysed how it channels its innovation process. We've seen three roles that can play a part in innovation; the innovator, the innomanager and the innoreceiver. A requirement for an innovation's success is that there is harmony among the three. Innovation generates problems and it is critical to be able to adapt the challenge of the problem to the stock of knowledge of the individual.

Innovation produces uncertainty and to combat this you need to be agile. One condition necessary to becoming agile is to implement JIT in services, and this requires the *anticipation* of problems and *methodologies* for their solution. Finally, we've presented four actions that can help to achieve these two conditions.

A few questions upon which to reflect:

- Who are the innovators in your company?
- What role do you play?
- Do you have adequate problems, challenges and stock of knowledge?
- Is your company swamped by rules and guidelines?
- Are your Operations agile?
- Can you implement JIT in your service?
- Do you possess some of the necessary characteristics to achieve JIT in your service?

XV
Rehearsal and Training

The next two chapters are dedicated to two activities critical for the success of service: rehearsal and training. They go hand-in-hand with innovation as they form part of the problem-diagnosis process, by trying to anticipate how a problem might have an effect on service. But they are also the result of one of the Teatro Real's objectives: 'Zero defects. We are a five-star hotel.'

An opera at the Teatro Real is the result of an exhaustive process of rehearsal and training. As Daniel Bianco says 'The final objective of all this work is to arrive on-stage, and to arrive with no defects.' They strive hard to achieve this. 'You have to arrive with the prototype practically finished; you can't start improvising.' And this is achieved by rehearsing and training. In what follows, we will associate rehearsals with experiments, and review the characteristics of those experiments. We will consider the different types of rehearsals in order to show the process of experimental design that this leads to. Each rehearsal is carefully defined in the 'theatrical common sense'. Who's in charge, who's rehearsing, what repercussions this might have; all of this is perfectly delimited and (almost) nothing is left to chance. Or maybe not...because there is always a residual uncertainty, that must be dealt with in other ways. Everybody trains to be able to deal with residual uncertainty, considering the possible repercussions and the actions necessary to prevent them.

How is this managed in the world of business? How do we manage uncertainty? For example, Operations in service companies are characterised by the considerable uncertainty of demand. What steps must be taken in companies to reduce these uncertainties? Our proposal is the DLAI approach (Debug, Learn, Anticipate and, as a result, Improve).

Our interviewee in this chapter is Daniel Bianco, and we are concentrating on the structure and significance of the rehearsals.

What is the rehearsal room for?

The set rehearsals are done in the rehearsal rooms; the full set isn't there, but there is a pre-set which, in addition, gets further developed throughout the rehearsals.

The senior stage manager attends all the rehearsals and it's in the rehearsal room that we work out many of the *tops*. The ones we can't do there are the lighting cues, which need to be done on stage. Let's suppose that the Stage Director says 'Ah, very good, then right now is when I want the wall to rise, and the smoke to come on-stage from Felipe's side and the monitors get switched off, because they become visible at that point.' Well, the senior stage manager notes all this down and assigns a *top*.

What's the rehearsal room like?

[At this point Daniel turns on a television monitor, on which we can see the rehearsal room with a built set.]

This is the set of *Macbeth*, built in the rehearsal room ... Look, look, there's the stairs, the whole set. But this isn't the real set; it's just the pre-set. None of this has cost us a Euro! We do it all with wooden modules that we already have, previously bought and prepared.

We make the stairs, the platforms ... but the real pieces are 12 m high, whereas these are only 5 m so they fit in the room; we only have a limited ceiling height, obviously. Nevertheless, it's a real space to rehearse in. This is fundamental, for our way of working. But don't go thinking that many people do this; it's only typical of this theatre.

Why is it fundamental?

Well, can you imagine if you had to spend a month rehearsing in a set that wasn't spatially correct? Imagine that the singer has to sit at table like this [*he gestures towards the office desk*] but, instead of having her sit at that desk with this space and a swivel chair in which you can adopt this posture [*he leans on the desk*], you make her sit at a small desk and then say to her 'No, not like that! The real desk is bigger!'

So, in order to rehearse you need to have everything as close to the real set as possible?

Maybe you don't give her the actual chair, because the actual chair is made of white leather and it marks easily, but we'll certainly give her one that swivels. The singer also has to create. She probably knows how her character would use the swivel movement, and she can experiment with the amount of time it takes her to approach another character, and so on. But we don't give her the actual things. The stairs, for example, there's no point in building them from bricks – what's the point? But we do have to give them realistic representations, so that, when she rehearses the aria during which she has to go up the stairs, the tempo as she's ascending can be identical to the performance. And all of this represents time that we've saved.

We've already said that a minute on stage costs much more than a minute in the rehearsal room. Imagine a theatre brought to a halt because the singer needs to practice going up the stairs. And, of course, the first time she rehearses in full costume and on the real stairs she trips, and says the stairs are rubbish, she gets cross...So if you do this in the rehearsal room, then the entire theatre doesn't have to stop. Losing time costs thousands of Euros, so 80 blokes waiting for this lady to go up some stairs.

We do the same with costume. Nobody wears their definitive costume in the rehearsal room; for example, if the singer has to wear a dress with an 8-m train, then we'll give her an 8-m train so she can practise and figure out how to sit down with this thing dragging along behind her.

And this sort of thing is only done in this theatre?

There are many places where they don't do it. First, many people don't have a good rehearsal room like ours, and second, because this really is a question of our own take on things – the rest of the world does it when the Stage Director asks for it, but here nobody needs to ask. Here we surprise people; they say 'I can't believe it!' But this is only because they arrive with a different mentality to ours.

We're happy doing it too, because it saves us time and work. And everybody starts to get this consciousness of the set, which also saves us complications. See, there are two days of absolute catastrophe; one we've already mentioned, the day of the full dress rehearsal. But the other is the day of the set rehearsal. If we didn't have the rehearsal room, this would be total chaos!

And when do you reach the proper stage?

The final objective of all our work is to arrive on-stage, but the stage is another world. In this type of theatre, with this infrastructure, with these dimensions and so on. In the rehearsal room, you talk without microphones because the distances are small. On a stage you can be twenty-something metres away, so you can't talk 'personally', it's a different connection.

You have to arrive with the prototype practically finished; you can't start improvising...well, in fact everything changes as you go along because many things happen, but you must try to have everything as fixed as possible. Now is when everything we've been doing in the rehearsal room starts to make sense. For example, in *Macbeth*, the stairs have a certain protagonist element; they're not simply decorative. So in the rehearsals we used stairs that, although decoratively different from the definitive ones, have a very similar 'set behaviour' in terms of the rise and depth of each step and the position of the banister. Therefore, the way of walking 'musically', how the singer ascends the stairs in time, will already have been fixed in rehearsal.

Arriving on-stage messes everybody up, because it's the moment when the artist is exposed to reality. And I'm not only talking about the Stage Director, but all the artists: the singers, chorus, extras, the ballet and so on. Consider the case of a ballerina. She has rehearsed in the rehearsal room with all the obstacles in the final position, but when she gets to the real stage, she realises that it has a certain slipperiness, and she has to adapt to that.

Our work begins with bringing up the set from the sixteenth floor below ground, where we built it. Then, on the stage itself, we set up the lighting. This theatre has an excellent characteristic, which was one of Tamayo's ideas.[1] In the majority of the world's opera theatres, the lighting bars, where you hang the lights, are fixed. The theatre designer originally determined the initial position of the lights and there they stay for eternity. Typically, this means there's a lighting bar at the front of the stage and another at the back for backlights... more or less. Whereas here everything is flexible. It's like a TV studio floor, where you can do what you like. The rolls of cable are placed high up above the stage so that you can power whichever bar you like. Between shows, we 'clean' all the lighting and start again from scratch. This avoids the creation of the unhealthy dynamic that you can find in other theatres, where the spot is always hung from the same point, full of dust, no lens change, no bulb change, nothing. It's not healthy.

Here we demolish the entire 'house' and build a new one each time. This requires a lot of preparation on the part of the head electrician, who will have already received all the information from the project department, prepared his plans and given his people all that they need. He will have also made sure that, in his workshops, they've prepared all the trolleys with the apparatus specified for all of the sectors of the stage where they're going to be set up. Everything must be prepared in the sixteenth floor below ground, ready to bring up to the stage and start to set up. In this stage, as everything needs hanging, we'll take two days to do the complete lighting set-up.

The majority of the props, almost all, will have been in the rehearsal room for use in the rehearsals. Now it all gets taken to the stage, also on trolleys or carts, and distributed throughout the set. During this month of rehearsals you'll have had a chance to see all the characters' entrances and exits, what props they use and when.

Now we reach the first day of the set rehearsal. The objective is that everything must already be prepared for this first day. This is the objective, but you know you're not going to achieve it. You're not going to achieve it because some things are not yet finalised, and you have to give a certain amount of freedom to the artist. The artist must be able to watch from the stalls, from a distance, and say 'No, it doesn't work for me if he comes on from here – let's try over here instead' or 'we need more snow', as was the case with *Macbeth*. The Stage Director sees it live, and if he doesn't like it he'll change the set.

The Stage Director is on-stage from the first day of rehearsal. And the Musical Director too, even if it's only the *ante piano*. The Musical Director has also been in the rehearsal room, because he has to lead the musical

---

[1] The reader will recall the interview with José Luis Tamayo in Chapter IX.

tempo for the singers, and this tempo is developed with the pianist. He, the Musical Director, doesn't play; he directs, while the pianist plays. But he works, just like the actors.

We do on average four or five rehearsals, and typically, we go in order of the acts. We start with Act One, then Act Two...This requires very careful programming of the timetable because there are many people and many different working agreements. We have people who work very different hours; each staff level with its own problems.

During the rehearsal days, the Stage Director can stop as many times as he likes and can do what he likes. He can work for three hours on one scene or he can whip through several quickly. The Stage Director has absolute power. Now is when everything that we've done in the rehearsal room comes together, and he can see if it works in the final situation. There are many things that you really can only see *in situ*.

Normally during the morning ,we set up and direct the spots. All lights that we've hung up need to be directed, that is, we need to mark the positions where they're going to go. Directing the lighting is not yet a simple case of recording a sequence in the computer. First, we have to point the spots exactly where we want them, and maybe put on the gels that give them colour. Then we have to record their positions and, if we're using mobile spots, then we need to record not only the position but the movements too.

In the afternoon, we do the set rehearsals, with the actors. Once they're finished we start with the 'Italian'. There is no set activity in this rehearsal. The chorus and the singers are on the stage, with the orchestra, and we go through the entire opera with them playing and singing. That's when we make any musical adjustments. Previously, in the orchestra room, the conductor has 'read' the opera, which means he has played the score through with the orchestra three or four times.

But without the singers?

No. Normally, the director of the orchestra has worked with the singers in the rehearsal room, or in a small studio with the help of a piano, to work on particular passages. But the 'Italian' is the day when you hear the complete opera.

After that we come to what is known as an 'ensemble rehearsal' or simply an 'ensemble'. Normally when there's an ensemble in the afternoon, the morning is spent on the first recording of the lights. For this, we need a lighting guy and perhaps the Stage Director, depending on the artistic team and on the stage manager. The stage manager marks the lighting effects on the score, and also the entrances and exits of each effect, so that the whole lot can be recorded on the lighting desk. Typically, we record most of the first act and later we see it in the afternoon in the rehearsal. That's how we correct it because, of course, when you're setting the lights there's nobody on stage, and so the lights are not necessarily positioned correctly, but there soon will be loads of people. Although, in reality, it's the singer who'll find the spotlight – if you're in shadow, and you've only got a sliver of moonlight in which to sing this or that, then you're going to go and find that patch of light; it's not going to come to you.

If everything keeps coming together ok, then you say 'Right, in the morning I'm doing the lighting for the first act and in the afternoon I'm doing an ensemble for the first act, and that way it's easier to fine-tune.' Then you do the lighting in the morning, then in the afternoon the ensemble, in which you have the orchestra, the chorus if there is one in the production, all the singers and the extras.

The ensemble is where we start to bring the scenes and the orchestra together. Of course, an opera with piano is not the same as when all the instruments start playing. First, because this is where the orchestral director's authority surpasses the Stage Director's. Second, because it's not the same for a chorus to attack, to come in on time, with a piano as with an orchestra. In the latter case, the maestro has to coordinate his 50 or 60 professionals with the 60 in the chorus. Third, because the singers need support, maybe by holding a note a little longer to allow them time to breathe. And all of this needs to be perfectly integrated with the scene being played out on stage. The first day of ensemble is precisely when the singer starts to worry about the musical side and forgets to act the scene, although often the Stage Director will step in with reminders.

Do the Musical Director and the singers have to agree on everything?

Yes, it's strange...I suppose because they get together alone and talk, but from the outside it looks very easy; there's a great understanding between them. It must be very complex, I suppose, but they seem to understand each other very quickly. Of course, it always turns out that there are certain points that they do not understand. Sometimes, very rarely, the 'star temperament' will appear; who's more important, the singer or the Director.

Once the ensembles are finished, and when the orchestra has a day off (in our case a Sunday), we do another, different rehearsal, the 'ante piano'. This is the entire opera, exactly as it has to be, with make-up, wigs, costumes, set changes, singers, chorus, extras, everyone and everything, but only with piano accompaniment. This rehearsal usually lasts much longer than the opera, because they stop now and then to check the costumes, the changes, how it all comes together, and to discover any problems of coordination. It's the Stage Director's last opportunity to correct things, because after this we go to the pre-general rehearsal, and the pre-general is the same as the performance, including the orchestra.

Then we go to the last rehearsals, the generals. It's considered 'good theatre' to do generals 'open', with an audience. No audience comments are allowed, though, and the singer can choose whether to sing or not, or to sing but only gently. The singers really need to look after their voices at this point, so they're still able to sing the entire opera in the performances.

Finally, the premiere. Once you reach 'curtain-up' you've finished one job, but now you need to get through the performances. You've been building up the energy to get to opening night, get there, get there... and once you get there, ok, if everything comes out well then great. But after that climax, you still have eight or ten performances, in which you need to maintain the tension. It's just as important to maintain as it was to get there. And, in this theatre, on the day after the premiere there's one group of people who continue doing the performances, and there's another group that starts to work on the next opera.

XVI
The RT Concept

Innovation and efficiency

Two chapters ago, we saw how the Teatro Real is an innovative company in terms of product. Because of this level of innovation, it is exposed to the effects of chance – to unexpected results. Every time they introduce something new, and when they don't have comprehensive experience of the result, they're opening the door to unexpected problems. It is impossible to completely control something novel, with which we are not familiar, and many occurrences can cause a disruption to the normal process of a service (in this case, a performance).

Combining innovation and efficiency is an arcane art that very few companies know. When there is a lot of innovation, there tends to be a lot of chaos. And order always goes hand-in-hand with stability and efficiency ... or at least, that has always been one of the basic premises of Operations.

In the past few years, this premise has been much discussed and argued. Some maintain that world-class companies should be capable of surviving chaos. But to do this the company should be able to control chaos. And control is always a form of imposing order on a system. Of course, the company that manages to be efficient and chaotic at the same time will have a major competitive advantage over the rest. It will be able to do everything, and make money. This is a very powerful inducement to try to combine the two (un-combinable) sides of the coin. But to do this we must understand the essence of the phenomenon.

In a low-innovation company, in which the environment remains more or less constant, everybody has time to refine processes, and the operational variables in general, until they can be assured that there are no surprises lurking. By repetition, it is possible to optimise the production of a factory. You need to use only an iterative methodology; possibly examining one variable per iteration. Important variables are selected and tests are carried out to find the optimal value of each. When one has been adjusted, you move on to the next, and so on through all the variables.

However, when there is a high degree of innovation, this is very difficult to do. The iterative method of optimisation is a *local* method; it only considers the environment local to that variable. You change things bit by bit (*céteris paribus*) and see what happens. But by the time you want to change a variable in a highly innovative environment, the system state has probably changed and the results cannot therefore be compared to previous ones. To be able to adjust the system, you need to design experiments that are more elaborate. The iterative methodology doesn't work, and you have to resort to procedures that deal with the situation in a *global* manner.

Rehearsals

This is the role and purpose of rehearsals; their name says it all. A rehearsal is a sophisticated experiment designed to improve a system. Would it surprise you if we said that a rehearsal is equivalent to debugging in computer programming? Or if we likened it to a simulation? No, of course not; neither of these comparisons is surprising because they're all aspects of the same reality. In a simulation, let's say a spreadsheet for financial modelling, we emphasise the 'what-if?' We repeat the analysis various times, changing the suppositions. In rehearsals we simply emphasise the 'What happens if we do this normally?'

Why rehearse? To find the *faults in the system*. Also, because everybody can gain *familiarity* with the show in preparation; that is to say, to increase the *knowledge* of everybody involved. And, finally, to reduce the *uncertainty*, anticipating the results such that everything that can happen has already happened before we get on-stage, where fixes are very expensive, or where perhaps there is no remedy.

> **Should you introduce rehearsals to improve your service?**

The theatrical professions discovered the art of experimentation many years ago. The sequence of rehearsals at the Teatro Real contains nothing arbitrary; it satisfies the best norms of experimental design.

And did they invent it themselves? No, not really. This is another evolutionary phenomenon, that of Darwinian Theory. It has developed over many years, introducing innovation after innovation into the process, obtaining mutations, and selecting those that are successful. Now and then an innovator appears, such as Tamayo or Bianco, who breaks the previous schemes and redesigns the entire process, removing what's not needed and rationalising the whole. The result is then wrapped up and put back into the evolutionary stream.

This has to be the case because, in local optimisation, sustained over a long time, errors build up that need period 'spring-cleaning'. Technically, we say that the optimisation has reached a local optimum, an optimum that cannot be improved by simply making small changes. To improve in such a case, we need to resort to big changes, major reforms. Essentially, you have to go back to square one and start again. Daniel recognises this when he says 'With Tamayo we said "let's go and make the theatre that we've always wanted"'. Yes, Tamayo, Bianco and their colleagues are innovators, but they are fundamentally the inheritors of a long tradition of experimentation, whose battle cry, if a little too wordy, could have been 'Let's do it *well*, now that we know how to do it and we are able to do it!'[1]

Innovation in theatrical processes has traditionally been minimal, and there has been a lot of time in which to optimise the iterative debugging process of the theatre performance. And really, it is well optimised.

The current system of rehearsals, as in the best approaches to experimentation, takes into account the cost of experimenting. It is cheaper to experiment in the rehearsal room than on the stage, because to perform the experiment on-stage you have to disrupt the entire factory. The stage is a speeding train; to stop it, you have to overcome the vast inertia that it and the 200-odd people around it have accumulated. And this is very expensive. The closer the experiment in the rehearsal room is to reality – the more similar it appears to the reality in the factory – the better the results of the experiment will be. Stairs of the correct dimensions allow the soprano to judge with a fair degree of accuracy on how to arrive at the landing in time to safely hit the high notes. Because once there on the landing, she can concentrate on the song, and not on the operation of going up the stairs.

The process appears to be carefully studied to control uncertainty and complexity. It's interesting to note that they introduce the components of the system one by one. Once they have completed the analysis of one phase they introduce the innovations into the next. They begin first with only scene movement in the rehearsal room. A physical experiment on the impenetrability of bodies; oriented to the feasibility of movement of all the participants.

Then they put the scene movement aside, and they concentrate on the music. 'Let's see what can happen with the music; let's do the Italian.' After the Italian, they put together the two central aspects: the music and the action. And they do that in the ensemble rehearsals. But they still don't bring in the singing. Operatic singing is exhausting for the singers, and it's never a good idea to kill them off too early.

Now, yes, now they bring in the singers, but they leave out one element that would introduce additional complexities: the orchestra. The orchestra has a lot of inertia, so they don't want to introduce them until the end.

Finally, they go to the integration of the whole system. They introduce the orchestra. And they include a simulation of the full show, complete with an

---

[1] This echoes Isaac Newton's modest words to Robert Hooke: 'If I have seen farther it is by standing on the shoulders of giants.'

audience. It's an inoffensive and tame audience, to be sure, but at the end of the day it is an audience.

RT: Rehearsal and training

The rehearsal strategy appears to us to be so important, we've given it a snappy name, which also provides us with an appropriate pun for a book about opera: the RT strategy (go on, say it out loud ... 'arty strategy'. See?) RT for Rehearsal and Training. The T of training recognises the explicit role of a rehearsal as a permanent personal trainer for the Teatro Real (of the company in general). It's the learning achieved by the experimenters, not the objects of the experiments. In a laboratory experiment, it isn't only the mice that learn, but also the people involved, increasing their knowledge in the same way as they would by solving real problems. This is virtual problem-solving; experience away from the operational reality, but no less valid for all that. At the Teatro Real the rehearsals fulfil the same purpose as flight simulators. They allow people to have an experience of what could happen, without any danger of grave consequences that have no remedy.

If the rehearsal isn't meticulously prepared and carried out then doubts will immediately appear. 'No, it can't be, that's wrong. In reality the soprano is taller than you.' A bad experiment doesn't produce conclusive results. There always remain doubts about their validity. The rehearsal has to be meticulous and definitive. And it must be designed to be so. Can you imagine the anguish that the tenor would suffer if he doesn't think that what he did in rehearsal shows him in the best light? If he changes it, he destroys his relationship with the rest of the production. Rehearsals, by the end of the process, must be the definitive commitment of the action. Rehearsed and decided. Notice how the Stage Director 'loses' his authority once the ante piano rehearsals start. It's over. What's done is done.

The complement to rehearsing is training. The acquisition of non-formalised knowledge that helps prepare for possible pitfalls. The perception derived from the rehearsal is not enough in itself; you need to stop and talk about what's happening. In the ensembles, the Stage Director can spend as much time as he wants on whatever he wants. And the participants have to talk about what has happened, their perceptions and what they've learnt.

We want to champion the role of RT in the company. In your company, and in ours, mountains of experiments are performed. And their objectives are those we mentioned previously: Debug, Learn, Anticipate and, as a result, Improve. But, in the majority of companies that we know, the rehearsal methodology leaves a lot to be desired.

> Debug, Learn, Anticipate, Improve (DLAI).

They don't follow a rigorous and controllable sequence like those in the Teatro Real. And all of this is a consequence of a lack of knowledge. In a person's professional development, little time is dedicated to the methodologies of observing the world, the experimental methodologies. Think about your own training and development... a lot of theory, but what about experiments?

There was a time when, to resolve this situation, specialists in quality wanted to convert everyone into a statistic. And they started to teach the methods of Taguchi.[2] Without doubt, Taguchi deserves great credit for having realised the problem years ago, and for having prepared digestible simplifications of advanced experiment–design methodologies. But wanting to convert everybody into experiment–design specialists is pushing things a bit far.

There are two key points about the RT strategy. First, you need to be sure that the poor quality of the experiment will not lead us to doubt the results (or, to put it another way, that the high quality of the experiment gives us faith in the results). Second, that the experiment gives rise to training, the corresponding *collective learning*.

Residual uncertainty

There is an additional concept that we have not taken into account in the foregoing, and that we must highlight. We have been implicitly supposing that the result of an experiment, or rehearsal, is *deterministic*. That is to say, if we repeat it twice under the same conditions, it turns out the same way. That if a motor works in one rehearsal and none of the operating conditions are changed, then it will work in the next rehearsal. That's a bit optimistic, though. It's well known that this is not the case. As Murphy's Law tells us, *anything that can go wrong, will... and at the worst possible moment.*

The reason is that there are countless *small causes* whose effect is very difficult to predict and that, together, introduce chance and uncertainty into the results of an experiment. Two repetitions of the same experiment give similar, but not exact, results.

How can we improve something by experimenting, if chance disguises or distorts the results? The trick is by considering, and reducing, the residual chance. Suppose that we want to predict sales. For the sake of argument, let's say that we have the feeling that the month's sales can be anything from 100 to 500 units, with an average of 300. We have a high level of uncertainty. One method of quantifying this would be to take the interval 500–100 and divide it by the average. Ok, let's do it. We get a variability of 400/300 = 1.33. This is high! But note that we are including in this variability certain effects

---

[2] Developed by Genichi Taguchi (Japan, 1924–), this is a method applied to the design of experiments, which takes external factors into account. This controversial methodology, which many say is flawed but most admit contains much of great value (such as considering the cost of poor quality), began to be applied in manufacturing from the mid-1950s, and more recently in biotechnology, marketing and advertising.

that we can foresee and predict. For example, if we sell ice creams then we know that the temperature affects sales. If the weather forecast is for a hot spell this month, then we could probably use the forecast temperatures to fine-tune the sales forecast. If we do this we can adjust our sales figure range upwards and end up with an interval of, say, 600–400 = 200. With an average of, let's say, 400, the residual uncertainty is now reduced to 0.5

> **Residual uncertainty is the randomness that remains when the effects of all possible causes have been removed.**

Residual uncertainty is the randomness that remains after having removed the effects of all the causes that we are able to identify and evaluate. It thus follows, of course, that as we eliminate more effects of more causes, then we will have less *residual uncertainty*. Let's see another example. In civil aviation, each accident is studied in the greatest detail to determine the cause or causes, and to regulate aviation design and practice to avoid another accident occurring for identical reasons. In the world of aviation, they can draw on more than 70 years of 'experiments' (unplanned) and countless rules and regulations that try to eliminate any possible accident. Despite this, accidents still happen. At the time of writing, it is estimated that the residual accident rate is something like two per million take-offs. And this number is not reducing. It is remaining stable, and has been so for the past few years, despite all the additional regulations introduced during that same period of time.

> **Tackle the residual uncertainty in your service.**

This means that, having eliminated all the randomness that we're able to, eliminating causes, we have reached a limit that we don't know how to reduce. None of the actions that we take, no matter how refined or esoteric, are able to reduce this 'residual' rate. We can say that this is the intrinsic residual *uncertainty* of the phenomenon. Something similar occurs in road traffic accidents. Governments try to reduce accidents through all sorts of more or less plausible measures. Of course, the ultimate measure, to reduce the accident rate to zero or nearly-zero, would be to prohibit the movement of vehicles. Luckily, this doesn't seem to have occurred to our ministers ... yet. But within certain limits, the accident rate on the roads appears to remain invariable. We are probably at the level of intrinsic residual randomness that won't go away, despite the best efforts of governments' campaigns to terrorise their citizens.

With this concept of residual randomness under our belts, we can better understand the RT strategy. Through the medium of experiments, rehearsals, we can continue removing all the causes that can provoke failure. In *Don Giovanni*, the singers had to climb onto a table with wheels, which was then moved. In one rehearsal at which we were present, the table wobbled and the 'passengers', through fright, ended up in less-than-elegant poses that would not have looked very graceful in the performance. For the next rehearsal, they had put bigger wheels on the table. Was a possible failure eliminated? No, they only eliminated one possible cause. With bigger wheels, the small irregularities of the stage surface no longer cause the table to wobble. But there is still the possibility that there is a not-so-small irregularity; some object left lying on the stage could spell trouble for the singers' bones! That didn't happen in the rehearsal, we're glad to report, but the theatrical gods can always find some surprise for us mere mortals.

No matter how much we rehearse, residual uncertainty will always continue to exist. If it's very small we can afford to ignore it and accept that one time in a million, let's say, something unexpected is going to happen and this will cause a failure. Fine, those are not bad odds. To reach a million performances, at the rate of 150 per year, would take a while...about 6666 years, in fact. But what if the rate is higher? Or what if we haven't reduced the failure rate to those sorts of acceptable levels and we can have something fail every, say, five performances?

Incidentally, all these probabilities can be calculated. Lleonard Garuz, Operations Director at Barcelona's Liceo theatre, does a failure analysis of all the operas, through which he is able to calculate the probability of disaster striking. This doesn't fix the problem, of course, but at least it helps him to know what to look out for.

Conclusion: Failure can always happen. This is always true. In every company and in every situation, you cannot eliminate the possibility of failure. But you can minimise the effect; first, by calculating the probability of the failure occurring and, second, by preparing your people to react as rapidly as possible to limit the damage. And we've already seen that this is the purpose of rehearsals, to fulfil the two functions of experimentation and training. It'll come as no surprise when we say that training helps to solve the problems that crop up in rehearsals. Again, we see problem-solving in its dual role; as an improver of operations (Efficiency) and as a provider of knowledge (Attractiveness).

What should you do in your company?

Here we offer some advice on how to obtain the best results from the RT approach in your company:

1. Create a rehearsal or experimentation methodology.
2. Document the results of all rehearsals. It is common in companies to repeat the same experiments various times simply because people didn't know of their existence.
3. Evaluate existing uncertainty by performing an analysis of failures.
4. Establish ways to reduce residual uncertainty.
5. Train people in ways to avoid residual uncertainty damaging service.

Let's look at each one of those in more detail.

1. *Create a rehearsal or experimentation methodology.* Learning even a few basics in the analysis of experiments can be very rewarding. Get your people used to using ideas such as variables, controls, degrees of freedom, statistic significance and so on. Remember that a frequent cause of experiments being repeated is the lack of confidence in the results. As far as possible, clarify all the errors that can interfere with each phenomenon.

2. *Document the results of all rehearsals.* All experiments should have a list of conclusions reached, with a clear description of the purpose and the methodology of the experiment. Remember that in the Teatro Real, all the conclusions are noted on the score and then become part of the *tops*. Thus, they are always accessible and well-documented.

3. *Evaluate existing uncertainty by performing an analysis of failures.* Find an expert who can show you the basics of error analysis. A simple method of assigning variables to probabilities in complex situations would be sufficient. If necessary, there are also software applications that can help in this task (even if you don't trust the software industry – those who write software tend to be technical people who don't know how (or don't want) to help us; what they want is to sell programs, which is very different).

4. *Establish ways to reduce residual uncertainty.* Get your people used to thinking about the causes of failures and about the effect each failure has on the result. Often a simple cause-and-effect table will prove sufficient to help you understand how to reduce uncertainty.

5. *Train people in ways to avoid residual uncertainty damaging service.* Train your people. Perform simulations, drills or whatever other problem-solving activity that can help to maintain a high level of service quality even when undesired events occur.

Conclusions

In this chapter, we've seen how rehearsals and training are essential to obtain excellence in service. The objective of rehearsing is to be able to debug the provision of service as much as possible. In a rehearsal, we can detect errors, analyse possibilities and foresee potentially problematic circumstances. Training goes hand-in-hand with rehearsing, preparing people to deal with emergencies, learning not only how to solve problems but also how to solve them rapidly, filling gaps in knowledge and being prepared to solve the problems that are *going* to happen. Training is one of the critical tools in achieving excellence in service.

Even so, the possibility of failure remains; the residual uncertainty or randomness that remains after having removed the effect of all probable causes.

In this chapter, we've proposed five actions to tackle it. We urge you to start applying them before your competitors do.

We'll end with our regular questions to help you reflect on the foregoing:

- Should you suggest including rehearsals as a necessary means of achieving excellence in your service?
- How can you tackle residual uncertainty?
- What is the role of training in your company?
- Do you have a DLAI strategy?

XVII
The Creative Process:
The Opera *Don Giovanni*

Creativity has become one of the hot topics in the business world. It's as though companies suddenly need to have brilliant ideas.

What is creativity? It's the generation of ideas. Creativity, innovation and problem-solving make up the basic short-list of the learning process. To innovate is to implement, and implementing generates problems that need solving. But the ability to innovate requires the generation of ideas, and that's where the creativity comes in. Creation must go hand-in-hand with implementation, and having one without the other makes no sense.

To understand what creativity is requires us to understand how the creative process takes place. In this chapter, Lluís Pasqual, the renowned Stage Director, provides us with a wonderful example of the creative process. His explanation of how they staged Don Giovanni *helps us to understand a little better how creation and implementation work.*

There are people capable of creating intuitively. But they are few and far between; the majority need to learn how to create. Then the creativity increases and becomes customary. But not by using simplistic or infantile techniques, as appears to be typical among many aficionados of the subject, but by the generation of new structures, new approaches, that support the development of new ideas. Indirect actions that boost the production of ideas.

The creative process is the subject of the next two chapters. The objective is to provide managers with an approach that can accelerate the generation of ideas throughout the organisation, not just in those who are already intuitively creative. We advocate daily creativity that leads a company to constantly generate ideas (although not necessarily brilliant ones!)

This chapter is based on our conversations with Lluís Pasqual, the world-renowned Stage Director of theatre and opera. Lluís Pasqual has been a distinguished figure in the creation of Barcelona's Teatre Lliure, in which he collaborated from the outset with Fabià Puigserver. Lluís Pasqual has worked a lot with Daniel Bianco and José Luis Tamayo, and within this esteemed trio it's sometimes impossible to decide where the ideas start and where they finish. The three of them are incredibly in tune with each other, and as Pasqual says 'As we had to make it all up as we went along, we have no choice but to convey what we were creating.'

The plot of *Don Giovanni*[1]

It will perhaps help the reader, to better understand this chapter, to present a brief synopsis of the plot of *Don Giovanni*. It is yet another work based on the legend of Don Juan, as were those of Tirso de Molina, Molière and Zorrilla, among others, but this time with music by none other than the late, great Wolfgang Amadeus Mozart (hats off, please). At the start of this wonderful opera, Don Juan has just had 'relations' with Donna Ana, the fiancée of Don Ottavio, in her father's house. It is not clear how, and it appears that Donna Ana had nothing to do with it and that Don Giovanni seduced her against her will. The outraged father of Donna Ana, the Comendatore, makes a poor estimation of his own physical prowess and challenges Don Giovanni to a duel while Donna Ana goes for help. As a result of the duel (and could there be any other outcome?) the Comendatore dies. When Donna Ana returns with Don Ottavio and finds her father dead, she wants Don Ottavio, who is apparently not much use in a fight, to swear that he will avenge her father's death by killing the unknown murderer. Being head-over-heels in love with her, Don Ottavio agrees to this.

As Don Giovanni and Leporello, his servant, arrive back at Don Giovanni's palace, they bump into Donna Elvira, a woman who Don Giovanni recently took liberties with. And she's very angry because the scoundrel had the audacity to run away after the deed. Another one who seems to have missed the plot ... Trusty Leporello, to help remove any lingering doubts Donna Elvira might still have, decides to read her the list of all Don Giovanni's conquests; a list that contains 2065 names. Donna Elvira sees that sharing her man with 2065 other women won't be easy, and really begins to see red. So she also vows to get her revenge.

Meanwhile, our man comes across a wedding procession. As he's a lad with a good heart (and he's attracted to the bride), he offers to help the groom and make the bride happy by hosting a wedding celebration at his palace. In short, he sings to the bride, Zerlina, a pretty, little song, she's starting to melt, and it's all going swimmingly .... Until the killjoy Angry Elvira arrives to thwart the best laid plans of mice and Giovannis. She is soon joined by Donna Ana and Don Ottavio who are still on the trail of her father's unknown murderer.

Later, since he is apparently incapable of keeping out of trouble for even five minutes, Don Giovanni tries to seduce Donna Elvira's maid, serenading her just in front of the aforementioned's house. This plan is also thwarted by Donna Elvira, who is really starting to be a nuisance. She apparently wants to convince Don Giovanni, whether through shouts or recriminations, that he should love her. But all she manages to do is bore him. Don Giovanni returns home, but passing by the cemetery where the Comendatore is buried with a commemorative statue over the grave, he decides to have a laugh and also scare the life out of Leporello by getting him to invite the statue to dinner. Leporello, despite several attempts, is too scared to complete the task and so Don Giovanni invites the statue, thus sealing his own doom. The statue, being by now fairly talkative, replies 'I'll come'.

In the final scene, Don Giovanni is dining peacefully when Donna Elvira arrives again to be a pain in the neck, asking him to change his ways. The poor guy only wants to be left in peace to enjoy his dinner, and so you can't really blame him for not seeing her point of view. As Donna Elvira goes to leave, a scream is heard and she runs back in. Leporello goes to

---

[1] This plot summary is the work of one of the current authors, which allows the reader a certain freedom to form an opinion about the characters; a freedom that the other author doesn't share.

> investigate and cries out, saying that the statue has come to dinner as invited. Don Giovanni opens the door himself and in comes the statue. Our boy can't really believe his eyes but, keeping a cool head and remembering his manners, he says 'I'd never have believed it myself, but there you go. Leporello, get another plate.' The statue starts pressuring Don Giovanni to change his lifestyle but Don Giovanni gets bored with the sermon and says no way, he doesn't want to and, anyway, it's not his fault that he's such a good-looking lad. Well, the statue gets angry, grabs Don Giovanni by the hand on the pretext of shaking it and takes him down to the toasty netherworld. The opera finishes with a moral delivered by all the protagonists; the moral was probably originally included to satisfy the *nihil obstat*[2] to allow the opera to be performed.
>
> For many of us Don Giovanni is a likeable chap who just couldn't stand the tears of one woman, and whom women pursued and offered themselves to. And as Don Giovanni has a good heart, he has no choice but to surrender to their wishes. To Don Giovanni we might apply the words of his colleague, Don Mendo, he of the Vengeance, when he says 'Unlucky is the man who is born while I'm so handsome.' But, surprisingly, there are other interpretations... especially that of the other author, who doesn't seem to be much in agreement. Oh well...

The role of the stage director

What, in your opinion, is a Stage Director?

The Stage Director is an *energy catalyst*; he is the leader, the boss, in my case, of the opera. This leadership is shared with the Orchestral Director. It's not exactly shared, but there is a point where I pass the reins to him, and he takes control. We can say that there are two parallel processes; the Orchestral Director prepares all the musical side of things, while I prepare the dramatic side. Then comes the moment when he takes the reins, and is the boss. My role is therefore the energy catalyst.

And it's not at all the same doing *Tosca* as to do a Rossini, I can assure you. It's nowhere near the same to spend all day hearing the guffawing echo of Rossini, to hearing the dark drama of Tosca. Not the same at all, the people work in a completely different way.

I take the lead from the moment the opera is handed to me, from before we start the rehearsals and during the rehearsals. In the case of this Don Giovanni, we even start talking about the types of singers we want to have. In other cases, the casting is done by the theatres themselves. The personal trajectory of each Stage Director defines what each one can come to demand; this is what they call 'career ladder'. That's what it boils down to at the end of the day; getting to the point of having better working conditions.

From there the Stage Director chooses what we call the 'artistic team', who are the people who do the sets, the lights, the costumes... and they're

---

[2] *Nihil obstat* is official approval that a work dealing with faith or morals does not contradict Catholic teaching.

a hugely important part of an opera, more so than in 'normal' theatre. Opera supposes huge dimensions, figuratively and literally: a lot of space to manage.

The project has to be realised in various stages specifically designed for various reasons. For example, you can't rehearse the opera for ten hours a day because the singers can't physically manage it nor can the musical director. So there are some rehearsal hours in which all the teams are learning; they're there, talking about things and doing the show. *Narrating and doing.*

Narrating, describing, is very important. Because the rehearsals are done in the rehearsal room, where there is no complete set, just a pre-set that gets developed as the rehearsals progress. An example: In my *Don Giovanni*, there's going to be, on the stage, a revolving set. But not in the rehearsal room, because it won't fit and it's not even ready. Donna Elvira enters from the right. Let's suppose that at that moment I think that the revolving set should change, because her entrance changes the music. It should then become melancholy music, because she can't come on like a war-horse! As the rehearsal room doesn't have the revolving set, I say 'Stage management, here the set changes.' The people in stage management then know that at this moment the set has to change. Similarly, if I want Donna Elvira to come on with a lace mantilla, then I have to tell the costume people that. *Narrating and doing.*

And so it goes, the same with props and everything else. I go along *telling and doing*, telling and doing. Everything that happens doesn't need telling, but everything that can't be done in the rehearsal has to be said. I have to explain to everyone the reason for everything. I can't just say to Donna Elvira, 'Enter' because she'll ask me 'Enter? Where from? Left, right, back, front, through the door, the window...?' And this needs to be done second by second throughout the opera, beat by beat, note by note. I go with them through the rehearsal, I accompany them.

There are things that can be done in the rehearsal room. For example, when Donna Elvira comes on we can measure the amount of musical time there is from the door to the moment when she begins her aria. And this time has to be sufficient for her to get into position.

However, the person who directs this timing is the Orchestral Director. He really is the one who, literally, marks time. Generally, he has to be at rehearsals because the tempo conditions everything. If the music's going quickly, tap-tap-tap, and these three beats mark time for the singer to take three steps, then it's a very different proposition than a slower tempo of tap...tap...tap...This can change everything, even the feeling or intention. Good maestros mark time from the beginning, because that way we can know whether the action should be more or less passionate. Everything depends on his interpretation of the music.

After the rehearsals' room, we go to the stage. And there we have to adjust ourselves to the dimensions of the stage. The rehearsal room has a 5 m-high ceiling, but the stage has something like 14 m clearance, in which the voice needs to breathe completely differently. That is a fundamental moment; when the name most frequently used is that of the Stage Director. Everybody needs him. 'Lluís, what costume should she wear?' 'Lluís, does the car come on here?' Lluís this, Lluís that, constantly.

And, bit by bit, you start to hear the name less, because you begin disappearing, disappearing... you start taking a step back, leaving things alone, letting go, until the rehearsals with the orchestra. Then you have to watch the whole thing from the outside to give it the final tweaks and touches.

This is when we add the lighting. Lighting is fundamental in an opera because it fills the gap between what's seen and what's heard, so there is no divorce, no 'seven centimetre' gap between them. It's not just the costume nor the set, nor the colours. The lighting is what applies a filter to everything. You know that people lower their voices at night and raise them during the day, right? Well it's the same for the audience, the lighting accompanies the spectator, accompanies the score. Those 'seven centimetres' are our responsibility. When there's that gap there, that's when things aren't going well.

Foresee and adapt

I have to imagine this world and detect the problems. The most stressful part of an opera is having to detect them so far in advance. You have to foresee things and later be sufficiently flexible to be able to change, according to the resources you have available in the theatre. Particularly if you don't know those resources beforehand.

There's a whole load of determining factors that must be remembered, from the people to the machinery of the theatre. In the theatre, one of the most difficult things to manage is the coordination of the various groups of people that make up the show. Timetables of the chorus, orchestra and technicians that overlap and often contradict. The orchestra has to have an hour's break, the chorus has 20 minutes' break and the pianists only a quarter of an hour, and you have to get them to coincide because if not then we'll be doing nothing by breaks.

This is why, in some theatres such as the German ones, there is a planning director. This is a person whose only job is planning. He or she plans everything, from the arrival of the singers, or organising the people who go and get the necessary rights for a concert, to the timetables of all the people involved.

In *Don Giovanni*, I had only worked with two of the singers; the rest I'd never met before. Some of them I'd never known personally, having only seen them on stage, but it's like window shopping – such basic things as having a Donna Elvira who's really tall at 1.91 m, but luckily I also have a Don Giovanni who's also tall, at 1.92 m. But what would I have done if he were only 1.70 m tall?

Another example: Don Giovanni and Leporello, they have to swap clothes because at one point in the action they need to pass off as each other. It's a theatre trick, suspending disbelief – you put my hat on, I'll put yours on, and that's it, we've swapped. But for this to work you can't have a Don Giovanni who's 2 m tall, and a Leporello who's 1.5 m, because then the audience will say 'What? Do you think we're blind or stupid? What's going on here?'

Everything is convention, I know, but up to a certain point, because the contemporary audience member is very well versed in imagery, whether from the cinema or television, you still have to find certain credibility even within such conventions. In this sort of case, I've intervened in the casting. But sometimes I've found myself with singers who've put on 30 kg from the time we hired them, and others who've lost 30 kg. And you can go from such basic things as these up to finer points such as how to interpret a song. One Donna Elvira is furious; another is much more sorrowful, acting in a much more heart-broken way to the first who is just really angry. The two sing the same notes, both very well, and both act very well. Therefore, if I've already got fixed ideas about Donna Elvira, I'm going to end up clashing with one or the other, and it mustn't be like that. My ideas of the role must always be made-to-measure for each singer.

Do the majority of people in the Stage Directors' profession share your views?

No, mainly because I maintain a principle that goes against my profession. I believe that a blind person can go to the opera; they'll miss a lot but they'll still enjoy the opera. But a deaf person can't. Therefore, if I have to choose between someone who acts well or another who sings well, I'll always choose the better singer. This might not be in my own best interests, but if not I have to ask myself why am I doing opera? Nobody makes me … No, I have to be true to the music, whether people agree or not.

You can do anything on a stage if you have a purpose. I've seen a Salomé singing naked and it was so well done, *so* well done, that it made no difference. It was just like that and not another way. And in another opera I've seen the entire chorus singing while hanging from the flys like legs of cured ham. And it was fantastic. And Jonathan Price, about 20 years ago, set *Rigoletto*[3] in a 1930s Chicago neighbourhood, complete with violent

---

[3] *Rigoletto*, by Giuseppe Verdi. Perhaps, alongside *La Traviata*, one of the most popular by Verdi. Who hasn't heard 'La donna è mobile'? A tragedy set around the eponymous hunchbacked jester of the Duke of Mantua (it was originally King François I of France, but this was censored). The jester has a daughter, Gilda, who is seduced by the Duke, who passes himself off as a student, thinking that she's Rigoletto's lover. Rigoletto wants revenge and hires an assassin to do away with the Duke, while this latter is visiting Magdalena, the sister of the hired assassin. But Gilda, Rigoletto's

gangsters, and it was a miracle. Anything and everything can be done, so long as it serves the purpose.

I have to take this, my personal interpretation of *Don Giovanni*, and move it forward, getting as close as possible to Mozart. I have to understand what Mozart put into the music, and work on the libretto of Da Ponte.[4]

In the opera, people always argue over whether it's the libretto that's important, or the music. It's the famous Italian polemic of 'prima la musica, prima la parole...'

I believe there are appalling librettos with sublime music... and occasionally you'll also find the reverse. This is not the case with *Don Giovanni*, but in general, the libretto is inferior to the music. In general. This has led me to believe that the musicians, in reality, are not embodying the words, but the sentiments that lie behind the words: what the poet wanted to say, not what the poet said.

The music has a more metaphysical dimension than the spoken word. If you do *Romeo and Juliet*, the theatre play, you can make the famous balcony scene really passionate, sad, despairing, about two losers who know that they can never be lovers, or you can do it as two naïve innocents who believe that their love with be eternal. I can do it how I like; I can breathe it how I like. But when you do *Romeo and Juliet*, the opera, there is nothing to decide in that sense, the composer has already done it, and has permanently embodied those feelings into the music. Therefore I can't trust the libretto as the starting point of my work, I have to trust the music, on the interpretation that the music gives. If I have to trust anyone, it's going to be the composer.

In my case, I have to know the opera off by heart – any opera I do, if I don't already know it like that, then I'll learn it. I get to know it note by note. I can't work in any other way. I read music but not as fast as a professional musician.

... so you spend time listening to the music?

Exactly, the first thing I do is put it on the record player. I'm not so young, so I now know many operas. But if it's one I don't know, or I don't know it so well, then I'll play it and play it and play it, while I'm cooking, bathing, driving... often without knowing the plot, without reading the libretto. I play it until it's completely familiar.

---

daughter, finds out that they want to kill off the Duke, and she sacrifices herself for her lover. When they deliver the body in a sack to Rigoletto, who believes the corpse to be the Duke's, he discovers with horror that it is in fact his daughter, mortally wounded. Nevertheless, they both find enough energy to sing a beautiful duet to end the piece.

[4] Mozart's librettist.

Once I know the music, I get the libretto and I say *let's see what happens, what they say*. I try to join the two parts and then I'll see the gaps, because I already know the music. Then, intuitively, I have to interpret the music and I have to imagine how to do the opera. I try to follow the libretto, but above all, I think in colours. The music will suggest tonalities of colour, of light, of space and so on.

It's very important to know what the composer intended. Or try to imagine it, anyway. In the case of *Don Giovanni*, I don't believe for a moment that someone of such unquestionable genius as Mozart would have spent so much time and written so many notes, just to explain that bad people go to hell, which is what the ending seems to suggest. That ending is without doubt just paying lip-service to the church. Like in plays by Calderon de la Barca, where the King always turns up at the end to fix everything, because otherwise he wouldn't have been paid for the work and the performances wouldn't have been allowed. This also takes the blame away from the authors, rather cleverly, when they have characters say daring things such as 'Long live liberty!'[5]

Let's take an example of understanding the opera, above all philologically. In the libretto of *Don Giovanni*, the protagonist invites these poor country people to his palace, so that they can see a real, luxurious house. These days everyone has seen the inside of a palatial home, at least on the television, but back then, when the piece was written, this was not the case. And why? There is a clue. They arrive at the part, and they're offered 'cioccolatte', 'caffè', 'sorbetti' and 'confetti' – chocolate, coffee, sorbets and sugared almonds. In the eighteenth century, coffee was banned by the Vatican for 30 years and chocolate for 35, because they invited excess; and sorbets because these were 'exclusive' to the King of England and the Pope. So, for these country folk to be offered them was a way of dazzling them and winning them over.

So how would I translate that? In the first place, you don't break things if they're not broken. We're dealing with a product of the eighteenth century composed in the eighteenth century. It's an antique that I have to hand down carefully to those who will come after me. But it is an antique; it's not a model of design. It's not a Mariscal.[6] It's from the eighteenth century and you can only push it up to a certain point without it breaking.

But there is something that you cannot convey to the audience, I believe, by doing an eighteenth-century *Don Giovanni*. If I do an eighteenth-century

---

[5] In the second act of the opera there is a party, in which Don Giovanni starts on a libertarian discourse which must have been extremely risky and provoking in those times, which was clearly the intention of the authors.

[6] Javier Mariscal (Valencia, 1950). Spanish draftsman, painter and designer, whose style is characterised by the angular simplicity of stroke and form contained within a very advanced conception of the image. Perhaps his most well-known work is Cobi, the mascot of the 1992 Barcelona Olympics.

version, the public wouldn't understand, in this particular example, the offence caused by the chocolate and coffee. There would only be the formal historical part, and that can't be, because this formal part is for telling a tremendous story, a myth, a thriller. And that's the eternal and insoluble problem of *Don Giovanni*. No staging, which is always composed of concrete elements, can ever 'fly' as high as the music. The depths and heights only come from the music and the singer's voice. At that point, any staging is 'small'. For this reason, and because every opera lover who comes to see it with their own personal and distinct version in mind, there has never been, and I believe there never will be, a perfect, 'comprehensive' staging. And it will never satisfy the audience 100 percent, much less a critic, and even less the Spanish public, who unavoidably arrive at the theatre with their Don Juan cliché, which is above all the *Don Juan Tenorio* by Zorrilla. And that has very little to do with the Don Juan/Don Giovanni of Mozart and Da Ponte.

What I've done is bring it sufficiently up to date to be able to recognise and understand the characters, but keep it sufficiently distant so it doesn't appear to be set in our present day-to-day lives. So, I placed it in 1940. But not to make a story about the Spanish civil war. *Don Giovanni* is a work about Eros and consequences such as love, sex and flirting, and all the energies contained within. Above all, it's the story of a person who, as he goes through life, leaves his mark on people. Wherever Don Giovanni goes, people are affected, one in one way, another person in another. It's set in 1940 because, for us, 1940 is a time that most of us have lived vicariously through someone who is still alive, who was young at that time, perhaps a family member. But it's still far away, something only known in 'black and white'. Maybe twenty years ago it wouldn't have worked, setting it in 1940, but now it does. It's history, sufficiently far, but at the same time sufficiently close to be able to recognise, and so that we can understand a certain type of moral order and, as a consequence, the high level of depravity in Don Giovanni that Mozart so clearly brought out.

At the beginning, Don Giovanni kills the Comendatore. He is a criminal; there's no doubt about that. But often the 'baddy' in the movies is the most attractive. Everything is ambiguous, a purely mental exercise. I can't tell you exactly where Mozart is ambiguous. Donna Ana is an ambiguous character, though. We don't really know what's happened to her; yes, we know that she's been marked by Don Juan, but we don't know to what degree and whether for good or bad. But the singer has to know for herself; that's the dichotomy. In *Don Giovanni* there is no one character who isn't in love with someone. Everybody loves. Don Giovanni, of course, in his own way, clearly. But all of them love in their own way.

Don Ottavio is a strange case. He has a problem, caused by having an extra aria, which Mozart added later. The problem is that he talks more than he should. I think that Don Ottavio is a man of few words. He's often been seen as a limited character, short on intelligence and slow to react. And he is without doubt a character who can be well-defined by the first line of his aria, where he says 'If my wife is happy, I'm happy; if my wife is unhappy, I am unhappy.' Just with that you can write a treatise on psychology. He's noble and practical. His love is not a naïve love, it's an intelligent and mature love. If it were not, he couldn't sing so sweetly, and with such extraordinary music. Don Ottavio is someone who says little, but enough, and who knows that he very much loves the person at his side, and if she's fine then he's fine, and that's all. He is exactly the opposite of Don Giovanni, who is constantly unbalanced, in a spiral, running away, dizzy. By contrast, Don Ottavio is the type of person who wants to go and live with nature. And he doesn't just want to go, he'll be happy when he goes.

And once you have your concept, you explain your ideas to the Operations Director and the Set Designer. Is it a big effort to translate your vision for them?

I explain it to them, but it is one thing to explain to Daniel; it's quite another to explain it to another Operations Director! Daniel and I have been working together for many years. He knows me very well, I know him very well and so we just don't have problems. We're of the same school, he and I; we share the idea that theatre, no matter how hi-tech it becomes, is still at base an art form.

Theatre is craftsmanship. In theatre, all the products are prototypes; everything is crafted. Maybe later it's moved by motors and controlled by computers, but the point remains. In the background you're still making a made-to-measure costume for each singer; made-to-measure physically, and artistically. Everything is an adventure, a world in itself.

I understand it by dividing it into two distinct parts; one is the imaginative side that explains the 'whys', and the other is the common language. The theatre is a trade, and we have a common language. If I say 'In the first act, there's a point in which this wall has to rise,' then Daniel will say 'ok.' Ten minutes later, and I'll say 'Daniel, how are we going to do it?' and he'll reply 'Well, motorised, because it weighs about 1,500 kilos.'

'Ok,' I'll say, 'I'd like to move it in time with the music.'

'No problem, then we'll use variable speed motors.'

I want the wall to take 22 seconds to reach its highest point, because I have 22 seconds of music, and I know that, for my security, he's going to assign two technicians to rehearse it to this exact timing. This understanding, this thing I've explained so easily, is the result of working together for many years.

I know what can be done on the stage. The Set Designer says 'Where do you want Don Giovanni to exit at the end?' and I'll say 'I'd like him to go through the floor, just to disappear downwards' and Daniel will just mention 'Pasqual, remember we've got the revolving stage' and I'll realise that he's right – you don't want to use trapdoors when you've got the revolving stage. If I didn't know that, if I didn't have the stagecraft, I'd then start to look like an idiot by saying 'but he's got to go down through the stage, because he's supposed to be going to hell, so I want a trapdoor, got it? I want a trapdoor!'

until they actually went and installed one and then ask for €60,000 more because, yes, you can do it, but it's stupidly expensive. You have to re-cable the entire revolving stage along the edges, which is a really complicated task. But because I understand that, I don't ask for it.

And this happens because, fundamentally, you're both men of the theatre?

Yes, it's a trade you learn. One can have more or less talent, but you still have to know how the flys work. I remember one of the funniest things I heard was a theatre director who said 'At this point I want cave light' and the lighting guy from a distance responds with 'cave by day or cave by night?' Obviously... I know how the flys work, I know their possible uses, but this is a trade. I need to be well in-tune with the Operations Director, as with the Orchestral Director and the rest.

The Operations Director stamps his own character on the production, as does the Stage Director. The Operations Director is the boss of a group of people who spend many hours locked in a place without seeing sunlight, working for these lunatics who think they have great ideas. And this is both very difficult to achieve and very important work.

I was the first person in Spain to ask for the job of Operations Director of a national theatre to be officially named and recognised in the BOE.[7] Until then the post didn't officially exist.

The Operations Director fulfils a critical function. It is very important, *very* important that somebody, as well as distributing the work well and respecting the associated norms and guidelines, can convey without explaining; can make everybody understand that detail is what matters; can get everyone – for example, the who spends so many days fixing shades to the thousands of lights on the carousel in Don Giovanni – can get even this guy to feel that what he's doing is important for the show. If that guy doesn't feel that what he's doing is of great value, then we're all going wrong. Rubinstein,[8] the pianist, put it beautifully when he said 'God is in the details' and it's true: a show, like almost everything in life, is in the details.

---

[7] *The Boletín Oficial del Estado* is a daily Spanish government publication of new laws, directives, executive decisions, public-sector appointments and contracts.

[8] Arthur Rubinstein (Lódz, Poland, 1887–1982). A pianist, born in the same city as Chopin, his sublime concerts resonated throughout the world, reaching even the most remote places. His biographers observed that, during the time of his numerous concerts and recitals, he used to study and practice his interpretation and technique on the piano for between 12 and 16 hours a day. His interpretation style places him among the romantic pianists, yet at the same time among the exotics. During most of his life he specialised largely in the works of Chopin, with some of his interpretations being considered the representative pinnacle of Chopin's music.

XVIII
Basic Concepts of the Creative Process

Innovation and Creativity are two indispensable factors for a company to remain in a competitive position.[1] In Chapter 13, we presented the Stage Director as the principal source of innovation in an opera theatre. This role as a source of innovation is coupled with that of being the creative element in pursuit of excellence. In this chapter, we want to analyse not only how a creative process is generated, but also how this process can help to create an environment in which the creativity of others can flourish and in turn complement the process. A third aspect to analyse, and one that's complementary to the previous two, is his role as custodian of the materialisation of the idea, of its shaping in reality.

A Stage Director is a professional innovator. By definition, and for the greater glory of the theatre that contracts him, he tries to do new things, things that nobody has done before. His mission is to set aside the old, and strike out on new paths.

The creative process

Pasqual has a problem 'to create a production of *Don Giovanni*, different and high quality'. And in the face of this, as we know, he has two alternative extreme processes: applied and exploratory.[2] But, since the problem is a new one, then by definition the applied process won't work. Instead, he has to opt for exploration. We've already seen that this is a way of getting somewhere where nobody has ever been before, but it is resource-intensive, and vice versa. If a time limit is imposed, then the quality of the obtained result is reduced, and not proportionally; clearly, a solution won't be found on day one that is half as good as the solution found on day two.

---

[1] As we've already said, these are not differentiating factors; rather they are necessary for survival.

[2] We trust you'll remember chapter X, where we defined the difference between an applied process and an exploratory process.

Pasqual doesn't have all the time in the world. He has a deadline, as a result of which he needs to employ all the tricks he can to explore the problem as far as possible without missing that deadline. This means preparing and implementing 'exploration aids'; in this case, 'creativity aids'. These structures enable the rapid processing of new ideas, without having to manage a potentially infinite exploratory process.

How should Pasqual focus on his creative process? First, he has a clear objective: *'The first thing I ask myself is "What am I going to do with this opera?"'* Then he starts to soak up the music of the opera; to live it, by making it part of his daily life, he forces the music into his head. He says *'I have to learn it'*. It's a process of osmosis. He's going to feel the different states of musical animation that will give him clues about the different alternatives he can employ. If Donna Elvira has melancholic music, she can't come in galloping on a horse. It's obvious, but important. He absorbs this musical knowledge to be able to generate an infrastructure that will support him in the search for his creativity.

Pasqual tries to live each note in an attempt to understand what inspired the composer in creating it. The score ends up being almost his own; he feels as if it is penetrating his mind. Pasqual talks of colours and says, *'The musical pieces suggest tonalities of colour, light and space.'* Pasqual tries to interpret the music in terms which are more familiar to him, allowing him to later create ideas about how to stage the opera. He tries to *synthesize specific elements*, melodies and colours that he finds easier to handle to create the concept, to start to 'smell' how it is going to be staged. It is a process of looking for anchor points, related to the musical pieces, but more familiar to him, which will serve as a foundation for the creation of his own responses.

Once he has created this 'warehouse' of mental objects, he seems ready to solve the problem itself. He says, *'You have to interpret the music intuitively and imagine a way of making it'.* He starts his search for a solution by focusing on the reality of the concept of opera. Without the previous process of coming up with more familiar objects, the problem would still be thought of in very general, abstract terms, in such a way that it would become burdensome. Where would the reader start from if he was to design *Don Giovanni*? With familiar objects in mind, he would have better-known pieces to start *combining* in different ways.

Pasqual, like so many other protagonists of this book, seems to go through these processes very intuitively. He is considered an excellent Stage Director because he is capable of creating interesting new designs. Yet as we have just seen, behind this quality lie both a *methodology* and his own *combinatorial skills*.

In terms of *methodology*, it is clear that he follows a systematic process. First in his creation of *helpful objects* and then, only having done this, by starting to *explore* the problem. He has great skill in creating these objects, the new bricks which will make it possible to build a 'different' house. Pasqual projects the initial problem onto new ground which he knows better, has more control over, giving him the construction material he needs. Now he can start to combine those materials. These two aspects, the ability to *create objects* and capacity to *combine them* in innovative ways, are the most important in his creative process.

The whole process is not linear, but recursive. As he goes exploring, getting closer and further away from the solution, according to the needs of his brain, from time to time he will go back to creating new pieces to stay in the game.

The creation of new pieces is very important to move on to the real, creative process itself. A way of helping our collaborators to carry out creative activities is by allowing them access to 'libraries of pieces' of *'pre-inventive'* *structures,* as some call them; nice name ...

Something for the reader to consider: How can you help your collaborators to generate new concepts which work as new bricks in the creation process? Where are the 'music and colours' in your company? There are companies which have meeting rooms painted in bright colours, furnished with comfortable chairs so that people can relax, talk, share and think. There are other companies which support the idea of 10-minute naps to boost alertness and creativity. What do you think? Maybe too hippy? One of the current authors at least thinks that this is nonsense, that more tangible initiatives are needed such as libraries or databases of *pre-inventive struc-*

> **How can you help your company to create a new environment that favours the generation of ideas?**

tures. However, the other author says, 'Or would these be attempts to create 'the colours of the music'?' Going into unknown territory with only the help of a walking stick of unknown characteristics is very difficult. We all agree on the need to look for familiar elements, found in familiar universes, which help us to jump over the huge chasm on the threshold of a problem that requires a 'creative' solution. The attempts described may be just that, attempts, but they underline the existence of a need. The question lies in how help can be provided that is systematically adjusted to the reality of each company.

We have to recognise that some people are born with the innate ability to create. They are capable of generating more bricks, more *pre-inventive struc-tures* and particularly those which are *more suitable* to solving the overall problem. This ability allows them, apparently easily, to solve problems which escape the rest of us mortals. However, this is not to say that others are incapable of doing similar things. It is possible that there are geniuses[3]

---

[3] For example, it may be that among the current authors, there is only one genius (or half a one), but how awful it would be if we both were!

with sufficient intuition to discover the suitable piece for each moment, but there are only a few of these around.

The fact that Mozart was apparently capable of writing *Don Giovanni* without a single correction, without having to go back in his exploration process to take a different route, evidences only one thing: that his virtual exploration process was very strong and that when he got around to writing the music, he had already explored the problem in his head, until he found a solution. This is the opposite of Beethoven, who scribbled and crossed out, almost 'fighting' with his scores. However, this is not the evidence that Mozart was a genius. That lies in the result of his process, the solution found, because *Don Giovanni* is a work of art of exceptional calibre, like the *5th Symphony*. These works are done by geniuses.

It is not in the interests of companies to have too many geniuses; we tend to have more than enough with a couple of them. What we do need are many people who are capable of generating small new ideas which take the company forward. This is what Margaret Boden[4] called *simple creativity*. To achieve this it is not enough to just take on good people, you have to also support them.

Nevertheless, let's get back to the story of our protagonist. Once the music is done with, and the structures which arise from it are finished, Pasqual attacks the libretto; specifying it, understanding the meaning, the reality of the moment which it describes and the reason behind each detail. '*I try to bring together one thing with another and see the disparity between them, because I don't know about music.*' The libretto itself offers little as a facilitator of creativity because it is too specific. Donna Anna is called 'Donna Anna', and Don Ottavio is in love with his wife, in a straightforward, reasonable way – full stop. The libretto describes the specific relationships between characters. Pasqual is going to make them into *relationships* between his *pre-invention structures*. And the way he does it is by increasing the level of *abstraction,* moving away from the anecdote to concentrate on the meaning of the concept in Mozart's time.

It's an interesting methodology, generating concepts from the libretto and presenting them through the idea of 'not *transgressing* the meaning'. Understanding the *context* to create new *relationships*. For example, if chocolate was a luxury in the eighteenth century, today we should look for another type of luxury, so that the staging reflects the same contextual reality...that's it, we'll use a Rolls-Royce! With this, Pasqual has added a collection of new structures to his portfolio, structures that go beyond the limits of the libretto's author in his own creation process. A sort of reverse engineering of the libretto. And armed with all this, he goes back to the search process.

---

[4] Boden, Margaret. '*The Creative Mind: Myths and Mechanisms*' Routledge London 2004.

As he moves forward, he has to take the details into consideration. It would be difficult to bear them all in mind from the beginning. Details which seem to be trivial are important for the creation of a virtual world that should be credible to the audience; whether a mantilla is needed or staging which revolves with the soprano inside. The details can make an approach or a solution and force you back to the drawing board. There may be contradictory situations, perhaps due to the principle of impenetrability of bodies. He needs to deal with the uncertainty of implementation and foresee various adaptations. This *foresight* and *adaptation* makes use of Pasqual's combinatory abilities. Here 'combining' means *organising* the different *structures* in such a way that we *get closer* to the desired *result*. At this specific time in the process, this is easier to achieve, because his *pre-inventive structures,* the pieces he handles to reach the solution, are, by now, nearly physical entities: a tenor, a soprano, a chorus, a chair and so on. It is easier to contemplate the desired result and combine the elements he has to hand to fine-tune the solution.

Pasqual carries out a simultaneous process; he tries to imagine the repercussions of the realisation of the concepts he is handling, while constantly evaluating the quality of the solution he is getting close to. It doesn't always fit, and sometimes he has to go back. *'You have to foresee it and then be sufficiently easily influenced to having got there, be able to change, depending on what the elements throw at you.'* The concept is adapted and transformed, meaning that the original idea is modified. The creative process is not focused on the staging plans, but takes place over the duration of the production, from the initial humming of the score in the shower through to the dress rehearsal. *'Narrating and doing'* says Pasqual. Big and small changes arise as the exploration goes on, making the real, physical idea more concrete.

The Stage Director as promoter of a creative environment

A second aspect within the creative process is the need to generate an environment favourable for simple creativity of all the other agents involved. When we asked Lluís Pasqual what his role as Stage Director is, he responded, *'I take the lead from the moment the opera is handed to me; from before we start the rehearsals and during the rehearsals.'* However, what does he lead? Yes, he creates the concept, but then what? He leads by ensuring that the concept is passed onto all those involved and, as such, he creates environments in which his people take the original idea and make it their own, or even *modify* it.

Pasqual creates a space, a suitable environment for the implementation of his ideas, surroundings where the agents (and particularly the actors) can dwell credibly, with stage logic and have sufficient effect on the audience, since those who transmit the purpose of the staging are the agents, not the Stage Director.

The Stage Director not only has to create and devise, but also accompany everyone involved, minutely explaining every detail. He should give them the *logic* of the world the action is to take place in. *'I have to explain the reason for each thing to everyone. This has to be done second by second of the opera, minute by minute, bar by bar, note by note.'*

It was tremendously interesting for us to see Pasqual in action, and see how this Stage Director explained, explained and explained. He spent a huge amount of time in the rehearsals explaining the reasons and details of things. All rehearsals are a constant source of explanations, in an attempt to transmit the ideas in his head through words and movements. One moment Pasqual is in the auditorium, the next he jumps onto the stage, takes a singer by the arm and takes them to a place he thinks is better for them. Then he shows them the facial expression they should be making at that moment. He moves around the whole theatre. Due to all this, the others become absorbed, making the context their own. Pasqual calls this, 'narrate and do'. *'I go around narrating and doing, narrating and doing.'* It is about making them understand, transmitting a concept so that they can live it or change it within the purpose. It is about creating environments which ease the transformation of the concept into a credible reality. For example, in a rehearsal for *Don Giovanni* there was a table laid with tablecloth which made the work of the singers more difficult. The baritone drew attention to it, 'This tablecloth is a nuisance.' Following much discussion between all involved, the tablecloth was removed and replaced with a more suitable setting. Could this be called creativity? Yes, it is, it is *simple creativity*. It is part of the whole process of exploration, creativity which seeks solutions to minor problems.

> How do you create an environment that encourages creativity?

All those involved contribute small creative influences. Nevertheless, it is thanks to the existence of an environment which encourages them to do this that they are able to do so. Individual creativity can remain suffocated if the environment is not suitable. The big concept, the big idea behind it all is developed by the Stage Director, but the small adaptations, the transformations which make the idea a reality, are carried out by all the participants.

> Do you restrict peoples' capacity to think?

How does the Stage Director manage to get his spirit of creation across? Pasqual told us that the Stage Director is an energy catalyst. His idea is passed on to everyone else. Therefore, in the beginning, they all ask him to explain himself, to tell them about it. His name is the one most often heard; everyone needs him. He is the *'factotum de la cittá.'*[5] However, as the concepts

---

[5] Translated as, 'I'm the factotum of the city', as we are certain the reader had deduced. Another sign of our culture. Taken from the Figaro's aria in the first act of *The Barber of Seville*.

get inside each person, his role diminishes and eventually disappears. Pasqual consciously lets go, *getting rid of the burden*. He has succeeded in getting them to absorb the idea and make it their own; he is no longer needed.

Here Pasqual formulates one of the favourite phrases of one of the current authors. When he lets go of everything, lighting is what is left. *'Lighting is fundamental for an opera because it is what fills up the seven centimetres between the hearing and the eye, so that there is no discrepancy between what is said and what is seen.'*

> **How can you become an energy catalyst in your company?**

Pasqual is left with getting around this discrepancy to achieve harmony. This is his final responsibility. In the *Don Giovanni* rehearsals we were able to see how lighting becomes an obsession and how the lighting box, where the rig is controlled from, becomes a hive of activity.

> **Who watches out for the 'Seven centimetres' in your company?**

Can we apply the idea of 'eye-ear distance' to worlds outside the specifically operatic? In reality, this is the distance between *what we say* and *what we do*. It is the internal consistency of management actions, a key component of Attractiveness. The Stage Director needs to find the harmony in those 'seven centimetres'. If the manager wishes to attain Attractiveness, he needs to know where these 'seven centimetres' are and become obsessed with them. Not only does he need to become obsessed with them, but the whole company must also focus on this consistency. It really is an interesting idea.

What is the role of the Orchestral Director within this creative process?

> **Who keeps the tempo in your company?**

Pasqual gives us a concise answer to this; his role is to mark time. Pasqual emphatically states that the timing in an opera is set by the maestro. *'Good maestros mark time from the beginning ... This can change everything, even the feeling or intention.'* So how is it possible that the timing of a piece of music can change the meaning of a performance? Pasqual tells us *'If the music's going quickly, tap-tap-tap, and these three beats mark time for the singer to take three steps, then it's a very different proposition than a slower tempo of tap ... tap ... tap ... .'*

This is another interesting concept, the concept of tempo. We could translate this as the style or character that we want to instil. The scene, the behaviour of the singers and other participants is given by the Stage Director, but the rhythm is defined by the Orchestral Director. This rhythm is fundamental to the perception of the audience, the client. The functions of the Stage and Orchestral Directors are complementary, the former passes control to the other and the Orchestral Director becomes the person in charge of the opera. In setting the tempo he makes his contribution to the creation, and in taking on the day-to-day running of the performances, he becomes the custodian, the guardian of the show's consistency.

The materialization of the idea

Therefore, we reach the last topic, the process of materialisation of the idea. An ethereal idea brings nothing tangible to the world of theatre. Creativity and the creative process have no sense without the materialisation of the result.

Does the reader remember the idea of the Operations Director as a translator? Well here, we will find the complementary vision. The materialisation of the idea needs a translation from the language of the Stage Director to the language of screws, cables, motors, spotlights and so on. It is a translation process on several levels, which means there is increased danger of distortion. To avoid this, Pasqual tells us that it is essential to understand the origin of the idea. *'I explain it based on two perspectives; one imaginative, trying to explain my reasons, and another practical using a common language.'* There is a common language to the whole process, which facilitates the materialisation of the ideas. This common language allows the ideas to be transmitted, but the imaginative part ensures that each person involved really understands what he is proposing. Where does this common language come from? Pasqual clarifies this in the following sentence, taking about Daniel Bianco, *'We come from the same school, that is, we have a concept of theatre, that, as technological as it may be, has an artistic foundation.'* The same knowledge base, the same 'theatrical common sense' enables us to easily 'imagine' what he's speaking about. An engineer from a large European telecommunications company recently commented to us that every day the distance between the engineers and the sales and marketing people seemed to increase. The problems caused by this are endless because the lack of comprehension between the two 'populations' generates losses and unacceptable delays. Because of this our engineer is becoming a translator, who makes an effort to give the non-technical people the indispensable concepts they need to understand the idea they are promoting and *vice versa*. It is about taking steps forward in the creation of a common language, a minimum subset which helps to break down the communication barrier.

Pasqual presents an indispensable idea to achieve the materialisation of an idea without huge setbacks, *'I have to know how a grid works',* that is, I should understand what a change means, what implications it has for the show. We go back to the idea that to direct you have to have 'washed paint brushes', have to dirty your

> **Do you value attention to detail?**

hands. *'If I didn't know that, if I didn't have the stagecraft, I'd then start to look like an idiot in order to get what I ask for.'* His understanding of the situation allows him to evaluate its eventual impact, and all this is vital to reduce the amount of time needed to get results. This in turn will allow better results to be achieved, given the exploratory nature of the process. This presence of a common language allows the creative to stay active throughout the whole process, from the idea to the premiere.

So how does this affect a company? We have already said that, over many years, the designer, the man from R&D, is not involved in the industrialisation, in the preparation of the production process. He throws his designs over the garden wall (a virtual garden wall, but nonetheless, real) and washes his hands of it. If the product is difficult to make, let the factory guys sort it out. This methodology brings increased production costs, due to having to do implausible things that weren't even that necessary. Unwittingly, the designer simply chose the worse solution from a production perspective.

Business research demonstrates that simultaneous design, collaboration between the designer and producer, reduces the production time and lowers the costs. When Pasqual says, *'I always rehearse with the technicians and the actors at the same time, because I think it is a joint thing'*, we get the idea of a step beyond this. They are all the *protagonists* of the opera. Making changes as they go along and understanding the repercussions of their every action.

His is a *permanent design* over the whole operations *chain*. The creator communicates with all the elements of the chain, from those who design to those who put the nuts and bolts in the set. However, for this to work everyone has to deeply understand the implications of their work on that of others. Moreover, this is extended to all the transversal processes, not only R&D and Production, but others as well such as Marketing and Engineering.

Sadly, in many companies it seems as if this 'fresh' approach has been lost, and instead of promoting this way of working the organisation restricts it. We have to go back to simplicity, generating the fluency of ideas that pyramidal organisations stifle.

Imagination and common language bring with them excellence in the small details. Pasqual make a Rubinstein phrase his own: *'God is in the detail.'* If the carousel in *Don Giovanni* has 10,000 light bulbs of all colours, they should be perfect. We assure you, dear reader, that they were all present and correct on the day of the premiere. We are not sure if there were 10,000 because we didn't get around to counting them, but there were a lot. The carousel was one of the main attractions of Pasqual's *Don Giovanni*.

The result makes all the effort worthwhile. Nevertheless, this effort is arduous since one of the roles of the Stage Director, like everything innovative, is to explore the boundaries, always asking 'can I do this?'; where each 'can I do ...?' may be a change which costs time and money.

What does Daniel Bianco think about how Lluís Pasqual is to work with? Daniel says, 'He is a Stage Director who transmits energy to everyone. He is very creative and does not fail to move people.'

A logical framework to understand the creative process

Lluís Pasqual's style is curiously close to the conceptual framework that we are going to speak briefly about, which tries to explain logically the creative phenomenon. It remains to be seen to what extent this is a result of Pasqual's intuition, or a product of the current authors' creativity, which have a tendency to fit it into well-known models. However, we would like to end this chapter by giving the reader an inkling of this conceptual model. Many of the topics we have seen in Pasqual's creative process are contemplated in this framework and have already been mentioned, but we believe a final synthesis will help fix the ideas.

It concerns the *Geneplore*[6] model. It is sufficiently simple to be applicable and sufficiently complex not to trivialise things to useless recommendations, as many other models do. Let's see how this model can be adapted to Lluís Pasqual's creative process.

Greatly simplifying things,[7] let's say that *Geneplore* proposes the existence of two parallel processes.

- An exploration process, seeking a solution to the problem in hand. As we have seen, creativity is always an activity associated with problem-solving; and since the problems tend to be new, there is little immediate knowledge applicable to their resolution.
- A process which *generates new pre-inventive structures,* which support the development of the exploration process above. These *pre-inventive structures* are created by the individual, handling and combining elements which either already exist in their knowledge base, or are incorporated as formalised knowledge. However, and this is an important aspect, this process does not necessarily generate knowledge which can be applied to the problem; it generates structures which can be used as pieces of the puzzle being solved in the other process at the same time. The structures create blocks which the individual can combine together in the exploration process.

Pasqual combines the two *Geneplore* processes, but what really distinguishes him is his innate ability to create new, interesting structures. This gives him the capability of imagining different answers to the problem he is presented with.

In short, creativity is not innate, but supported and generated. It is developed following a clear recipe, *'Don't support the exploration process, and support the generation process of new structures.'* Don't teach people search methods, such as brainstorming[8] and concentrate your efforts on helping them to create new structures which support the creative process.

---

[6] Finke, R.A., Ward, T.B. and Smith, S. M. *Creative cognition: Theory, research and application.* MIT Press, 1992.

[7] And we prey for humble forgiveness from its authors.

[8] As you know, people say they involve, 'a great deal of storm, and little brain'.

Conclusions

We will summarise the key ideas of this chapter. We have seen how the creative process generates structures to manipulate ideas in better-known contexts. Creativity requires environments which promote it, and questions and answers help to create these surroundings. Similarly, we have seen the need to develop an imagination in all those involved, which incites this questioning.

Companies should consider these topics as they look at how to boost creativity in their organisation. All this should be done after identifying the *energy catalyst* that will make the creative process work. If the manager wishes to achieve Attractiveness, he should become obsessed with the consistency between what he says and what he does (the famous seven centimetres!).

By the way, a question for the reader, who is the equivalent to the Stage Director in your company?

As always, we draw to a close with some questions for your thoughts:

- How can you help your company to create new structures which promote the generation of ideas?
- How can you create a favourable environment for creativity?
- How can you become an energy catalyst in your company?
- Who sets the tempo in your company?
- Where can the 'seven centimetres' be found in your company?
- What steps are you taking to develop the imaginative part of your company?
- Do you value attention to detail?

Part III
Unity

Now we can enter into the third dimension of the New Operational Culture. This is Unity, or the identification of the members of an organisation with its objectives. Unity ensures that the principles and values of the company are the same across the entire company. Moreover, to achieve Unity is to manage; and to manage in such a way that all the talent in an organisation can emerge. The 'brain power' can only emerge in a coherent environment, where people feel they are contributing to a common objective. In the following chapters, we are going to look in more detail at these concepts.

We will start by looking at the type of talent dealt with when producing an opera. How it is managed, what has to be done to ensure it develops to its full potential and how to support it are some of the topics that we are going to discuss. Shortly we will consider how in theatre in general, and in the Teatro Real in particular, the technical personnel fully take on board the relevance of their role in the company's attainment of goals. They completely understand the impact of their actions on the final service. They are conscious of their individual role in the opera being successful and put the group's interests above their own. In the Teatro Real, you do not work on your own, 'here we work in plural'.

The professionals tend to refer to their people as 'theatre people', and to them they attribute the above-mentioned qualities. Here we will try to define the expression 'theatre people', to ascertain whether any of their virtues can be passed on to the corporate world. The most important is total integration with the final purpose: the success of the opera. But how can one achieve the integration of all involved in a common purpose? Read on and we will find out.

XIX
Relevance and Operational Culture

In this chapter, we are going to talk with Daniel about how he manages the 'brain power' in the Teatro Real.

You always recount an anecdote about a Wagnerian tenor ...

It's true. We were working on Wagner's, *The Twilight of the Gods*.[1] It really is very hard to find a tenor who can sing this and although we normally have understudy singers, this time we didn't. Then the day before the performance, the one we had came and told us that he had a very bad voice and wasn't sure if he would be able to sing the next day. He said he would try to sing to see if he could do it. The production people started searching and searching. At this time nearly all the Wagnerian tenors were in Japan, doing a Wagner season; there was no way they would be able to get to Madrid on time. Finally, they found one on holiday in the Netherlands, who we didn't know at all. He told us that, yes, he would come, and we sorted out his tickets to get him down to Madrid. However, the performance started at six in the evening, and he couldn't get there until 7.30 p.m. So we spoke to our tenor and he said that he could do the first act, he had no idea how he would

---

[1] The last part of the work *Der Ring des Nibelungen*, also known as the 'The Ring Cycle', by Richard Wagner. Heaven forbid that we were to try, albeit briefly, to describe the plot of these four interrelated operas. We will simply say that it recounts the fortunes and misfortunes of the hero Siegfried, who competes against the gods Valhalla and Wotan and their men, for world supremacy. The Ring Cycle is made up of four operas: *The Rheingold, The Valkyrie, Siegfried* and *The Twilight of the Gods*. A total of 15 hours of music and song, in which all sorts of curious creatures intermingle, including gods such as Wotan and his consort; giants like Fáfnir; dwarves such as Mime and Alberich; Valkyries such as Brünnhilde, and other everyday types that you see on the morning train. *The Twilight of the Gods* is a nightmare for a tenor. A Wagnerian tenor has very little to do with a tenor of the Italian repertoire. They need big voices with a superhuman power to breathe and project the voice in the high notes which are most uncomfortable. Wagner had no pity; he not only killed Siegfried, but also managed to martyr all future tenors.

sing, but was going to give it a try. We had the whole operation in place, a car waiting at the airport to bring the tenor to the theatre, so that after the first act and following the half-hour interval, we were going to make an announcement: 'we are going to substitute the tenor' and then the other would appear.

However, as he went on stage and tried to sing, the main tenor, stood with his mouth open, gesticulating, unable to make a single sound. He had completely lost his voice before even hitting the first note. We swiftly brought the curtain down, and announced that he had to be substituted due to illness. Yet this meant waiting for half an hour. Of course, we could not tell the audience that we had another one at the airport, who was on his way. Anyway, we made a first announcement that due to vocal problems we had to suspend the show until further notice, we made another announcement 15 minutes later, and finally we said that in half an hour we would restart the opera. Those who wanted to could stay and those who didn't want to were offered their money back. Very few people left. Meanwhile the other gentleman arrived, with no luggage or anything, in a pair of Bermuda shorts and a t-shirt. He got into the car and while the production girl was on the phone asking him (or measuring) his foot, chest, etc. sizes, for a dinner jacket, another person was putting his make-up on. Then at one point, the man said, 'But gentlemen, I have to warm up my voice before singing.' And our team said 'Well you go ahead and start right here in the car.' So anyway, he started to warm up, making booming sounds. He got there at top speed and when he got there we allowed the public back into the auditorium and in less than five minutes he was dressed in a dinner jacket (held together with Velcro at the back), shoes, bow tie, the whole lot; they did his hair and out he went to the stage. He was positioned at a music stand on the side of the stage, and from there he sang the three-and-a-half-hour opera while the other, the one who'd lost his voice, acted out the movements and mimed. An actor who hasn't been in rehearsals can't get involved in the action because he has no idea what he's supposed to be doing.

In all this, the thing that really struck me most was what happened the following day. We had to issue a press release, so we asked the communication department to prepare the exact words that we should use. I remember the image very well; the press girl, while preparing the releases, looked at me and said that she didn't understand why we didn't just cancel that performance. At that moment, I said to me 'It's completely logical that she should think that, but this would never even occur to "theatre people"'. I don't know why, I really don't have the answer. I don't know, but it never occurred to anybody to even think of cancelling.

And were you there throughout all this mess or did other people fix it?

No, I wasn't there, because really this falls to the artistic and musical management. The stage managers got involved for the announcements that needed making. Really, it was a terrible day; for the artistic director of a really important opera theatre, one day in the morning a singer pulled out, then in the space of that morning they had to find another singer who could arrive in time to sing. Some people asked him 'How can you stand the nervous tension?' and he said 'Because they pay me my entire year's salary to deal with a day like today.'

The show must go on…

Exactly; it's weird though, because you ask 'Why, if husband of one of the actresses has died this morning, should she have to go on with the show? Why? I don't know why, but I do know that she does. That's the way it is; it cannot stop. The farce, the comedy, the drama; it must continue. You may have to do the impossible, but you must go on. It's similar to live television. When you're live on TV, you can't stop. Here it's a bit the same. Bringing the curtain down during a performance is the last resort. In other types of activities you can stop. In accounting, I imagine that if the computer goes down then you can say 'fine, I'll continue tomorrow'. Well, here you can't continue tomorrow. For us, if the computer goes down, everything goes down. There's a phrase we use here a lot: 'With my teeth; I'll raise the platform with my teeth if I have to!' And you go, and you raise it manually. The other day we had a problem just before we started. Finally we solved everything, but it was a frenetic half-hour: 'What do I do? What do I do?' 'No, look, can you prepare this, or the other?' 'Yes…' We created an emergency plan and put into practice in just half an hour. I think that this, seen from the outside, is probably impressive, but what should be more impressive is the level of commitment that the people here have to their work.

That, that is vital; the level of commitment…

Of course, because we work on something that gives us a lot of headaches and makes us suffer a great deal, but *we like it*. We are lucky to work on something that we like and we feel *committed to*. Generally, everyone feels that way. You notice the folk that have a day off because they've got a cold, and those who come in anyway, even at death's door, because they know they have a performance to do and its better they do it than someone else.

Why? I don't know. Maybe because it's unrepeatable, because it's today and that's not the same as tomorrow. Because I do the performance today, and I want to do it, because that's what I was destined for. Maybe because it's a very artisanal thing. It's like you're making a pottery bowl…I don't know, but it's like that. It's not very scientific, but when you're interviewing someone for a job you know if the person has that theatre instinct or 'smell' about them.

If it's true what they say, that people are not committed to their work, then maybe it is the bosses who are much less committed. But the level of commitment here is really high…I suppose that must also have something to do with the fact that perhaps in a company somebody is doing something that they don't enjoy, and maybe they don't even know why they're doing it.

Do you normally have understudies?

When it's a double cast, yes. There are many operas for which you have a double cast, or understudies; 'covers' as they're known in the opera trade. In fact, in *Tosca*, every time she was going out to sing, dressed, wigged and made-up, the lead singer would ask us for 10 more minutes. We had to tell the public to wait ten minutes more, and we'd get her cover dressed and made up in the dressing room next-door, so obviously, that the first singer knew perfectly well that if she said anything at all, her cover would be able to go out immediately.

I'll give you an example. We had *La Traviata* all prepared; Angela Gheorghiu[2] was going to open and her cover was Norah Amsellem.[3] We also had a third soprano for certain performances. Well, Ms Gheorghiu 'left' the production – she pulled a diva number on the theatre, and the theatre told her to leave. Therefore Norah Amsellem was in line to open the show, ok? She had been second, so now she's first. But, on the day of the opening, there was a strike that affected her and she couldn't get here, so the second cover, the third soprano, ended up opening the opera.

There's a famous anecdote that happened many years ago at the Zarzuela theatre, in Lluís Pasqual's debut with *Don Carlo*. They brought in a tenor, from some eastern country, who had lots of problems on the day of the premiere. The day before he'd been very ill, he went to the doctor, who gave him some suppositories and, instead of administering them in the normal way, he swallowed them, as though they were tablets.

Poor man... Are the singers all divas?

Not now, no, that attitude doesn't really exist now. Look at Nadal,[4] the Roland Garros[5] winner, is he a male diva? I don't know if he is, but of course

---

[2] Born in Romania, 1975, Angela Gheorghiu is a soprano of international standing and a great interpreter of some of Verdi's characters. She is widely held to be the best Violetta (from *La Traviata*) in the world. A woman of great beauty, mettle and energy, she sometimes loses herself and has a tendency to act the diva, and perhaps not only because she is one in the classic sense. Her (second) husband is the French tenor, Roberto Alagna.

[3] A young and promising French soprano, born in Paris.

[4] Rafael Nadal (Manacor, Spain, 1986). Spanish tennis player, specialist on clay court who, at the time of writing, has won the Roland Garros three times.

[5] Roland Garros, also known as the French Open, is a tennis tournament in Paris; the most important clay-court tournament in the world, and the second of the Grand Slams in the annual tennis calendar.

he must receive special attention, because the pressure he is under makes it necessary.

I think that someone can say, please, I don't like the air conditioning, the draughts, cigarette smoke, I want the piano tuned, I want to rest between performances... without being a diva. It's just part of the trade. You need to be in very fine physical form to sing an entire opera. There were divas before, because there was a very high professional level. I think that Montserrat Caballé was a great diva because she was capricious; being capricious is something else. Montserrat Caballé was a diva because she was unique, because there was a world of difference between her and the rest, but capricious types, no, I don't think they generally exist now.

And what about people like Plácido Domingo,[6] Ruggero Raimondi;[7] don't they feel this...?

I think that the two you mention are great, but only because they're great men. Plácido Domingo is one of the easiest people to work with, and one of the most professional. He is a person who always knows what he's doing, he has studied and he's respectful to his colleagues, to the technical staff, to the theatre... the same as Ruggero Raimondi. In reality, this happens a bit with rich people, don't you think? One thing is to be rich and another is to be *nouveau riche*. It's similar, the rich people treat those at their service with, naturally, respect because they were born with service. But when you've never had service in your life before, and suddenly you do because you're rich, you treat it badly. Well, this is a bit the same.

And what about younger people such as Marcelo Álvarez?[8]

These are people who look after their instruments: their throats. Juan Diego Flórez[9] is someone completely ready and willing to work, but he has his 'things'. We did *The Barber of Seville* here and he asked me to buy him a flask

---

[6] Plácido Domingo (Madrid, 1941). Spanish tenor. Known as the King of the Tenors, he has broken all the records of operatic longevity and productivity, always on top artistic form and with a tremendous quality and consistency in his performances. He is also a multi-talented person, being also an Orchestral Director and administrator of several theatres throughout the world.

[7] Ruggero Raimondi (Bologna, 1939). Bass-baritone and actor; one of the greatest bass-baritones of the twentieth century. He is especially well-known for the film *Don Giovanni* that he made with Joseph Losey in 1979, in which he presented an aggressive and evil *Don Giovanni*. Moreover, he's the brother-in-law of Marta Maier.

[8] (Córdoba, Argentina, 1963). One of the recently emerged tenors in current musical theatre, Álvarez is already a star and sings in the best theatres of the world.

[9] (Lima, Peru, 1973) One of the new great light-lyric voices coming onto the scene, at the moment he is singing tenor *spinto*, or light works such as *La Fille du Regiment* and the entire repertoire of Rossini. His appearances are always successes. Interestingly, he started out singing covers of Beatles and Led Zeppelin hits.

for water, which we should disinfect and then could only be touched by him. He had to use it in a scene. But it's true – why should he run the risk of catching some virus and ruin eight performances? Especially when he's the one who'd have to go out and sing even if he's ill. Nevertheless, he's a person who, if you book him in to rehearse, he'll turn up for rehearsals and he'll be ready to do costume tests and everything else, too. However, do we have to treat him well? Yes, him too. Dolora Zajick,[10] the *mezzo-soprano* who's singing now in *Don Carlo*, she's highly allergic. Fine, no smoking is permitted in this theatre, but I've seen her in a theatre in Italy where people were allowed to smoke, and she asked them to please not to. I understand if people then say 'that diva...', but it's normal for her to ask that. For me the nuisances are the ones who you can't work with; the people who come along but don't deliver, but luckily there are very, very few.

I expect you have a protocol of how to treat these people – taking them to good hotels, collecting them...?

No, they get their own hotels, and nobody collects them. We look after them only when they're within the production itself. Artists have a contract for an amount, a sum of money, that is paid per performance, an agreement for some rehearsal days, and what the theatre does is to help them find a hotel according to their budget.

Once they get here you look after them, you look after them in every aspect; I don't know, if, say, they get robbed or they have any problem. But we don't go to collect them from the airport nor do we take them here and there or anything like that... They are people accustomed to that sort of life. What happens is that, quite rightly, since they are people accustomed to that sort of life, there are a number of things that you have to know how to do. For example, the theatre has a list of people with apartments in the area, and who are happy to rent them to us. We send the information by e-mail or fax to the singers or their agent, and they sort out the details such as getting the keys. Many singers have property near the theatres. For example, just next to here is María Bayo's apartment. Ruggero Raimondi also has one, just here on the corner... They use them when they come to sing here and, if not, they rent them out.

If you don't sing, you don't charge...

Right; if you don't sing, you don't charge. You can have spent an entire month rehearsing but if you're ill on the day of the premiere, you get nothing. The life of an artist is very insecure, above all because maybe tomorrow you wake up and your voice has gone. There is a very famous case in Spain, that of Enedina Lloris, a wonderful Valencian singer. At a key point in her

---

[10] (Oregon, USA) *Mezzo-soprano* with a powerful voice and enormous range.

career, just when it was taking off, just when the world had started to take notice and she had contracts lined up ... click. She never sang professionally again. She had an infection, I don't know exactly what but she never sang again. Now she's a singing teacher in Valencia.

Once you mentioned that people had booed Renée Fleming, and I wonder, how can it ever be possible to boo someone who sings like an angel?

It happened in Milan's La Scala in 1998, when she sang *Lucrezia Borgia*. I don't know why. Maybe because the gods weren't happy about an American singing there, or maybe she wasn't singing the same as on the CD or maybe she did some extra *coloraturas* that she shouldn't have, or maybe she didn't sing it like Montserrat Caballé did in nineteen-seventy-something. Poor thing, it got to the point where she couldn't even finish the aria, she was trying to sing and she heard the public booing and shouting how bad it was. It was terrible.

What does a singer or artist do in these situations?

If I were the singer, I'd leave but she, being a great professional, finished. Later she left the theatre and never went back. We had the same here with a tenor. When we did *Rigoletto*, the contracted tenor was Aquiles Machado. The Stage Director, Graham Vic, couldn't see Aquiles Machado in the role of the seducer Duke of Mantua because of his physique; he's quite a short, fat man. He managed to get the theatre not to contract him, and substituted him with another tenor who's reasonably well known internationally, with a big name and an exemplary career. This got into the press and I suppose that the friends and fans of Aquiles Machado exaggerated the whole thing, and the public didn't forgive it – they just attacked the new tenor at every performance and, at the fourth performance or thereabouts, he was asked to leave.

That's a horrible thing to do, it makes you want to go down and hit the person who's shouting

It happened once to the character of Liu from *Turandot*.[11] A girl was singing it, I don't remember her name. She was a great singer and with a good

---

[11] *Turandot* was the last opera by Giacomo Puccini, who died before completing it. It was later completed by Franco Alfano. Set in China, it unites the exotic surroundings with music inspired by the tonal system of that culture. Turandot is a Chinese princess who scrutinises her suitors through a series of questions. Whoever is capable of correctly answering three riddles will marry her. Otherwise, he'll lose his head, in the most literal sense. Calaf, a foreign prince, passes the test, but he is stupid enough to give Turandot an escape clause; if she guesses his name he will give up the wedding and his head. Everything works out fine though, because Turandot falls in love with him (although it's anybody's guess how). In passing, Liu, a young serving girl who is

international career. When she finished singing the audience started shouting 'very bad, very bad'. Of course, to have a good round of applause in the theatre you need at least a thousand people applauding, but to be booed, you only need four. In this case, when she came out for curtain call they started shouting 'very bad, that's not how it's done' and they booed her. Then she did something that I don't think you should ever do. She told the audience to be quiet, and told the people who had booed her that she'd wait for them in the dressing room. This could have provoked a worse reaction, but in the end, it worked out fine.

Another thing happened with the soprano at the premiere of *The Barber of Seville*, which was a massive success, massive. When she finished singing the aria, she heard one person's voice saying 'You have to learn how to sing in tune.' It was just one person, and I even know who it was – someone very well known in the opera world and a bit mad – and then that person left, as if he'd only come to have a rant. I remember going to the singer's changing room afterwards, and she couldn't think of the 1849 people who'd applauded her and shouted 'bravo!'; she could only think of the one person who had criticised her.

Does the Stage Director come in for a large proportion of the booing?

Yes, pretty much. Recently there's been a tendency to shout at the Stage Director, and I don't think it's because the productions are shocking or odd in any way. No, this isn't a theatre that puts on cutting-edge productions, so it has to be something much simpler than that. The world of opera is very complicated. Opera fans can be strange people; like any fans, I suppose. The other day, a friend told me that he had many operas and could copy some for me if I were interested. He said to me 'I'll give you a list of the operas I have.' Do you know how many were on that list? 425! Of course, I said to him 'Thanks anyway, but I'm going to buy the latest Julio Iglesias CD.'

When you talk with opera fans, you notice that they see things that we don't. They can spot a singer and know what he's doing, how he's doing it and how he sings it. I don't know if they enjoy it, because they seem to have a way of enjoying things that is different to mine. I'm sure there must be five or six of them who meet and have already decided how they're going to rate a singer. Sometimes we think 'They're going to have a right go at this singer, thrashing them to within an inch of their lives' and then the day of the premiere comes along and it's quite the opposite. It's unpredictable. Gerardo Vera's *Macbeth*, for example; you never would have

---

in love with Calaf, dies for having helped him to triumph. Well, someone had to die... Princess Turandot is one of the more difficult roles of Puccini. It demands a dramatic soprano, almost Wagnerian, but who is also capable of ready incursions into the highest registers. Despite that, she does need to be mortal, though.

thought that it was going to be booed so much, and I just can't justify it, I can't understand why.

Does the Musical Director also come in for controversy?

Yes, yes, very much. In *The Barber of Seville*, after the interval, when he returned for the second act, they started whistling him. But it was erratic. There are days when he does, and days when he doesn't. In this case, he thought, as he's a director of the Rome opera, perhaps they were people from Rome who had come specially to whistle at him, because this also tends to happen.

Don't all these things really affect you?

No, they don't directly affect me at all. Well, it would affect me if a critic said 'The set presentation was bad.' It affects me in a positive way when, in *Don Carlo* for example, in the *auto da fé*, we did a change of the view and the public applauded the change. Although to be honest the change wasn't really our idea; it was the Stage Director and the Set Designer who came up with it.

So they applaud some of the set changes?

Yes, in the United States, they always do. You bring up the curtain, they applaud. Here in *Aida*[12] they applauded, and in *Don Carlo*, in the second performance, they also applauded. This is appreciation. It makes you happy. Really, they're applauding the Set Designer, but you feel it too. Even for me, what really makes me happy is to get to the premiere and for everything to work; to know that that's it, you've managed to get there. You already know that we can see the premiere on the internal televisions, but we all know at which point we should start getting nervous, depending on the opera.

You get nervous?

There are some operas where yes, I get very nervous. I mean, very, very! And there are others where you don't. For example, *The Woman without a*

---

[12] Opera by Giuseppe Verdi, set in ancient Egypt. It premiered in Cairo for the inauguration of the Suez Canal. It is probably one of the most spectacular of Verdi's works, full of warriors, armies, slaves and odalisques. Radames, Captain of the Guard of the Egyptian army, is in charge of leading the fight against the Ethiopians, commanded by their King Amonasro. But Radames is in love with Aida, a slave of the Princess Amneris, the pharaoh's sister. Aida, just to bring it around full-circle, is the daughter of Amonasro. Of course, Radames wins the war and imprisons Amonasro. This, in turn, convinces Aida to help him flee. But in mid-escape, they trip over Radames who, to prevent Aida running away and leaving him, lets her coax him into escaping with them. Logically, they're caught and condemned to death. As the Egyptian priests don't do things by halves, they bury them alive. Ah, we almost forgot – Amneris is in love with Radames.

Shadow[13], is an opera that made me very nervous, because we had 25 machine operators working to change the set in 48 seconds, while the orchestra played ... and when the orchestra had finished, the change hadn't – we had to drop the curtain and give the order to stop. I felt terrible about that, just terrible. Every day we had done a technical rehearsal ... and at the end we were 15 seconds over, because the people had really got into the spirit and had taken extra care. It was all 'come on, let's go, all together, we're the best' but ...

This must be one of the few places where people really take up the challenge and say things like 'come on, all together'

Yes, this would be more difficult in companies. But I think it's because people don't generally work in something they actually like. Here, most people like what they're doing. They like to know that they have a minute and a half to do a change. That they have, let's say, to get to the window, close it, exit running and hide behind a column. Maybe it has something to do with playfulness, with the capacity to play games – a group of adults playing as if they were children. Perhaps because it's a group activity. Maybe because they're trying to achieve something that's objective and within everyone's grasp and, above all, because it is mainly vocational. This doesn't happen in normal jobs; I believe that there are many, many people in the world who work and don't see the result of what they're doing. We see what we do.

Don Carlo has been a big success, hasn't it?

Yes, in terms of the production and of the singers. This year (2005) we've had a lot of successful shows. I think that it's the best season that we've ever had at the Teatro Real, and this is one of the successes of the season. Yes, it's impressive, it's a super-veristic, super-real concept of opera. I assigned Carlos to *Don Carlo*, and he's practically killed himself for it. It's taken much longer than we thought and much more energy than we imagined. I wrote him a letter of thanks.

---

[13] *Die Frau ohne Schatten*, by Richard Strauss. This work, composed during the First World War, is one of the most ambitious products of the collaboration between Strauss and the librettist Hugo von Hofmannsthal. Their first intention was to produce a simple and colouristic work which, once the libretto was done, became one of the most difficult and monumental of Strauss's operas and, in addition, the one that needs a larger orchestra than ever seen until recent times. The opera tells the story of the beautiful daughter of Keikobad, the King of the sprits, who is captured by the Emperor of the South-West Isles, whom she agrees to marry. (This summary was taken, and translated, from the brochure of the Teatro Real, because neither of the current authors knows this opera, nor have they ever seen it.)

Is this a tradition?

Well, yes, it happens sometimes. For example, in *The Barber of Seville*, I was put directly in charge of a lot of things. After the premiere, at two in the morning, Carlos sent me a text message, saying thanks. I don't know, something happens, something different. There's a good attitude, maybe because here it's a question of teamwork.

What about people from 'outside' the theatre, do they feel this *bonhomie*? Singers, Musical Directors, Stage Directors... do all these people fit in?

I think that one of the best things this theatre does is to look after the people who come in from 'outside'. I don't know anybody who hasn't left here congratulating us for the attention and care that they've received. When they return, they reintegrate in the group; above all the Stage Directors, Set Designers, costume and lighting people, and singers. Not so much the Musical Director. He has a strong relationship with the orchestra, but not really with the rest of the theatre because he's not on-stage or backstage. This is where people get very involved and really become part of the family.

Who established this 'house style'?

Let's see, where did you get your manners from? It's more or less the same here; nobody really established it. It's a question of a way of working. Of course, there have been clear definitions of how we work; the first question I asked of Tamayo was 'Is this a "yes" theatre or a "no" theatre?' and he said 'a "yes" theatre'. Fine. Now we have the habit of going to the dressing room and saying to someone 'Hi, how are you, welcome to our theatre. I'm the senior stage manager; what you need is my telephone number – here, this is where you can reach me.' We have this attitude because we bring it from home or from school or wherever, but it's clear that if you have it and carry it out, then you instil it in others.

Doesn't this happen in other theatres?

No, not really. Sometimes it does, because there are friendly people all over the world, but not as a working concept. I know a theatre in Japan that also works like us, but I think that's more about the people – whereas in this theatre it's our philosophy.

Mind you, here the people are more or less of the same age, and the majority come from prose theatre, not opera theatre. We look after the shows as if they're our own. This is something really deep-rooted in our way of working; the shows are ours. We don't need the Stage Director to tell us it's a shambles and we need to do another technical rehearsal. It's not needed because if, for example, we see that the moon goes down badly, in fits and starts, we'll call the stage manager and say 'tomorrow we need to do a technical rehearsal for this' or 'we need to fix this'.

I like to manage groups, I feel comfortable doing it and I think I do it well. I see young people who work in the theatre, and the disposition they have, how they move on set, hiding so they can't be seen on stage, how they come out quickly for a change, who pays attention to detail. It is a job which requires great detail. Above all, I believe it's important to convey a good feeling to the group. I don't know if the staff speaks in such glowing terms as I do about the theatre, but if I'm sure of one thing, I'm sure that they say that the image we give as a team is solid. We always try to avoid bumps and hurdles, and if we make a mistake, it doesn't matter. We always have it clear that within these four walls we might want to kill each other, but we're all friends afterwards.

Are the orchestra and the chorus strange elements in all this?

Yes, they're a world apart, especially the orchestra. The chorus has more dealings with us because of the costumes and the make-up; after all, the wardrobe people see them naked. But with the orchestra there's more distance. It's another world. The orchestra is full of people who have studied for 14 years and dedicate 6 hours a day to playing the violin. It's another world. The orchestra only sits in the light. Each time we go to the first ensemble rehearsal they complain because there's not enough light. They want to have the entire theatre lit up. The also complain, every time we start an opera, that the seats are uncomfortable, that the music stands are too small, or the place is too hot or too cold, or there's a draught on their necks or in their ear, and so on.

All that said, the group functions alone and perfectly. The chorus? The chorus are people who, if you call them two hours early for make-up and hair, they don't want to come. Then, once you have them dressed, they want to go down to the canteen, dragging the trains of their dresses, which is forbidden. They come back to the dressing room and they think their wig looks bad, they want to take it off, and you have to chase them around making sure they don't...same as any activity where there are groups.

In this theatre, the chorus people are young. I suppose that eventually they all want to be soloists. They're professionals, yes, and all have studied music and singing, and all of them have passed auditions as soloists.

What about the dancers and extras?

The dancers are contracted as dancers, and the extras as extras. If you want be an extra you leave a photo and a CV. They'll make up a file that says 'Man with beard, 55 years old, 1.80 m...' If the Stage Director comes along and says 'I want all the old ones', then they'll call you. Then they'll do a test, whatever the Stage Director wants...Now, if they ask you for a lookalike, or a fire-eater, or a juggler, then of course you're going to look specifically for those types of people.

The extra who performs any gestures on stage is normally someone who has studied theatre and dance. The extras never give us problems. They're good, maybe because life is very unjust and opera is very elitist and, if you're a nuisance, then you're not going to get hired again. There are people who want to play *Hamlet* and can't, but they go out on stage and they're happy and content. I think that's marvellous, very dignified and respectable. The extras always do things with great excitement, I mean really excited! And in the morning they act as lighting doubles – when we rig the lights, extras from the evening come along only to help us see how the light works on someone.

XX
Talent Management and Operational Culture

The two main topics which came up in conversation with Daniel are: why 'theatre people' *are so motivated and immersed in their work* and how to operatively *handle* the *talent* rife in this type of company. As we will see, the first topic has a lot to do with the immediate *feedback* which occurs in theatre, the most irascible form of which is booing. The second will take us deeper into ways of exploiting the *talent* for a company's success. So, like good Mediterranean people, we will logically start with the second topic.

Handling the talent

All companies have people with talent. We could go so far as to say that these types of people are in abundance in many companies. However, in most cases, bad use is made of them and they are not properly exploited. Talent should be exploited, and exploited in the most direct way. Companies' exploitation of the workforce gave rise to protesting factions and increased social tensions and disputes. The workforce with their market power diminished by the huge numbers of workers looking for jobs, demanded fairer treatment, confronting the company.

However, this is not the case with talented people, because talent likes to be exploited. It dislikes the opposite situation, where it is not given goals. When talent is challenged, it takes on problems and carries them around with it, even dreaming of them (and sometimes solving them in its sleep).

Another phenomenon observed in Daniel's story and typical of talented people is improvement through *competition*. In an opera, like many other types of theatre, where the professionals are of similar quality, if one really excels in, let's say an aria, the others also try to do better. The result is a type of catharsis which leads to true artistic events, achieved without thinking about it, and only ever so often. This happens despite the fact that the people involved may be the same as those involved in other performances.

It is just that in one of the shows a struggle is established which takes it above and beyond the others.[1]

This type of personnel, therefore, does not have the same characteristics as the 'workforce'. To a certain extent, people of talent are deformed. They have developed one part of their brain a great deal at the expense of other parts of their anatomy. We can all think of some extreme examples. A tale of Albert Einstein is told in which one day as he walked around Princeton, a little girl came up to him and gave him a kiss. Einstein stroked her hair and said, 'My, what a pretty little girl! What's your name dear?' and the child responded, 'Clara Einstein, Dad.'

Beyond the extreme anecdotes, to create a work of art or an excellent company through bringing talent together, you need to have the right 'glue'. We have to move on from the simple talent mix (very easy because it is enough to take talented people on and put them together) to a chemical reaction, a cooperation synergy which should give rise to an unrepeatable work of art, or to an excellent company.

---

[1] Many years ago one of the current authors experienced a catharsis like this in the Liceo in Barcelona. It was the beginnings of a great soprano, one of the greatest of this century. *Renata Tabaldi*. They were performing *La Bohème*. Gianni Poggi was the tenor – a young man with the ability to easily hit notes and with great style, who in the end did not have an extensive career, for reasons beyond the scope of this book. The baritone was Manuel Ausensi, a local singer and greatly loved by the audience. The end of the first act includes the three most beautiful pages of music that Puccini ever wrote; the tenor's aria 'Che gelida manina', that of the soprano, 'Mi chiamano Mimi' and the love duet 'O soave fanciulla'. The addicts in the audience know the opera back to front and greatly look forward to this part of the performance. In this case, contrary to audience expectation, the tenor started a masterly rendition of his aria, but his singing in the most effusive part (also the most difficult from a vocal perspective) was impressive. The passion he managed to impregnate it with reached the stalls with force. Upon finishing the aria the ovation was thunderous and lasted for ten minutes. It seemed impossible to beat what had been seen (and heard), but then Tabaldi the genius appeared. And without vocal displays, in a delicate, emotional voice, she sang the aria as only a privileged few can. No-one could remember having seen anything similar. When she finished half of the audience had goose bumps. The ovation was as never before. For 15 minutes the audience was madly cheering, completely losing their composure. Men in tuxedos threw their jackets onto the stage; ladies dressed up to the nines threw their bags in the air... Madness. So do we need to go into what happened after the duet? The reader can imagine it. What happened went beyond the confines of the theatre and out into the street. The rest of the performances of the opera were packed out with people hoping to experience a similar thing. But, however... it was never the same. They were good performances but not one was like the first. What brought about this result? A combination of factors, but underneath them lies a well-known and little understood concept, the determination of the artists to overcome the limits of the show and make it into a true work of art.

We will try to put forward some of the characteristics of people with talent, important to manage them properly. The list shows a number of these, taken from our own experience of working with 'brainpower'.

Some characteristics of talented people

1. Each person is a specialist, possibly highly trained.
2. Each person thinks he or she is the best at something.
3. All of them have evaluated everyone else.
4. Inconsistencies and arbitrariness are easily spotted.
5. They don't accept power, but will accept authority.
6. They all think that they would be able to do the task in hand better than their boss (and it is probably true).
7. They come into direct contact with high-level clients.
8. They place great value on personal progress.

Some of these traits don't need further comment. The fact that each person is a *specialist* is obvious from what Daniel says, but the same thing happens in your company, or at least, should happen. A consequence of this is the second characteristic of the list above.

Perhaps less well-known is the fact that talented people tend to have the ability to rapidly and precisely *evaluate* others. They are perceptive; they quickly know what their strengths, weaknesses and virtues are.

Related to this capacity to *evaluate* is the ability to *understand their surroundings* in a logical way, which makes it easy for them to identify any inconsistencies in it. Where, for example, someone of less merit is occupying a position with more decision capacity, they immediately detect arbitrariness, and sometimes they attribute the aberrant behaviour to the management team. 'Corporate incest' is one of the more polite phrases which might be used in this case.

The fifth characteristic says that they don't accept *power* but do accept *authority*. *Power* is the command *given to you* formally by the organization, from the state and attributions which define you within it. *Authority* is what is gained through your own merit, the ability to influence, considered as *the value of oneself.* It is not surprising, then, that authority is accepted where power is rejected. Authority means that commands are accepted in areas which the higher quality of the commander is recognised, although, on average, everyone thinks they would do a better job than their boss could.

Personnel with talent, who are highly qualified, often mix with *influential people,* whether from their own organisation or others. Typically, this comes about due to their *authority.* They are in contact with powerful people simply because they know how to best solve problems they are concerned with, for which others do not have sufficient knowledge. Think, for example, about the IT guy in your company and whom he turns to when his computer 'goes on the blink'. People (and companies) learn to distinguish between those who really know and solve problems, and those who just issue commands using their positions, both internally and externally.

Finally, talented people know that the *only thing they have is this talent*. Their main activity is what they have in their neurons and that is the reason their knowledge is worth what it is worth. As such, they place great value on personal progress.

Achieving talent integration

All these characteristics can be seen in many of the Teatro Real's people. In Daniel's words, the theatre 'is full of great professionals'. How are things sorted out to satisfy the aspirations of this kind of person?

First, we should bear in mind that these people will not actively *take part in* the development of a situation if they don't *come out having gained something* in the process. As we said in the first chapter, this is the idea of *win-win*. You win, I win; together we win. Just the idea of this was sufficient back then, but now we're in a position to go into greater depth, armed as we are with a more complete scheme with which to understand how this effect can be achieved. The *Golden Triad* is key to this understanding. Let's look at it.

> **How can you achieve the integration attained by the Operations department of the Teatro Real?**

a) *Efficiency*. In terms of *Efficiency* there are only a few things to add to what we already know. This has been the strong principle of previous chapters. We would simply add that in the conversation with Daniel one observes a great deal of what we have called the *'egoism' principle*.

b) *Attractiveness*. We know that the winning of agents may also come from *Attractiveness*, through the satisfaction arising from learning carried out in the action. And as can be deduced from their traits, this aspect is *central* for the 'brainpower'. Although the result in terms of efficiency may not be entirely positive, if one of these people learns more in a situation, it may be that the overall experience is very positive. A lot of the time we meet alumni who, when asked 'Why are you still with that company, when you earn much less than you could earn elsewhere?' simply replies, 'Because I learn a lot'. Naturally, if this were not the case no-one would ever pay for a professional development course.

c) *Unity*. Finally, for completeness comes one of the most important beauties of the *triad*, satisfaction may come from *increase of Unity*, from *integration* with the organization or the integration of *people* within the organization. From the satisfaction of *belonging* to a group of people who do an excellent job. All of this creates bonds which even become emotional ones between those involved, which we can clearly see in the Teatro Real, but which is rarer in companies. However, we have also seen other examples of this with charity workers. 'I don't get paid, but I contribute' some even say.

Are theatre people special?

When we talk about 'theatre people' we are not talking about the 'great artists', the singers, stage directors, orchestral directors and so on. We are talking about the talented professionals, those who make up the theatre's dorsal fin of Operations, people who appear in the interviews with Daniel, and are proud to define themselves as 'theatre people'. We are talking about the senior stage managers, stage managers, lighting people, mechanics and so on. Not so much about the orchestra and chorus. It is curious but in theatrical culture, these latter two are 'musicians' and not 'theatre people'. This is not only so in the Teatro Real, as we will see in the epilogue, Maestro López Cobos also makes this distinction. In the Teatro Real, it can be partly explained because the orchestra and chorus are sub-contracted and act as a single agent. The musicians in the orchestra, those comprising the chorus, take on their maximum expression as a collective, not individually. A chorister is not managed, the whole chorus is managed. However, in contrast, you do manage a stage manager, or a lighting director.

What are the main characteristics of these 'theatre people' that we have observed throughout the time we have spent working with them? Here is a list of five aspects which stand out, which is not intended to be exhaustive and builds on the general ones in the previous section:

1. They tend *to give different personalities a chance* no matter how esoteric their behaviour.
2. They are very aware of the *impact their work* has on the service delivered.
3. They place the *work of the group* above the work of the people.
4. They tend to be good *professionals* in their area, and think they are.
5. They are proud of *making the impossible attainable,* and making the possible easy.

We will comment on these five properties a little more.

1. *They tend to give different personalities a chance no matter how esoteric their behaviour.* Well-known talented people, artists in particular, do not tend to be conventional in their attitudes and behaviour. They have their ticks and they don't mind recognising them openly. 'I'm like this. If you want me to take part, you have to accept it, and if you don't, no problem.' If Juan Diego Flórez wants to wear gloves to open doors because he's scared of picking up infections, he has his reasons and the right to do so. 'Theatre people' have learnt to see though the façade. The little whims of a soprano have little importance. The important thing is that she is happy to collaborate and take part in the general spirit of the production; that she is a 'theatre person' and not a diva that is capricious and proud. So long as this is the case, she is accepted for what she is worth, for the value she adds to the service. This

value may be (and usually is) very great. This attitude extends to all the agents of the rich universe that takes part in the production. Specifically, *in theatre people are usually treated in line with what they contribute, for the talent they bring and not for what they superficially appear to be.* Behind the frivolous are a vital attitude and an Attitude–Aptitude balance. That is to say, 'We are willing to forgive your *attitudes*, because you contribute to our success with your *aptitudes*.'

2. *They are very aware of the impact their work has on the service delivered.* Perhaps because they experience it, they see it happen with their own eyes, *everyone knows what will happen if each person does not do his or her work well.* If a spotlight comes on a second after it is supposed to, the singer will start to sing the aria in the dark. The audience will see, and may laugh, and this will destroy the suspension of disbelief; the seven centimetres which Lluís Pasqual spoke about, which gives credibility to what the audience will witness. The suspension of disbelief is to make people believe, and create a virtual world, that the spectator comes to take as real, where the action takes place.

Suddenly the audience becomes aware that a motor is noisy. They become conscious of the existence of a motor, a strange element in *Romeo and Juliet* set in mediaeval Verona. And the situation becomes laughable. The spell is broken and this small detail makes the whole performance a failure. Daniel has told us various times that a single failure can destroy the whole show. Theatre people live this situation first-hand. In rehearsals, they are constantly going through the consequences of their actions. If a glass is not in the right place so that the tenor can pick it up at the moment of a toast, the singer will have to distract himself from his passionate toast to try to find it. And the person who put it in the wrong place will realise immediately; no-one will have to tell him about it. It is not strange then, that each person has a very clear vision of the value they contribute through what they do and how they do it.

3. *They place the work of the group above the work of the people.* Everyone knows that their role is to make their internal clients sparkle. Whether it is the Stage Director during the preparation of the production, or the singer, the musicians and the chorus during the performance. The technicians, 'the theatre people' do not appear to the audience directly and their roles are not as clear as those on other levels. Their success is *indirect.* They substitute their own ostentation for that of others, making their clients sparkle, because 'their success is ours'. There is also a *group* feeling in this situation. 'Theatre people' know that not putting their all into the project has a direct effect on the work of their colleagues. It can even get to the stage where the effort of everyone else is completely *useless.* As always, the weakest link in the chain determines the quality of the product. This is why the group rejects those members who do not give their all to the joint

determination. And they do so because their *failure* will be our failure. We are witnessing true teamwork, which is only comparable with sports practiced in small teams. In these, the wrong contribution by one of the members will ruin the result, because effort cannot be substituted. Does the reader recognise the role of *Unity* here?

4. *They tend to be good professionals in their area, and hold themselves out to be so.* The dictionary defines 'professional' as 'A person who exercises their profession with the relevant ability and application.' Dictionaries sometimes give strange definitions, but in this case the definition is precise, and highlights two components, 'ability' and 'application'. In other words a good professional 'knows a lot' about their area, and also has sufficient motivation to 'apply' it well. When Daniel says that Juan Diego Flórez is a great *professional*, he is saying that a) he is a great singer and b) he puts all of his art into the achievement of the *common result*. From this perspective, all of the agents of the theatre would be classified as good professionals. Daniel once commented in a conference that, in the beginning, if everything had gone well, at the end of a premiere he would congratulate his people. He would go backstage and say something like, 'Well done, it went really well. Congratulations.' He did this for a while, but stopped doing so when after one such comment, he heard someone murmur, 'Of course we did well. What did you think would happen?'

5. *They are proud of making the impossible attainable, and making the possible easy.* Perhaps the tail of the Wagnerian tenor caught the reader's attention, and perhaps the extraordinary fact, related by Daniel, that no-one even considered cancelling the performance to be a viable solution. Come rain or shine (or, for that matter, earthquakes) 'the show must go on'. There is the well-known case of Julián Gayarre, a tenor famous at the end of the nineteenth century. Julián had to sing *L'Elisir d'Amore* in Varese (Italy). Before starting the second act, which includes the famous romance *Una furtive lacrima,* a piece in which a tenor can really shine, he received a telegram informing him of the death of his mother. Julián went out on stage and sang. Word at the time held that he had never sung as he did that night, nor would he ever sing like that again. No-one thought of cancelling the show... An exceptional situation is a challenge, an incentive for all to work together to save the show, putting all their collective personal energy together. The story of the tenor demonstrates the passion to solve the problem on all levels of the theatre. No-one doubted it. 'Did we have to do it? Well we did it. Was it difficult? Yes, but that's why we are here', one of our protagonists told us. For another significant detail, the reader may remember the teamwork to the cries of 'come on, come on, all together...' during a difficult scene change.

Beyond the peculiarities of talented people, which we may consider innate in this type of person, the five conditions above seem to have been clearly acquired. They form part of the training of this new *operational culture* that we are constantly referring to and which we will expand on next.

The emergence of a new Operational Culture

How are these five qualities achieved in the theatre? What are the circumstances which determine the emergence of this new Operational Culture? What is behind this which might inspire us so that, despite the differences, we are capable of creating it in our companies? The truth is that no-one really knows. However, we have some pointers that we are going to share with you. Even though they are incomplete, we have seen them work and can affirm that they are a necessary condition for the appearance of behaviour like that exhibited by theatre people. Whether they are enough is open to discussion.

1. Immediate feedback on the result of Operations.
2. Knowledge *a priori* of the relevance of your actions.
3. Implicit recognition of each person's merits.
4. Integration of people in the working team.

1. *Immediate feedback on the result of Operations.* In the theatre it is very easy to know whether our work is getting results or not, although the experience may be traumatic if we are not. A rowdy and perhaps ill-mannered audience will simply tell you to your face at the end of the performance. And that's not even mentioning the expert critics' specialised criticism: they will all praise or insult you with the same fervour. It is difficult to find any middle ground and sometimes due to silly little things. It is ridiculous that a singer of great quality and prestige, like Renée Fleming – a great professional – should be booed for a small error, such as singing the wrong note, or because a few people take exception to her way of performing. But that's how it is. However, when the audience is well mannered it can be worse. Experts say that courteous applause is worse than the audience kicking up a fuss, because a sign of indifference is worse than antagonism. At least when they scream and shout it helps you to know what's gone wrong; indifference is grey. Everything has gone 'quite badly'. Fortunately, though, the audience is generally ill mannered, so they constantly help the creation of the right Operational Culture. No-one designed this *fantastically efficient feedback mechanism*; it has been like this since theatre began. It wasn't consciously designed to improve the system, it simply happened.

2. *Knowledge* a priori *of the relevance of your actions.* The constant feedback, from the audience and other agents within our operative world, gives rise in the long term to the appearance of another spontaneous and nonetheless fantastic phenomenon. As time goes by, as experiences are accumulated, the ability to foresee, to anticipate the relevance of the different actions which

can be taken is acquired. This is an evaluative capacity which allows the value contribution of each of the alternatives available to be determined, without prior experience of them. It is an *a priori* ability, with no need to hear the audience's boos, to evaluate the results a certain course of action may have. In other words, 'If I do this and it goes wrong, we'll be in trouble.'In the section above, we discussed feedback on results, not the capacity to anticipate and evaluate them. These only occur through a process of internalisation of experiences, specifically the knowledge acquired through experience.

This evaluative capacity, which we call *relevance*, occurs through two mechanisms. First, due to the target *result* being constantly present in everyone's' minds. In theatre, this result is almost trivial, but this is not the case in other business activities which are less event-focused. Second, *relevance* comes about through an *internal evaluation* of the impact each action has on the client. This evaluation is based on the existence of an 'internal model' of the phenomenon, a series of premises which lead to prediction, using cold-hearted reasoning. When in the last act of *Don Giovanni* Lluís Pasqual placed a Don Giovanni dressed in the military uniform of Franco's era, and projected images from Franco's propagandistic newsreels – which included images of the lead character – he knew that either the audience would react in the way they did, or he had the wrong model of the situation. We think the former hypothesis is correct: the model was right. The reader should remember the anticipation, 'they're going to thrash him to within an inch of his life', that the theatre people predicted beforehand.

3. *Implicit recognition of each person's merits.* Mutual respect and professional recognition should pervade all professions. It is not about nominating an employee of the month and sticking his or her photo up on the wall, because this is not respect. It is simply a tactic invented by human resource 'experts', in an attempt to motivate the workforce. For professionals, for talented people, it is verging on the ridiculous and almost insulting. The recognition has to be carried out in the day-to-day Operations. A round of applause is, of course, one form of recognition, but in the interview in the previous chapter other more continued ways were brought to our attention: a letter, an answer-phone message and so on. To do this, the appreciation of all people for the virtues of their colleagues must be developed. Peoples' recognition comes about through the dissemination of their knowledge and virtues. Dissemination and acceptance of the fact that the actions of a professional cannot be confirmed by anyone other than another professional, equally or more professional than the first. Specifically, get them to use their *autoritas* rather than their *potestas*.[2] *Flattening the organisation,* and

---

[2] Latin terms, *autoritas* refers to moral influence based on prestige and dignity, while *potestas* is power based on coercion.

not *meddling in the professional areas,* and *accepting the decisions of others* as your own are all key elements of this point.

4. *Integration of people in the working team.* Theatre people know each other and know the capacities and abilities of others. Within a work environment, they form a team, and, perhaps strongly, this group will let others considered to be peers of the original members join. Stage Directors, Set Designers and all sorts of passing talent, are admitted to the group which watches the premieres on television. Also, since this group also exhibits most of the characteristics of talented people, they don't allow deceit or covering up.

How can we apply this to a company?

So if we are not running a theatre, where these things seem to happen spontaneously, how can we create the right environment for the development of this Operational Culture in our company, a normal business with talented people? The answers that we can give come from the analysis in the previous section. Of course, they are not an exhaustive list, but are simply intended to suggest paths of action to be followed to progress.

Five actions to help to create the right breeding-ground for the new Operational Culture:

---

1. Use a substitute for the audience.
2. Manage relevance.
3. Professionalise.
4. Implement RT.
5. Work in plural.

---

1. *Use a substitute for the audience.* The audience tells the truth, because they have paid to get in and are not in a frame of mind to be politically correct. So, we will not be politically correct in our company, we will be *aggressive but honest.* Initially we will enrage everyone; people will be offended because they are told some home truths. However, as a famous singer-songwriter says, 'The truth is never sad, but it can't be avoided', so if it can't be avoided we should bring it to the table. In traditional companies, doing this has always been difficult, because you have to tread on too many peoples' toes. Nevertheless, this should not be the case when we are dealing with talent. Talented people should be capable of accepting criticism where it is rational and justified, or at least of understanding it, because they have a more objective view of the world. Be careful, we are talking about criticism, not blame. Blame always implies some kind of penalisation. Blame can and should not be allocated. Like in the Teatro Real, no-one is blamed; there are just problems.

In knowledge-based companies, this can and should be achieved. We have seen it implemented with good results, but management has a huge responsibility. First, they should ensure that the surgical *incision* is made, and then, that *this doesn't have bad consequences*. Well, perhaps it is best that not too much blood is spilled, but then surgery is always bloody, and this cannot be avoided. We should always start by creating a suitable climate for the *incision,* accepting criticism and uttering it reasonably. If something is not done right, this should be made clear openly, at the same time as explaining why it is wrong. It is about handling *facts* not *stances.*

However, prudence is a great virtue, particularly in the beginning. Can the reader imagine a traditional company, with a great deal of talent, suddenly starting to play 'spin the bottle' and having to tell the truth? The death toll could be enormous. At the beginning of its implantation, this strategy requires a limit on collateral damage. You probably have to start with concrete *feedback,* not with everyone, and go on to the cascade. Perhaps it will be worth taking on external *help* so that the aggressiveness is blamed on these external facilitators, who can be made to disappear, while everyone else remains friends. Whatever the case, the well of knowledge has remained and the culture has changed.

2. *Managing relevance.* Hoping that a 'normal' organisation will develop relevance through evolution, as theatre has done, is a little slow and insecure. Pretty much no-one is willing to wait 3000 years until a culture like the theatrical one comes about. As Don Juan (the one from *Zorrilla,*[3] not *Don Giovanni*) says, 'I'll believe it when I see it!' The mutation and natural selection have to be speeded up so that the evolution takes place over a shorter time period. One way of doing this is by using *abstract knowledge;* knowledge which is developed to be formally transmitted. To do this we need to materialise and formalise the knowledge acquired through the experience of boos and cheers, and pass it on through education and training. This is what some business experts attempt to do by, for example, establishing criteria for each position in the company, which are derived from the mission of the company. Some call this technique *Management by Missions.* However, these actions always, always have to go in tandem with flooding all the participants with ideas.

A second line of action is to *achieve mimicry,* as a substitute for a long, theatrical tradition that is passed from father to son. Ensuring that no-one thinks about failing, working shoulder to shoulder with the employees, so that they see first-hand the type of criteria we are dealing with, what we all expect of each other and what we expect of ourselves. As we shall see, this is tightly linked to the role of the manager as educator, a role which should be the quintessence of all managers.

---

[3] Ramón Gómez de la Serna says in one of his aphorisms, 'Espronceda is a piano played with one finger, Bécquer is an accordion played by an angel, and Zorrilla is a pianola but the one who has got tired of peddling is him!'

A third line is insisting on the *'objectivisation' of everything objective.* Not working with opinions, but *with facts.* We should create non-involved meditation mechanisms that present information in an unbiased way. By spreading this information, we are creating a feedback mechanism without the need for an audience. Now there is no booing or confrontations. The cold, hard reality of the data shakes us, with no need for shouting. As a complement to this system, a fact-interpretation scheme should be developed, so that everyone can work with a common basic knowledge. In particular, 'business common sense' should be created.

3. *Professionalise.* Specifically, this involves ensuring that each employee of the company knows their area of work, that they enjoy the recognition of others and have the right conditions to be able to exercise their capabilities with passion. Of course, the first task is to *train* people but that does not mean sending them on courses. The manager is the main trainer, so you should get ready to work on training your people. Second, it is about making sure that people *get the most out of* their problem-solving. To do this you have to *share* the result of the effort, and that is the knowledge acquired. Some companies have created solution forums where employees present and discuss their problem-solving experiences; sharing and accepting suggestions. A good manager *knows how to get the best out of his people.* It is all about people growing and developing because of their work in the company.

In one company we worked with, we witnessed an interesting experience along these lines. They were dealing with a multimillion-Euro contract to provide the armed forces with a spy-plane. The company needed a technological partner, because it did not have sufficient knowledge of the necessary technology. Essentially, there were two possibilities: working with an American company or an Israeli one. The American company would deliver the plane pretty much finished, and the contracting company would carry out the integration and tests. In the other option, the Israeli company would deliver the parts and the Spanish company would have to assemble and test the system. The first choice was safer, but the second brought with it more knowledge. The manager leading the project was a young expert, with little experience in contracts of this magnitude. He favoured the American company because it gave increased assurance of meeting the client's requirements. His boss, an older gentleman, preferred the Israeli option because to his mind it gave the company a better future. The situation was analysed for a while. In the meeting in which the definitive option was to be decided on, each person stuck to his guns. After a few hours, the senior manager stood up and said, 'Ok, we'll go with the Americans.' The young project manager sat with his mouth open, because he expected his boss to exert his authority.

The project was a success, particularly due to the interest, dedication and learning the young manager put into it. When the senior manager was asked why he decided to back down, he said,

I did not have a great preference for the Israeli option, and I thought, if I decide, it will be my project, whilst if I let him decide it will be his project, and he knows how to do it far better than I. I'm interested in the success of the project and his learning, which is why it was obvious how I should act.

Obvious, but not hugely so.

4. *Implement RT.* The philosophy of RT emphasises the search for the causes of problems. This is why decisively taking part in the creation of a model gives a predictive mental image of the world, which is probably filed in the 'theatrical common sense'. So many important things are kept in this bag carried around on theatre peoples' backs!

5. *Work in plural.* According to Daniel, in the Teatro Real they work in plural. Everything needs the contribution of various people. It is natural that to work together efficiently people consider questions such as what motivates others? What do they like to do? What do the work colleagues enjoy? It is much better to work in a team where you know the preferences of your colleagues. In theatre there are huge opportunities to get to know these preferences, the way others are and feel, through the intensive coexistence it entails. The reader should remember Daniel's phrase, 'We eat together.' The level of coexistence is high and interaction is born out of knowing each other. The need to talk about, understand and take on board the satisfactions of other is created.

Nevertheless, this should not turn into paternalism, or into the ridiculous attitude that 'we are all friends here'. We know of a company whose director has the motto 'We fail together.' This is all very well, but it creates an immediate reaction of distrust in the employees. 'Fail? Who wants to fail? And if I do, we'll see the fuss that gets kicked up despite the guy's silly little phrases...' Scepticism is part of a healthy culture. You have to convince people, not stick flowers in the barrel of the guns. This was fair enough, not to mention romantic and emotive, in Lisbon during the first days of the Carnation Revolution. However, in the long run the carnations will wither away, spring is not always in the air, and the people need to feel that the result of it all is, once more, mutual winning. Make sure that this happens!

Conclusions

In this chapter, we have defined some of the characteristic of talented people and looked at how to manage them. We have analysed the importance of their integration into the company and how to make them function together. We have presented the concept of *relevance* as the ability to evaluate the impact of possible actions *a priori*. We have also seen how to apply this to the company. In the same way, we have looked at some of the traits of theatre people, which help instil *unity* in the whole organisation. Finally, we have presented five action points towards achieving this *unity* in the heart of your company.

We have one final comment. Daniel spoke of the similarities of theatre with the act of playing and many of the characteristics of playing being present in theatrical work. Someone said that 'theatre is a game before the gods'. So why can't these characteristics of play be present in companies? What are they anyway? *Enjoyment*, a few clear *rules*, transparent *relationships* between the players, no offence is taken in *winning*, the *impact* on others is understood and the results are *tangible* and easy to see. Do these things remind you of the concepts we have discussed in this chapter? Let's play then!

We will end the chapter with the following reflections:

- How do you manage your talent?
- How do you achieve their integration into the company?
- How to you ensure they work in unison?
- How could the five qualities we have seen in the Teatro Real help you to create a new Operational Culture?
- Could you put in place any of the suggestions on how to create the right environment for the new Operational Culture?

XXI*
The Management Style of
Teatro Real's Operations Director

In the next couple of chapters, we will analyse the management style necessary to engender Unity.

The Teatro Real's Operations Director has an interesting management technique, similar to that found in world-class companies. The 'Wednesday meeting', where the director deals out tasks and draws attention to future issues, is a key part of this technique. His management style revolves around letting his team get on with their work, while applying the maxim: 'don't worry about it, just solve it'.

The management style of a New Operational Culture is directly opposed to the classical approach: now it is not a person's power that is valued, but rather his authority. Governing by authority transforms the role of the manager. Yet to manage is not to order, 'to manage is to serve and support others'. The manager should become a manager-educator and, for this, the manager must be well aware of the complexities of the company. He should use this knowledge to support problem-solving, rather than to give orders on what must be done. Getting others to do something requires an understanding of this, so take a moment to think about it...

What is the 'Wednesday meeting'?

It's a meeting which all the section heads who report directly to me attend. In this meeting, we lay everything out on the table and coordinate our work. We give out the week's information to all the managers and they in turn pass it on to the backstage people. This ensures, for example, that all the technicians know, platform by platform unit and block by block, how the stage must be set, using exact measurements and specifications. These

---

* The only interviewee in this chapter is Daniel Bianco.

are striped; these are in black. This folder [he shows us a folder containing a stage plan] tells us all we need to know. A block painted black goes here [shown on the plan], here's a red one, these are blocks finished in tile, these in wood... anyway, and you can see all this from the plan. When the head of stage mechanics and his team are putting together the set, they use this plan and all the specifications. We have coordinates defined on the stage to help position the staging on the floor, and these are linked to the adjoining constructions. For instance, X has to be 3.5 m from Carlos and 2.75 m from Felipe. That's not to say that after all when the stage is set, someone doesn't come along and say, 'no, this bit here needs to be a little more to the left' and then you have to change it. But you have to start with the plan, otherwise it'll never work. This form of documentation is probably unique in Spain. But I can't really take credit for it though; it's thanks to everyone at this theatre. Since this tool was introduced, people have changed their attitude towards working in theatre. In Spain, where no leading theatre boasted state-of-the art technology, it was all: 'Manolo, chuck us that rope and let's hope for the best!', whereas now everyone's working like us!

The way of working in the Wednesday meeting developed on its own, without us pushing it. When we first started the meetings, we actually thought of calling them off! To begin with, we served coffee and croissants, because it seemed the sophisticated way forward, we liked to think of ourselves as top executives... but it didn't work. Then we tried to remain impartial... nothing. We've had massive disagreements, called off meetings, screamed and shouted till we were blue in the face and about to hit each other.

Nevertheless, over the years, everything has been sorted out and we've been able to put things into perspective. You have to learn to *use* these meetings. The meeting is not for you to go on about personal problems, which no-one is really interested in. *It's a work commitment where you present both the common problems that affect everyone else, and your thoughts on those problems.* Everybody does the same and as a result, ideas arise. The goal is not to be caught out by issues. We've learnt a lot. Now we are at a perfect stage, the meeting functions like a dream and then everyone goes off and gets on with their own tasks.

Planning the week is not the only function of the Wednesday meetings; they are also a time for us to discuss things that are worrying us. Together the team brings the current status of each production to the table. We have a master *schedule* that I draw up a year in advance, and then update it every week. The *schedule* includes the ins and outs of everything that happens in a week in theatre. On Mondays, for example, from eight 'til two, get the set in position, from two 'til four, set up the orchestra and so on. You have to have this schedule because by law you have to file the timetable a week before the production. In addition, it helps me to talk about the following week. I take the line 'Gentlemen, we are going to do it this way.' For example,

'I need lots of people to build the set for this production and, let's say, only a few for the concert.' Or 'the concert itself is not so important, but this particular part of it is ...' In the meetings I give a general outline of the week, and the rest of the attendees, the managers, are obliged to pass the information on to their people. They should also bring up any issues they're facing, so that they can be shared by everyone. The head of mechanics might say: 'watch out, or such and such will happen because I don't have enough people', or 'careful, we've got a problem with the stage and I need you as head of set mechanics, to set up the set-change motors.' Company problems, trade union issues, personal problems and the experiences of each attendee are brought to the table ... but it would be a mistake to think of it as some kind of psychiatrist's couch!

How long does one of these meetings last?

The meeting is split into two parts: logistics and other organisational matters. Last Wednesday, I spent 40 minutes saying that we had strayed off-course, I'd gone down to a rehearsal and everyone's attitude was disgraceful, we weren't in control of the group. All because when I was down on the stage, I saw a load of things that weren't right. *Everyone was so relaxed.* They had no idea of what was in store, nor had we foreseen the need to plan the work ahead. I said to them 'Gentlemen, we've started the season; it's come to my attention that the stage is highly disorganised and it's obvious there has been insufficient control. If we start the first opera of the year like this, by June, when it's summer, we'll be using the stage for nothing more than making paella.'

When I finished my sermon, we handed out the information on the operas for the next month and explained their structure. It was a long and intense meeting – normally they only take about an hour.

Then we tend to talk about what's going on with the performances. In *La Dolores* the set is highly motorised and in the Wednesday meeting I said to them, 'You've got to have the people ready, because if the motors fail, we'll have to move it manually.' Normally, they've already done it, or foreseen it at least. We discuss what's going to happen and what we can't let happen. To tell the truth, if I make any comments, most of the time they say, 'Yes, I'm already on it'. It's really unusual for them to say they hadn't thought of it. Sometimes when Carlos and I make comments they say, 'Oops, I hadn't realised' or 'I didn't think that you could see it from over there.' But never, never, never, have I made some comment on something *obvious* that they hadn't already noticed.

In many ways, I deal out cards in this meeting. I deal them a hand each and then it's up to them to play them and come back next Wednesday with their tasks done. Do you know why this works? Because one of the secrets, I think, is that *people believe that power is having it all,* but it's exactly the opposite, *it's giving everything away.*

Can you expand on this idea?

When you have everything, you don't have power because you can't really make use of it all. It *overwhelms* you. Power comes from *delegating* things to others so that they deal with them; this is where the real secret lies.

I think I'm pretty good at delegating. Not passing the buck, but delegating, knowing how to get someone else to do something for you. If you're a kitchen worker you do this, or if you work in a laundrette you do that; it's all about passing tasks on to each person and making sure that they all know what the objective is. It's not about washing your hands of the problem. No, it's more 'This has to be sorted out; it can't be put off forever. And if you're going to sort it out, then I have to give you the means.' Someone might answer: 'I can't, I don't have time.' My response to this is to say, 'OK, I'm going to put you on night shift, I'll give you more hours, or I'll let you work overtime.' Then I'll assess what this involves. I'll also see if I should have waited until they asked or whether I should have taken steps before. But there's no other option, it has to be sorted out.

I've seen, in managers of mine and in other Operations Directors I've known, that when they have power, and they have their desks piled high with paper, they're in a constant state of anxiety. Yet they are surrounded by people who look at them and don't do anything. This, I think, is one of the reasons why the pack of cards must be dealt out. I always use the example of the umpire in tennis. It's not by chance that the umpire sits in a tall chair; he needs to see the game from above, and in the event of any doubt, get down. A tennis umpire is not in the middle of the game like a football referee, who busily runs up and down and often doesn't see the foul. In tennis, it's crystal clear; the umpire has a bird's eye view, one with a global perspective. I call this the pyramid. The only way of working is to create a relational pyramid. But *it mustn't be perceived to be a pyramid of 'command', but rather a pyramid of 'I tell you what I see.'*

Both Carlos and I spend a lot of time down on the set – neither of us is a pen-pusher, and we spend very little time in the office at our desks. If you're always stuck in the office, you can't control the game. I never get tired of saying this to the stage managers; they're the ones I'm always chasing up on this. If the stage manager, who has an operational job, gets too involved in what he's doing, he becomes bogged down in the details and doesn't see what's going on around him and he could easily ruin the set! This is why I go down to the stage from time to time, I look at everything and tell the stage manager, 'Wait, step back, *look at it from the outside*, because if you don't see it from another point of view, you won't get a *global* impression. The section managers are there for the detail.' The stage manager must observe from a higher viewpoint. This strategy plus delegation are fundamental.

So, is your management style in place because you don't have any other choice?

No, no, it's the only way, it's the only way. And because in good theatre, in the technical part of good theatre, you're providing a *service*. You work for others. Bearing this in mind also helps a lot. Maybe in other lines of work it's different, but here you work to get the show on stage, so that when the curtain rises, it stays up. You know that in the theatre world, the curtain only comes down at the end.

What are the salaries like here? Does a manager, for example, earn a lot?

No, for the work he does, not really. He is quite well-paid, but he's not getting rich, no, no, not at all. This is not a place for people motivated by money. Here you can pay for your flat and live your life, but that's it. Let's see, if the job were as simple as that of some executives, on the salary of a stage or section manager, then maybe we'd be well-paid. If I knew I could have the day off on 6 January (an important national celebration in Spain and other Catholic countries), and that I could go home on Fridays and not have to come in until Monday morning... If I knew all this, well, yes my salary would be ok. However, when you need to be available all the time, when you have to work on Saturday and Sunday, when one day you're in at 8 a.m. and the next you have to stay until three in the morning, and you have to juggle that with doing the shopping or the laundry... in short, when you consider that you can't organise your life like a normal family, you really earn very little. You can't even choose when you take your holidays.

Isn't that hard on your family?

Extremely hard, what happens in reality is that your partner is expected to adapt to the theatre world. It is very tough though.

I've already said that there's a great atmosphere here. It just came about naturally with this team. Pretty much all of us who go to the Wednesday meetings eat together every day at the same table. At one time, I would go home for lunch, to relax, take a step back or whatever. It didn't work, so I stopped doing it. I have to eat with them; plenty of stuff goes on at lunch, especially *getting on well* and *building the team*. But it's not planned – it just happened *by accident*. I think there's also a good element of team-building, because at two in the afternoon everyone starts going 'Come on' 'Are we having lunch?' 'Where shall we go?' 'Shall we wait or see you there?' There's something intangible, something more than just a bunch of people working together.

There are many other good things as well, such as Secret Santa[1] at Christmas. Each time a show is premièred we each put in some money for

---

[1] Each person in the group draws, by anonymous lottery, the name of another person in the group. They then buy that person a Christmas present up to an agreed

some drinks and snacks or we bring in Spanish omelettes, ham, that sort of thing...it's something we Wednesday meeting people have always done, and we enjoy it all while watching the opera on the monitors (we're not allowed to see it any other way except on the monitors). In fact, it was funny yesterday because the premiere was in the morning, it was a TIE (theatre in education) show at 11 a.m. and the stage manager said, 'Hey, how about bringing in breakfast?' But these things come about because we've built up a team, a way of working. It's not by design that these things happen, but it's not by chance either – the best thing is to take advantage of them.

Is there anything else you can do to motivate people?

I only have two tools to do this. First, give them all the work resources they need, which normally has a very positive effect. For example, I give the lighting man the best stuff on his wish list and tools and systems to make his work better. I give him everything that signifies a *technological advance*. Well, at least I try to give him everything! The second thing is *flexible working hours*. I don't monitor people's work schedules. However, it's true that normally between 10 a.m. and 7 p.m. everyone's here. It's a 'meeting point' timetable. And on the Sundays when we do the *ante piano* they're here, and if there's a final pre-general run-though or general dress rehearsal they're here, even if it's a Saturday, Sunday or public holiday. But I'm never in the mood to control their hours. They clock in because they have to in order to get into the theatre, as do we all, but I'm not concerned with the time, I'm interested in getting the job done.

The only thing I can give them is *quality of life,* not money. What happens is that they are all here by vocation. They like their work. And naturally, after all the companies you've worked for, all the places you've been where you haven't had a good ladder to climb, where there's been no acceptable tools, not even a pair of decent gloves, or anything, suddenly you're here where they give you everything. Why would you leave?

I believe that you allow some departments to lend part of their budget to others, is this normal in the theatre world?

No, that's an invention of ours. What happens is that I have a sum of money and a number of budget areas; I am free to divide the sum between them as I wish. I have a budget area which is called 'stage expenses', which encompasses everything which can't be directly allocated to the production. And within stage expenses, there's another budget area called 'inventoried material'.

What I do is distribute the money from these budget areas to each section, because they are the ones who spend it, not me. I only authorise them, it's

---

price-limit. Everybody knows only the person for whom they're buying a present. Oh come on, do we really need to explain this?

not me who buys the wood, because I have no idea about buying wood. I don't know if we need wood for tomorrow or fabric, or if we're ok for everything. The only condition is that they can't go over the assigned amount. They have to reach the 31 December at zero.

For example, in the last tax year, wardrobe and make-up were €14,000 over budget, so they had to borrow it from other departments. Audiovisuals, for example, lent wardrobe some of their budget. For me, the accounts have to balance. On the thirtieth of each month, in the team meeting, I give each area their *bank statement*, how much they have, the *invoices* that they've received during the month and how much money is left in their budget. And they control it. This is brilliant, because you can only make savings when you have *control of the money* and you can see the expenses incurred. The section heads realise where the expenses are, and why exactly they are buying wood, fabric or whatever. That way they really value what they buy.

What's your typical working day like?

In the mornings, I'm mostly in the office, but in the afternoons I'm down on the stage a lot. Yesterday we had a crisis meeting; I called it an 'urgent crisis' meeting. At 12, we all went down to one of the meeting rooms because we had a problem with one of the motors. I said, 'Guys this is where we are, you've had four days to sort out the problem on your own, but now we've run out of time and have to make a decision – don't worry, I'm going to take it, but I need to know each of your opinions'. Both the head of stage management and the head of stage machinery – the overall manager responsible for the motors – gave me their opinions. They said, 'Hey, Daniel, can't you wait 24 hours more before taking the decision to replace the system? Because we think we've nearly fixed it.' Their reasons were clear, 'Look, you're right, but we have to premiere the show, and this means moving the set, even if we have to do it with our teeth.' They were more worried than I was, and added, 'Daniel, previously we had eight failed motors. We've been fixing them and working stuff out, and now we only have two that don't work. We've really moved forward. Give us 24 hours and we'll come up with a solution for these last two. And if we can't... Well, we'll stay here all night and change the motorised system for something else.' And I said, 'Ok then, the idea is very logical, I'll give you another 24 hours' and I did. By midnight that night they'd moved the scenery 36 times and it worked. From time to time, it still breaks down so there's always a possibility it might fail but now they're working on that.

Has anyone ever said that you've made a mistake?

I don't think so, no. They've probably thought that I've been wrong on some things, but they've never told me so directly. They have said things like, 'I don't think so, and I don't think it's what you're telling me, not really...'

I don't want to give the impression that I'm never wrong, because I've been wrong many times. It's just that the relationship I have with my team is one of an ongoing dialogue. We think out loud. I don't get to *make mistakes* because I don't *jump ahead* of them.

They are perfectly aware that in the end, the person who takes *overall responsibility* for everything is me. But I don't *impose* on them. I relieve them. I'll give you an example. Imagine that the director of the theatre tells me that at the last minute we must broadcast the show via television and therefore we have to use television lighting, no ifs, buts or maybes. So I get everyone together and say, 'Gentleman, we have to rig television lighting.' They may say, 'Sorry, I can't, I don't have enough people, the rigging's already been done' or 'I haven't got such and such.' But I reply 'Gentleman, use all the necessary resources, but make sure that we have television lighting by tomorrow at 8am.' OK. All the 'necessary resources' means that they are allowed to work overtime and get paid for it, and that they are authorised to make any necessary disbursements.

Here everything is 'in plural'; there is 'plural' thinking. Everyone knows what being the boss means and where their responsibility lies. So I've never had to impose something on them like this, because it really does all come down to teamwork.

Despite this essential team-thinking, where you've got a staff framework like this with 250 technicians, it's essential to have a very clear *pyramidal* structure although there must also be 'plural' thinking. You've got to say things out loud, establish a *dialogue*. Especially with the Technical Management of the project, the design people, stage managers, floor managers and level-one managers.

However, if we're talking about all the staff, well I obviously can't have a dialogue with *all* of them, otherwise it'd be ... well, this isn't a *commune*! But for me it is vital to think out loud with my team. Why? Because they are the ones who have to *convey my thoughts*, you know? If I say we're going to do such-and-such and that something else is important and I give some guidelines about the work we're going to do, I don't want them to convey my message incorrectly. It is vital they pass on the correct message. What concerns me most is that the *communication* is good, because we humans tend to distort things without realising it.

Some strange things have happened to me. Here's one about hair-styling. The singers often need to have their hair cut or dyed for the production. But sometimes a close relationship is formed between the singer and the hair-styling staff. The singer, who has spent a month wandering around the shops because she still hasn't decided what hairstyle she wants, finally becomes exasperated and asks the stylist, 'Hey, could you do this or that to my hair tomorrow? Tomorrow I'll come to the salon and we'll do it.' Well, I've had to ban these activities. I've said to the stylists, 'Look, you can cut or style for production but you can't bring in additional business.' Why? Not because it might upset me but because it creates a problem. If a singer becomes accustomed to this, she'll feel put out when comes the time that it can't be done because the stylist has too much work for the production.

Of course, a stylist might say, 'Sure I'll do your hair, why not? I'll talk to Daniel Bianco about it.' And they say to me, 'Have you banned it? Now what do I say to the singers?' I reply, 'With the singers, you do only what needs to be done for the performance, and nothing extra.'

'But I want to know if you've banned it or not!'

And I answer, 'Is there a sign that says that it is prohibited to urinate on the stage?'

'No!'

'Well,' I say, 'it's the same; we don't need to put up a sign saying that private things can't be done during work time.' But the comment is always, 'Daniel's banned it.' If I say at the team meeting what I want to do with the hair salon, it's important that the hair salon manager, Ovidio, conveys the idea clearly. In fact, on that occasion he conveyed it very well. He didn't say the word 'banned'. He simply said, 'You don't need me to tell you that you can't do that during working hours.'

Imagine if you had a manager who said to his people, 'Daniel's gone mad and banned this or that!' That's why there's the team meeting, to avoid situations like that, and achieve common thinking and almost a common language. Just one way of communicating things, in common. It's not always done successfully but, for me, it's fundamental. Because the profession, the work, everybody knows how to communicate...but how do you persuade a person to actually do it?

Another example: Álvaro, the props manager. He's a person who plans a long way ahead and he doesn't like improvising. For example, the Christ in *Tosca* which took so much time to make. You can't improvise a statue of Christ overnight, because it's not just the material, it's the work done in the mind. Raquel, the girl who made it doesn't start making a Christ in the morning as soon as she comes in; she has a coffee and then starts to chisel. No. She has to analyse the Christ, she has to see the photo, calculate it, study it, and get it fixed in her mind. It's not something you can start today and finish tomorrow. When things happen that aren't in her schedule, Raquel says to me, 'Daniel, please, explain it to Ovidio', and that's where *I come in*.

Normally I stay on top of the stage manager, because I have an advantage that none of them have. I'm the only one that can see *things from the outside*, and that's wonderful. I'm not there 24 hours a day but when I go down to the stage, I see it. I go down to the rehearsal and I say, 'Do you realise that this doesn't...?'

The other day I went down to the rehearsal. It wasn't really working for me. I could see it from the outside, and I saw that nobody was really in control. So I took the floor managers aside and I said to them, 'Do you realise that you have to take the reins? The Stage Director is lost and you have to guide him.' And they took the reins and did just that.

You know, sometimes I have much more contact with the Stage Directors than they do, so I get much closer to some than to others and they all tell me things. In such a situation, I'm like a hotel owner. If someone reserves one of my most expensive suites, I'm going to give him the best service, and I'll tell my people, 'Keep on your toes, he's a vegetarian, or he loves a good steak or whatever...' That's what I try to do.

Allow me an aside here. Things aren't really that black and white, perhaps because of the type of team we have created. Carlos and I have worked together for many years and we understand each other very well. He knows exactly when he has to *consult* me. He comes to me and says, 'Look, we can't do that,' or 'What do we do?' Not because I necessarily have the answer, but to bounce ideas around. The other day, he came to me and said, 'Daniel, I need you to step in – I've sent thousands of letters and the people in this theatre aren't answering me. There's nothing more I can do, now you've got to do something about it.' Then I attack.

I once read a report, 'thousands' of years ago, about Felipe González [the Prime Minister of Spain from 1982 to 1996]. He was talking about the *lone-liness* of his job and he said that whenever he looked at telephone in his government office, he would think, 'Well, this is the last telephone in the chain of command, and only I pick it up. Trouble is, there's no other telephone for *me* to call...' It's the end of the chain of authority. I have a magnificent relationship with my assistant; we understand each other perfectly. He handles many issues. But suddenly one day he says, 'That's as far as I can go.' And he passes it on to me. Then I always think that *there's no other phone for me to call*. I've already answered the 'phone and now I have to make a decision'. That wears you down.

Are your people's people empowered to propose changes to the things they are told or do they have to simply do what they're told?

No, not really, but they do have a say in HOW they do it. I'll give you a practical example. The other day, we went down with Emilio Sagi, who's the director of the *Barber of Seville*, to see the props they were making. He had stipulated, 'The leading character's armchair, at a particular point while he is singing, needs to suddenly collapse so he falls onto the ground. You can do it however you like, whatever's the simplest way.' To which I replied, 'Well, the best option is if the chair legs were to splay out like this, because that's the best way to fall to the floor, but if you do it like that the audience won't really see it. It would be more spectacular if the back of the chair suddenly fell backwards, SMACK!'

Then Álvaro, the props manager, said to me, 'Well, it would be better if the character fell to one side, so he doesn't bruise his backside. If he hangs on to the arm of the chair, he'll go sideways and the chair back goes backwards.' OK, perfect, we'll do it like that. Then Emilio, who is the artist, piped up with, 'Hey, make sure the chair isn't heavy, because he's got to move it around a lot.' Then I said, 'Álvaro, make two chairs, one as a backup, because it's 14 performances and at least 15 rehearsals. Imagine what would happen if the chair broke and you couldn't repair it in time for the next performance.' 'Oh, great,' said the props manager, 'Where am I going to find two identical chairs in the second-hand market? The only alternative is making them, and now there's not enough time.' But Emilio said, 'Don't worry; it doesn't matter if the chairs aren't identical – I just need the other chair as a backup.' Great.

So Álvaro started working with his staff to fix the chairs for the fall. Obviously, the fixing is done by the handyman who's good at this kind of thing. So what did Álvaro do? He *assigned* the task to someone who he knew was good at it. And he'll keep assigning different tasks to different people, distributing the work according to their abilities and skills.

XXII
Management Style

This chapter forms the crux of the book, despite its late entry on stage. This has been done deliberately so that the less tenacious readers don't get this far and therefore don't benefit from the pearls of wisdom to be found here ... ahem. Anyway, this chapter is a summary of the management style of the Teatro Real's Operations Management, and draws on various points (some from this book, some from elsewhere) that seem to us to be the most relevant to how it works.

Rationale of the management style

The management style of the Teatro Real's Operations Management can be summarised under the following structure:

1. We must separate what can be foreseen from what cannot be foreseen.
2. What can be foreseen is included in the formal control system, which culminates in the scheduling system.
3. What remains is residual uncertainty. Disaster can always strike!
4. To consider this uncertainty, it is necessary to develop an informal system. The only way to solve what is unforeseeable is to be ready always, alert, five minutes before it happens. Everyone has to be taut, ready to act.
5. During critical times, and as a consequence of residual uncertainty, messages must be communicated quickly and accurately. Therefore, people must be used to saying what they think and saying it clearly.
6. Each manager must have a global view of the status of his territory, so that all the parts he is responsible for fit together.
7. So that people can get things done, it is necessary to 'let go' of all that one can and to concentrate on helping the lower levels and on making their lives easier.
8. The boss's job is to serve his team.
9. The manager must educate everyone in his company.

10. The way to convey Operational Culture to everyone is by means of the cascade effect – getting all levels to buy-in.

Some remarks about each of these points.

1. *We must separate what can be foreseen from what cannot be foreseen.* What we can foresee is every event whose outcome can be predicted from the causes. To separate what is predictable from what isn't, we must perform experiments, rehearsals, with a clear and precise methodology, while keeping all the external factors the same otherwise the results will not be comparable.

2. *What can be foreseen is included in the formal control system, which culminates in the scheduling system,* for example, in the *tops.* Inclusion in the formal system presupposes definition of a series of rules of procedure. The Emergency Book is an example. We have defined certain problems, and the messages that must be sent out if those problems occur. These problems have been discovered through extensive testing. Of course, we must always have an entry in our Emergency Book that reads 'Unknown error', as in software manuals. It shouldn't happen in an ideal world, but it will happen in the real world because of residual uncertainty. The *tops* system is one way of taking into account the rules that must be applied in a specific performance.

3. *What remains is residual uncertainty. The winning number can always come up ... or not!* We can't afford for anything to go wrong. If possible, we need to rig the system in our favour before anyone notices.

4. *To consider this uncertainty, it is necessary to develop the informal system. The only way to solve what is unforeseeable is be always ready, alert, five minutes before it happens. Everyone has to be taut, ready to act.* The formal system processes the rules, but this same formal system cannot anticipate the rules that will be required for imponderables. They must be developed, improvising as they come up. This is only possible if you have a suitable informal system with the right *Operational Culture.*

5. *During critical times caused by residual uncertainty, messages must be communicated quickly and accurately. Therefore, people must be used to saying what they think and saying it clearly.* Politically correct language can be confusing and time-consuming. In a crisis, things must be said honestly and clearly. And if anyone is offended, then frankly that's their problem – one has to be able to live with an operating culture of clarity.

6. *Each manager must have a global view of the status of his territory, so that all the parts he is responsible for fit together.* With each person concentrating on solving his own problems, there are always gaps to fill. The fact that each motor works is no guarantee that the set will move; rather, this depends on

the interaction of the motors. If all the motors pull in opposite directions, there will be no movement. Sharing solutions requires a higher-level vision and, as with the motors, it is necessary not only to consider the parts but also to consider the whole.

7. *So that people can get things done, it is necessary to 'let go' of all that one can and to concentrate on helping the lower levels and making their lives easier.* We cannot expect anyone to have sufficient control of their entire subsystem to create all the processes that transform the action into a routine. You've got to let go of the problems and controls so that each operator can handle his own sail.

8. *The boss's job is to serve his team.* To serve others, always within the principle of subsidiarity – if *they* don't decide, I will, but don't worry, because where they can't reach, I can. This is one of the basic management paradigms in the twenty-first century, and has even given rise to the aphorism 'To manage is to serve.' This approach surprises many people, but there's nothing else quite like it, particularly in organisations with highly qualified personnel.

9. *The manager must educate everyone in his company.* This is a new role for the manager: the manager-educator. His purpose is less about conveying knowledge and more about educating staff in their work. He shows them their weaknesses and helps them develop their strengths. It is a vital role; so much so that, again, there are schools that say 'To manage is to educate.' As we are impartial, we say, 'To manage is to serve and educate... among other things.'

10. *The way to convey Operational Culture to everyone is by means of the cascade effect – getting all levels to buy-in.* There's no other way. We have already said in another chapter that the raw materials for changing Operational Culture are the first-level managers. In this chapter, we will see how and why. They are the driving force and, at the same time, their mission is to cascade the Operational Culture down through the organisation. Each one is a mini Operations Director, but with the potential to reach higher levels.

Implementation

So far, so good, but the truly interesting part is seeing how an Operational Culture can be implemented, so let's take a brief look at the critical components. They are:

1. Problem-sharing
2. Keeping the organisation taut
3. The constant evaluation of relevance
4. The use of the subsidiarity principle in decisions
5. The necessity for cascade management
6. Trust in the other person's action

7. The use of power
8. Talent is motivated by the work it achieves
9. Motivation for service well done
10. Positive and negative rules
11. Clarity and sincerity

1. *The problem-sharing* and idea-generating at the Wednesday meetings is basically a Unity mechanism, although its results also enable efficiency to flourish. Everyone tries to understand each other's difficulties and priorities. On one hand, the Wednesday meeting is a normal management meeting and, on the other hand, it is a meeting for sharing problems. It is a professional, operational 'round table'. Daniel's style contains a significant diagnostic element; he raises problems and passes them to his team for them to solve. He tries to see the global problems that are difficult to see from the perspective of each section's day-to-day operations, and the cascading process begins here – each manager must pass on what he has received. In addition, the theatre's master-work programme is reviewed every week.

2. *Keeping the organisation taut.* The surest symptom of the forthcoming demise of a business or its management team is complacency. There are companies and managers who walk around like zombies. To wake up, the management must *innovate*, make changes and make sure that change becomes a constant in daily life. At the Teatro Real, change is part of the environment and all that the Operations Director has to do is to expedite it when conformism appears. Daniel doesn't have to see the future, because the future is already planned – for instance, he already knows the operas he will have to set up during the next 5 years. One of his greatest concerns is people becoming complacent (he even said that complacency would lead to them 'using the stage for nothing more than making paella') and it is something that must be avoided at all costs to maintain a five-star service.

To keep people taut by introducing tension is not the same as introducing frustration. The two concepts are separated, albeit by a very thin line. Tension is giving challenges to generate learning and growth, keeping people 'on their toes', ready to go into action and accepting that being alert is an absolute necessity.

The tension that Daniel talks about is like that of the 100-m sprinter on the starting blocks – tense in anticipation, not because of mistrust or fear. Tension allows a fast reaction when the unexpected occurs, as when the starting pistol sounds. It is the manager's mission to keep the tension positive and foresee what is 'headed their way'.

3. *The constant evaluation of relevance.* Daniel often highlights the relevance of problems, and this aspect is discussed in Chapter 20. However, it would serve no purpose at all without the cascade effect. Most problems are diagnosed and known by the person responsible for solving them. If no action

has been taken, it may be due to a lack of resources, which must be obtained from those who can give them, or because the person concerned lacks a global view and is not sufficiently detached from the problem to appreciate the situation's relevance. Daniel's remarks on what he sees, by *simulating* the customer's voice, serve as mechanisms to strengthen relevance.

4. *The use of the subsidiarity principle in decisions.* Operating power is the power '*to get things done*'; the ability to get others to get things done. In a complex task, despite having all the information, all the knowledge about the situation, if you try to get things done by direct assignment of elementary tasks you will come to a virtual standstill. The volume of information to be handled and the details of each problem will prevent you from reaching safe action procedures. The ability to *get things done* is achieved when you pass on the *information* and demand *action* from your people. Daniel believes that his job is to build the team and get the others to do the work. But not a cheerful, trusting team, as is sometimes portrayed by human resource textbooks, but an efficient, taut team, that makes maximum use of each individual's abilities to achieve Efficiency, Attractiveness and Unity.

'Anywhere you cannot reach, I can, but the service must be impeccable. As I have more influence within the organisation and handle all the resources, I have the power to reassign them.' But be careful – it is expected that everyone in the entire pyramid (each sitting on his 'tennis umpire's chair', the height of which reflects his rank) be able to allocate the resources he has and procure those he needs but doesn't have, to make work easier for the rest of the team. This is the profile of the manager as resource handler. Typically, the common resource that management considers most important is money, but this is often not the case.

5. *The necessity for cascade management.* We have an example of what is done with the 'sundries budget'. Daniel uses this budget as a common fund. But – and this is the important point – how it is used is negotiated by the different parties involved. Budget is 'lent' and 'borrowed' – a truly advanced system that is used in very few classical companies; instead, the budget has traditionally been a tool for wielding power. Typically, the budget is used to bind people to a certain way of operating; they're reined in tight and the result is mutual distrust. It is another example of organisational schizophrenia. The situation also gives rise to 'negative learning'. Senior management distrusts budgets because it knows that the departments will always try to inflate them and, sure enough, the departments always try to inflate their budgets because they know that senior management won't believe them and will try to reduce their budgets further; a magnificent example of how Unity is sacrificed to increase Efficiency. The Teatro Real's system is an attempt, albeit only an attempt and not necessarily the optimal method, to eradicate this type of unhealthy behaviour within the limits imposed by the total budget.

6. *Trust in the other person's action.* Daniel interacts with a team of about ten people. His goal is that each member of the team conveys, in cascade fashion, his management style and methods. Everybody's contribution is accepted and their experience and knowledge is sought to solve the problems. Think again of the problem with the motors. Daniel reminds them that the problem must be solved within a certain time. Once that time has expired, a final decision has to be made. Now comes the interesting part: they ask for more time because they don't want to be beaten by this problem, this challenge. And to get this extra time, they offer to work as many hours as necessary to implement another system if they can't get the present system to work.

This behaviour is based on the premise that if they can't solve the problem, nobody can. The problems are being solved by the experts, the people who know most about them. And the senior manager must have faith in their knowledge... but not blind faith. He must demand, as in the case of the motors, that contingency plans be put into place. It can always turn out that the problem really can't be solved. No quality control of the plan is needed – whatever it turns out to be, we must accept that it's the best they can come up with. The desire to control, know and criticise a plan is only justified when it is believed that the expert needs more training – then the manager may act as an educator, but not as a controller. Involvement in the details can be neither permanent nor absolute. In situations of uncertainty, when you are managing highly qualified staff, you must *delegate by trust.* You've got to trust them, give them room to manoeuvre and then let them decide. There is no other choice; it's the only way forward.

7. *The use of power.* The management of power is one of the key elements in the running of a company, and in society in general; who has the power, who wields it, how it's earned and how it's lost. Power was probably at the root of the irrational behaviour of the first ape that came down from the trees, and it's still there at the core of our society. If the reader looks at it objectively, there is something anachronous, primitive and threatening in the exercise of power, in the desire to control other people's lives. It is as though an ancestral mechanism evolved to ensure the tribe's survival, where the fittest should interfere with and regulate others' lives, because those others are presumably less suited for survival. Within our conceptual framework, it is perfectly clear that by wielding power with the excuse of efficiency, we are decreasing the effectiveness of the other components of the 'Golden Triad'. The exercise of power in a talented environment needs a new vision. And in this sense, what Daniel says is enormously suggestive: *'People think that power is having everything, but power is exactly the opposite; it's giving everything away.'* Food for thought.

There are organisations where power is wielded brutally, and at all levels. We know a large bank where the bosses are known for being very demanding, aggressive and 'tough', they say ... Woe betide the manager who's too *'tough'*! These 'tough' managers probably have very little personal authority or self-belief, and therefore have to over-compensate with snarling faces and fierce reputations. Some of these 'tough' managers talk about delegation and participation, but the fact is it's all a show. We've seen high-level managers quake in their boots when they have to give bad news to their 'tough' boss. No, many managers don't want to uncover problems nor do they want to empower people to solve them – opening that 'Pandora's Box' may lead to their subordinates disagreeing with them, or proposing actions that are not in line with their own plans ... And we all know that the boss knows best – that's why he's the boss! It sounds appalling and perhaps we're presenting it here a bit 'tongue in cheek', but the fact is it's true.

In many organisations, even in some highly successful ones, that's the way it is. A chain of high street stores comes to mind, in which the top boss's authority is absolute, unquestionable and unquestioned. Either you worship him or you're out. And the chain is making piles of money ... so in that type of company, you've got to be very careful not to open that 'Pandora's Box'. Getting people to think is fine when the power to act can be distributed, but it is disastrous if this power is not distributed. If your organisation operates through the straightforward use of power, and then you should read this book as an entertaining intellectual exercise, but don't even try to implement the ideas it contains; the outcome could be disastrous. Even with the best will in the world, you risk spreading scepticism and cynicism in your organisation. Better to wait until more favourable winds are blowing. First, think whether you are willing to give up power and then act in accordance with your beliefs.

Lastly, 'giving away' power, surrendering it, may sound like a romantic dream or an overnight revolution. But at the Teatro Real and perhaps at your company too, it is a necessity to meet deadlines. There is no alternative. And the crucial factor is the existence of highly qualified, talented staff in Operations. Is it possible that your organisation is in the same dilemma and you just haven't realised it yet?

8. *Talent is motivated by the work it achieves.* Leaving to one side the idiosyncratic view that theatre people have about companies, Daniel stresses that he cannot use financial motivation to compensate the personal difficulties imposed by the work. But the fact is that they love their work! The reader will have already seen evidence of this in the preceding chapters.

What can happen in your company is not that different. Money is a very poor motivator. We have always thought that talent-driven organisations must pay a fixed salary and, if possible, a generous one, but in any case one that is linked to the market and the needs of all parties. And forget about supplements and bonuses; these tend to distort everything and divert managers from their true mission. A leftover from the 'workforce' era!

Given adequate pay, we know that the essential motivation of highly qualified staff lies in the work's attractiveness. It is the satisfaction of a job well done that gives them pleasure in their work. That's very different from the motivation described by some experts in human behaviour. It is an intrinsic motivation, arising from the work's own innate appeal.

Has the reader noticed anything strange about Daniel's reference to 'freedom in working hours'? Working from 10 in the morning to 7 in the evening is 9 hours which after taking off an hour for lunch, gives a normal working day of 8 hours. It is a basic timetable that would fill a normal employee's working day. Nor could it really be considered a flexible time-table. But, even more importantly, on top of that there are other obligations. They have to be at the theatre on Sundays for the *ante piano*, pre-general dress rehearsals and so on.

'Quality of life' Daniel says. This is not really 'quality of life', at least not as it is usually understood. Quality of life is usually associated with quality *outside of the job*. But here it is *quality of work*. They like their work, and they feel fulfilled both as people and as professionals!

Sometimes, there is a tendency to present the *family* environment as something at odds with the work environment. Probably because of the loss of the 'craftsman' concept which, rather than viewing a personality as various compartments, viewed the individual as an indivisible whole, without distinguishing between his personal and professional aspects. When humanity started to sell its hands to survive, to companies that wanted the hands to gain profit, a perverse dichotomy started to emerge. Now, people even talk of reconciling[1] personal and professional life, as if they were antagonistic. It is assumed that *personal* life is the good life, the life that gives people their good qualities. And *professional* life is an odious necessity for survival.

Something must change. People must develop as individuals in all aspects, and grow fully in all their activities. Not just exclusively within the family or exclusively at work. The individual is an inseparable unity of many things, including talent and feelings. Let's cultivate talent in the company and exploit it; let's not waste time confronting other values and talking about reconciliation.

9. *Motivation for service well done.* There is another type of motivation that the Teatro Real is achieving. This is the motivation gained by taking part in a common purpose; motivation that appears as a consequence of Unity. Some call it *transcendent motivation*, probably because it appears when you are satisfied with those whose lives are shared with you, they in turn are satisfied with you, and all of you are satisfied with the results of your

---

[1] One of the unfortunate influences of the so-called Western world, whose business impact permeates all the services offered to companies, sometimes to their detriment.

interaction. It can be supposed that the Teatro Real has succeeded in developing Unity from the existence of ties of friendship. Friendship is sufficient for acknowledging other people's preferences, but it is not absolutely necessary – we don't need to be friends for me to take your well-being and your preferences into account in my decisions. All that is needed is for each agent or employee to be willing to understand other people's motives and include them in their own preferences.

10. *Positive and negative rules.* Operational Culture contains positive and negative rules for action. The negative rules should be minimised, but they are a mechanism for defining the limits of a situation. An organised group must impose certain laws that prevent common tragedy, that prevent someone from unilaterally profiting from other people's work, to their detriment. And sometimes rules appear spontaneously that place Unity in jeopardy.

11. *Clarity and sincerity.* An environment of clarity and transparency must be created. This means putting your cards on the table and diagnosing situations using the data; not working with opinions but with facts. Nevertheless, a forum is sometimes needed for expressing doubts and fears of potential problems. Operations Management has managed to create this forum in the Wednesday meetings. It is not automatic; it is not even easy. They have had to build it through trial and error, and they almost gave up. But through perseverance they have managed to achieve a high level of acceptance and problem prevention in the management of their operations.

In our experience as business consultants, it has always been vital to gain the team's commitment through loyalty and transparency. A space or forum must be built where comments and criticism are openly accepted, always knowing that when the meeting ends and we leave the room, there will be no recriminations about what has been said. It's something like what football players say happens on the pitch. Everything that happens or it is said on the pitch stays on the pitch. At the end of the game, it's all over, the slate is wiped clean and everybody starts afresh.

Do you have a special space where problems can be shared openly, with all the cards on the table? What should you do to cultivate both this capacity to foresee situations and honesty between peers?

Closing synthesis

A manager's job is not to 'do' but to have others 'do'. Achieving this goal needs a global view of all the tasks that are being performed and the ability to provide support in situations of conflict. Do you complain that you don't have enough time? This is a clear symptom that you are not correctly performing your management function. As Daniel says, you are not dealing out the cards and getting other people to get things done.

If this is so, 'work' less and, above all, change the way you work. You will achieve nothing alone, no matter how clever and skilled you are; you are but another pebble on the beach. Now think, why do you work like this? Don't you trust how well your people work? Don't you trust their professionalism, their talent? Or do you find it easier to do than to teach and support your people so that they can get on with things? Teaching may take up more of your time than doing. But remember – give a man a fish and he'll eat for a day; teach him how to fish and he'll eat forever.

If you don't teach your people, they won't learn. Thus the company's potential will not develop. The only way to attain an efficient, attractive and united company is to *teach* and *let people do*. Your function as a manager is to give focus to their actions. They will take care of the day-to-day operations while you are there to support them, to get the best from them.

Conclusions

In this chapter, we have summarised the management style required to become a world-class company. We have identified 11 points for implementing this management style, and attaining the New Operational Culture that we need to compete at a world-class level. In the next chapter, we will summarise the recommendations given in the course of the book in a manifesto with 20 key points for implementing this Operational Culture.

To close this chapter, a few final reflections.

- What is your equivalent of the 'Wednesday meetings'? How do you exchange and establish global vision?
- Do you have an informal system capable of handling unexpected situations?
- Do you keep your people taut, or are they relaxed, just following instructions?
- What procedures do you use to achieve this positive tension? There are managers who believe in shouting at people; that you must shout at people because fear will keep them on their toes. Are you one of those people?
- What is your attitude when you observe? Do you give orders on the steps to be taken to fix a situation? Do you point out problems?
- How do you delegate and how do you use the subsidiarity principle? Remember, delegating is not giving power; it is giving authority.
- What is your style of communication and leadership? Do you use the cascade effect? Do you believe in centralised mechanisms? Do they work for you?
- How do you handle Efficiency in your organisation?
- How do you handle Attractiveness?
- How do you handle Unity?
- Do you agree that to manage is to serve? How do you implement it?
- How do you educate your people? And do you get your people to cascade this education downwards?

XXIII
The 'Icosalogue'

All culture is subject to a combination of rules and values. In an attempt to summarise the rules of the New Operational Culture, as the final chapter of this book, we've prepared a list of the twenty basic rules that it must comply with. We are aware that this is necessarily done in broad strokes, but in this way we try to avoid the element of preaching that has so often tainted some of the more classical approaches. We ask the reader not to focus too closely on the aphorisms and follow them to the letter, but rather to meditate on the message. To help in this we provide an introductory commentary for each one.

These twenty precepts (and thus an Icosalogue, rather than a Decalogue – see next page) bring together the ideas that we've seen in this book, and present an easy way to evaluate whether you are on the right path to implement this new way of working. Read, reflect and ponder about how many are already in place.

In this last chapter we are going to summarise the principal rules that lead us towards the *Golden Triad,* in the understanding that this is only a summary – it would be folly to try to present, in just a few rules, something as important as the creation of a new Operational Culture. But perhaps, by calling upon the classics, we can justify our daring attempt. Sancho Panza, the wise friend of Don Quixote, usually summarises his robust wisdom in the form of sayings. Of course, even though our advice is not in the form of sayings, nor can we claim any literary pretensions, the reference is sufficient to justify the approach.

The title of this chapter deserves its own paragraph. The word Icosalogue is a small play on words,[1] if Decalogue is a list of ten precepts (such as the Ten Commandments) then, since we have twenty, we have borrowed the Greek word '*icos*', meaning twenty, and used it as a prefix. Thus we have an Icosalogue, the Twenty Commandments, similar to icosahedron which has twenty faces.

---

[1] Probably originated with Antonio Valero, the first Dean of IESE Business School, who applied it to the list of twenty basic rules for the running of IESE, way back in 1964.

- **Efficiency**
  1. We are 'Yes' Operations, not 'No' Operations.
  2. Keep it simple.
  3. The sense of Operations: Why?
  4. We don't want one million-Euro improvement; we want one thousand thousand-Euro improvements.
  5. Everything is questionable, until we reach an agreement.
  6. Everyone needs to be 'stuck to Operations'.
  7. You can be General Manager, from 0800 to 0805 each day.
  8. Five minutes in advance.

- **Attractiveness**
  9. Don't bring me problems; bring me solutions.
  10. We should be aggressive and bold, but honest.
  11. We work on facts, not on opinions.
  12. In order for improvements to work, everybody involved must benefit (a win-win situation).
  13. To attain World-Class Operations you have to have talent and give it room to flourish.
  14. A good manager must deal out the cards.

- **Unity**
  15. You should not 'do', but rather have others 'do'.
  16. I'm here for you if there is something you can't solve.
  17. A good manager knows how to get the best out of his people.
  18. We work in plural.
  19. To manage is to serve.
  20. To manage is to educate.

Efficiency

1. We are 'Yes' Operations, not 'No' Operations

At some point in our story, Tamayo, Daniel and colleagues affirm that 'We are going to be a YES theatre, not a NO theatre.' We can generalise – 'Are we YES Operations or NO Operations?' Once again, a parallel with IT can help to illustrate the point. There are IT departments in the world whose favourite response to any request is 'No, that's not possible.' Evidently this has variations, such as 'We don't have the budget at the moment' or 'You'll have to wait your turn', but essentially the request is refused.

This attitude is very comfortable for the IT department. We have our work plan and we cannot deviate from that because management won't let us. There is a certain logic. Management in many companies, when presented with elevated costs for systems that rarely work smoothly, tend to demand rigid project plans and that these are strictly adhered to. Incidents and detailed requests distract people from reaching their objectives. 'This year we're implementing Balance Scorecard,' an IT person told us recently, 'We don't have time to change the production programs.' And if they're needed? 'They'll have to wait their turn.' But the same thing happens in Operations.

'Hey, is it possible to bring forward the delivery date of this order?' 'No. It's already scheduled.' 'It's just that there's a new provider who's offering us this type of chip at a better price.' 'No, the purchase order has already gone' and so on.

We have to eliminate this attitude. Every IT or Operations person who responds like that must be removed from the company. We have to be YES Operations. Of course, that doesn't imply an indiscriminate YES, but instead a 'Let's study it properly.' Then really study it, not use that as an excuse to stop. It is not normally possible to attend to all requests. Some might go against the design of the system, or contradict others. If we divert budget from one production to another, then clearly it's going to be difficult to go back and increase the first one. It is a zero-sum game. But submitted requests ask for changes for some reason; not capriciously. And this reason is in all probability associated with positive changes in the Efficiency, Attractiveness or Unity (of a part) of the company. But it is clear that the person making the request is ignoring the effect that responding to it will have on the Efficiency, Attractiveness or Unity of other parts of the company; specifically, that part that has to deal with the request.

Care must be given to all requests because the overall effect can be greater than it first appears. But since requests introduce changes and these changes generate friction, the requester has the right, and the duty, to know with precision what the effect of fulfilling the request will be on all the people who must deal with it.

YES Operations take into account the global situation and the indirect effects of change. NO Operations are a short-sighted form of protectionism that only provides for the comfort of the people involved and generates excuses and bad relationships.

2. Keep it simple

This is a variation of the underestimated Murphy's Law, which is no less important for being folklore. The professional who ignores this rule the most is arguably the System Designer. They tend to implement systems that are too complicated for the users – sometimes even for themselves – and full of obscure characteristics, the working of which nobody really understands and, when somebody tries to use them, fail miserably due to a lack of testing. A perfect example of this may be seen in many ERP (Enterprise Resource Planning) systems. Nobody has a complete understanding of what he or she does, because they're too complex.

However, System Designers are not the only ones. Stage Directors are probably the second group of professionals in the list of those who ignore this rule. We have discovered this in our work with the Teatro Real. In the search for originality, many Stage Directors design overly complicated things.

Luckily, for them, and in clear contrast with our system-design friends, a theatre has a structure that guards against over-complication. The entire technical structure of the theatre is concerned with the *feasibility* of the product. And as they absolutely cannot fail, they concern themselves with guaranteeing the result. The action plan is very simple. In the case of *over-complication*, start *drastically simplifying removing things until it is feasible*. The complexity of an object causes the number of associated interactions to increase exponentially, and the possibilities of failure to increase in the same way.

This rule is central in all types of temporarily innovative processes, such as project management. As a process will probably only be used during a short period, there will not be sufficient time to *debug* it. If we want to eliminate debugging, then we have to make the system as robust and reliable as possible and, most importantly, as simple as possible.

For example, Lleonard Garuz, the Operations Director of the Liceo, assures us that the level of risk in a theatrical production is so high that no company in the world would allow it in their own Operations ... and it's true. Platforms weighing several tonnes rising and lowering, with people on, people coming and going at great heights without handrails or sufficient protection, holes in the stage capable of swallowing up anybody ... this entire set-up maximises the risk of something bad happening. Of course, the counterbalance of this is the extra care and attention of all the participants, with the result that very few accidents actually happen.

In situations of high tension, it's useful to maintain the principle of control unity. The *simplest* system. As a colleague[2] says 'Order plus counter-order equal's disorder'. The management structure, the command, during the performances is designed in this way to react quickly to any eventuality. There is one person responsible for the running of the performance, the stage manager, who takes decisions while the curtain is up. And really it is the same person who commands the function and, without whom, all the rest would feel overwhelmed by this. They all understand the need for this structure, and they work comfortably within it.

3. The sense of Operations: Why?

What is the most important question in Operations? Without doubt, it is 'Why?' Why do we do this in this way? Why do we do it here? Why doesn't someone else do it? Why, why, why ... It's an old idea. Taylor himself recognised it early on in his WWWWH technique, which proposes situation analysis by asking 'Why, Where, When, Who and How?' When faced with any operation, we must ask why are we doing this? Where are we doing this? When are we doing this? Who is doing this? How are they doing this? Of course, this is not just to add to our stock of knowledge; instead, it is to understand, to discover better ways of doing something. The original technique proposed asking 'Why?' up to four times. As a technique, it is

---

[2] Lorenzo Dionis, Emeritus Professor of Operations at IESE, and an ex-military man.

heavy-going and slow, and the questioner could explode at any moment. But the danger is in conforming; conforming with the explanation obtained by the first 'Why?' For example, when the question is asked in a company, the answer is often 'Because we have always done it like that', 'Because it works that way', 'Because it's done like that in this sector', 'Because everyone does it like this' or 'What's the matter, don't you understand?' None of these responses is valid.

The power of 'Why?' comes from the un-scientific nature of operational activities. One is forced by the question to formulate a mental model of the situation; to provide a logical argument that links the cause to the effect; and to submit it to questioning. One of the current authors had a technology professor who visited the United States in 1958. Back then, Spain had a level of development that, shall we say, left a lot to be desired. He returned dazzled by what he had seen. But his more precious discovery was on a badge, in the form of a question. He proudly showed us this badge and said 'Never forget the key to improvement; the basic question, Why?' At that time the young students made fun of him but, as always happens with the passage of time, we finally realised that that professor was right. Even though the professor's attitude at that time was a bit superior.

4. We don't want one million-Euro improvement; we want one thousand thousand-Euro improvements.

Operations can always be *improved*. There is always room for improvement of things, with less time, less cost, greater personal satisfaction or, in the words of previous chapters, in better Efficiency, Attractiveness and Unity.

However, the Operations Managers are not stupid. Indeed, they're very smart. They manage a complicated task that involves many people of a necessarily high level of ability. An example will suffice: the former General Manager of the New York Metropolitan was also previously its Operations Director. It is certain that the greatest improvements, improvements that give rise to profits in the multi-millions, have already been discovered, considered and probably implemented in the majority of companies. In our case, the theatre systems are sufficiently refined that improvements of this kind do not exist, at least not the kind that lead to massive innovations. Any new 'big bang' innovation can only appear through *technological change,* motors instead of counterweights; a *global repositioning* of the company, let's say simple productions based on lighting; or by a change in the *way of competing,* for example, by eliminating in-house productions and renting instead. But typically these things happen only once in a while. To trust in progress through improvements of this kind is hazardous and probably excessively optimistic.

The *typical improvements* found in Operations are those of *low unit result;* low result but high profitability, because typically they don't require investment. We like to tell the story of a company with which we recently collaborated. It's a big company with some 10,000 workers and various plants and operating locations. A presentation was made to the Management Committee about the improvements that had been put into practice in the previous year and those that were about to be implemented. The annual savings totalled some €2,000,000, although none of them exceeded €50,000 individually. When the Management Committee asked when the pay-back would be, the ROI timeframe, they were baffled by the answer: 'Approximately two months', said the plan's presenter. The investment cost was only something like €250,000. The ROI in this case was huge!

Improvements of this type have an important property. They are difficult to *describe* to management. But they are very easy for the operational staff to propose. Those who experience the situation first-hand know that, for example, a particular drill would be much better for this task, because it'll do the job quicker. One of us once visited a factory in which it was easy to see that the way of working had been designed relying on the immediate co-operation of the person who occupied each post. It was impossible that anybody, not even the most expert production engineer, could have managed to design the mechanisms, the hair-splitting details almost, that they employed to simplify the lives and ease the work of the staff. And there is something similar in the Teatro Real. It's clear that everybody has collaborated to better design the work environment. Not the big aspects of the system, such as the bridges, the lifting year and so on, no – this was all done by Tamayo and his colleagues – but rather in the way in which they rig the lighting, how they prepare their plans, how they give cues and calls. The Emergency Book is the result of the teamwork of many people, and it saves time and money, and brings consistency.

5. Everything is questionable, until we reach an agreement.

In our work and teaching, we use a diagnostic method, the KJ methodology, which requires us from time to time to stand up, spread our arms wide, give an almighty clap and shout 'That's it!' This is the signal that we have committed to not going back to discuss again what has been discussed until then. Have we reached an agreement? Right, then let's not go back over it again; let's start working on achieving the result.

We often lose time by resurrecting old ghosts or troubles. This is tremendously inefficient. In the first place, it requires a *communication* system to inform everybody involved that we are changing our way of looking at the problem. Second, we arrive at what some call *inaction by the analysis route*. We analyse the situation so much that we can always find new aspects that make us reconsider the previous decision. This can lead to us being incredibly busy without really doing anything, because there is no way you should leave a group of people reviewing what they've done, so that they discover that they had made mistakes in almost everything. This leads to a block; nobody takes any decisions.

We urge the reader to implement this rule in his or her company. Let's not dig up old bones unless there's incontrovertible proof that there's actually life in them yet. And this must apply to everything. Everything is arguable and answerable – there must be no taboos or forbidden subjects – but once something is agreed, it stays agreed.

The Stage Director must be questioned, and indeed, he is, but not with useless questioning for its own sake, but focused questioning that constructively criticises solutions by providing reasons. Why those solutions will take us over budget, or why it is difficult to achieve from a technical point of view. Remember the case of *Macbeth*. The Stage Director wanted snow. Ok, but who really puts snow on a stage? It's never going to be a good idea. So we have to ask ourselves what he really wants. He wants a sensation of cold. Ah, and can we achieve that without it having anything to do with the temperature? The most intense cold is the cold of the soul (we permit ourselves a little indulgence with that phrase), so that's it. Do we agree? Great, then let's move on and not go back again, because now we have to make the set and this is difficult to re-do in time. We'll portray cold in the soul, but won't have physical cold in the body. Decision made.

Questioning? Yes, for a limited time, but once a thing is decided, let's forget the questions and get to the operation.

6. Everyone needs to be 'stuck to Operations'

To be 'stuck' to Operations means to live alongside the problems of Operations and feel their results at first-hand. Daniel cannot direct Operations at the Teatro Real if he doesn't see, down on the ground and through his own experience, the results of his efforts. We remember the case of the mobile platform in *Don Giovanni* – how can you know about such things if you're not there in rehearsal?

Of course, nobody can be at every single rehearsal; that would be ridiculous. Let's think about the experience of our protagonists. They are capable of directing because they have been directed. One cannot direct without having had the experience previously of what the company's operators (or the people on the receiving end) are going through; without knowing what the singers feel when they have to move about on that mobile platform, perhaps even fearing for its physical stability.

There was a time when people believed that a good manager was capable of managing any *type* of company; that there was something like an art of management that existed in abstract and independent of the managed company. We think that these days few people believe that, and even fewer believe that Operations can be managed without knowledge. Finance is universal, but Operations, being the nucleus of service, does not share this universality. *'Shoemaker, stick to making shoes'*, as one of our protagonists says.

7. You can be General Manager, from 0800 to 0805 each day

People dedicate more time and effort questioning what can't be changed than they do in changing what can be changed. Yes, the production line is too big; no we shouldn't sell ice creams in Vladivostok but in Nairobi ... and so on, thousands of questions. Do the test yourself. Ask the checkout girl at the supermarket or the receptionist at your company, and you'll see how they're capable of criticising a whole host of things that are outside their area of action.

This practice of criticising and questioning leads to two things. In the first place, *frustration*, caused by the mental awareness that something needs to change and the physical impossibility of doing it because it falls outside of your reach. In the second place, *loss of time* and effort, wasted in discussing what to do, instead of trying to do it. Operations must implement strategy, not talk about it. Strategy is not up for discussion; it is accepted or not. The first person who decided to bottle sarsaparilla and call it this-or-that-Cola must have been considered an absolute lunatic by his neighbours. And what does that tell us about the first person who bottled water? What a strategy! But these strategies worked, and a group of people had faith in them. Strategy is always visionary. A group of people formulate a strategy that they commit to implement because they *foresee* it as a winner.

There are two possible reactions to a strategy; either you *integrate* with it or you don't *belong*. It is possible that the Unity of your company cannot be achieved with certain people, because of their beliefs or attitudes. If the collective has decided to follow a particular path and you don't want to follow it, then your clearest option is to exclude yourself and find an alternative collective with which you can identify.

However, all the foregoing does not represent blind acceptance of a strategy by the operators. If operators think that a strategy, or a part of it, is wrong, then they have the moral obligation to fight to change it. But this fight mustn't occupy more than the first five minutes of their day. Anything else can lead to inefficiency or, worse, inefficacy. They won't only waste their own time, but also that of the organisation, and it is from this that we reach the advice that we preach: let's be strategists for just a few minutes a day. But once we've fought within reasonable limits, let's either apply ourselves to the implementation of the common strategy or get out of the company.

8. Five minutes in advance

Five minutes before things happen. In the theatre Operations we've singled out the effort that the theatre people make to eliminate all types of harmful randomness. But when there is nothing else left to be done, there is always a residual randomness remaining that is impossible to eliminate. We know that, in the face of this residual uncertainty, there is only one option: to have all the elements prepared just in case disaster strikes. These five minutes in advance, these are what make the difference between success and failure.

How to be ready five minutes in advance is a relatively simple matter: analyse the *risks*, anticipate their *effects*, have *resources* prepared 'just in case' and have an *action plan* flexible enough to be changed at the last minute if necessary. And all these things must be carefully analysed and calculated because we cannot fall into the infinite resource trap. To maintain extensive resources signifies an enormous cost in capacity that is not normally sustainable.

There are alternatives in the provision of resources. The principal is *polyvalence*. A polyvalent resource is one that can serve various needs. As the events that need facing are by definition random and infrequent, it is usual that the 'just in case' resources are, like the fire service, unused for part of the time. They are also much specialised, because they need to be able to deal with each type of incident, and if they are separate, the cost is the sum of the costs. Polyvalence, if applicable, goes a long way to resolving the problem. You need to have firemen who can also be electricians, let's say, so long as their work as electricians doesn't get in the way of or cause interference with their fire-fighting activity.

To be ready five minutes in advance doesn't only apply to Operations with uncertainty. It also denotes a vigilant attitude on the part of management; something important that they have to do; to see the future. That's what they're paid for. Every manager must try to anticipate what's going to happen, not only in emergencies but also with all the factors surrounding their work, in the short- medium- and long-term.

Attractiveness

9. Don't bring me problems; bring me solutions
This is the golden rule and we have analysed it in-depth previously. When we get our people to resolve problems then we won't only manage to get rid of the obstacles, which is *Efficiency*, but we'll also manage to achieve *learning* in those who participate in the solution and, in the future, this can be more important that the former.

Getting people to solve problems is the foundation for *efficient talent management* in the company. Now we already know that this needs more than just wishing for it. It requires that the people have *initiative*, that they are capable of discovering problems through the use of diagnostic *tools*, that they have the solution *methodology* and that they have, especially, the *authority* to implement the solution. The story of the tenor in Chapter XIX shows what people are capable of doing when they have the initiative and are appropriately qualified.

The Teatro Real places great importance on providing its people with the right conditions for efficient problem-solving. They help them carry out *diagnostics*; the Wednesday meeting is designed for that. But the theatre has also put in place a powerful system for identifying and solving problems before it's too late and the effect is felt in the service. This mechanism is the *rehearsals*.

To be sure, the system could be made even more sophisticated. They could be optimised to further reduce the *cost,* and this will happen over time. The learning that comes about from problems caused by budget restrictions will result in our protagonists discovering new ways of reducing costs. An example – Garuz, the Technical Director of the Liceo in Barcelona, has introduced Pert and bar charts in the planning of productions. No doubt when he started to do these things some people said 'He's gone mad', as they said to Tamayo when he solved the problem of synchronisation by using the *tops* system.

No, we're not saying that companies should rehearse before doing. But we could, couldn't we? Because, after all, a rehearsal is an *experiment* in a controlled environment and observed by experts. Conducting experiments is common in many companies, especially in Operations. We know a food company that is continually experimenting with ways of making their factories more efficient. They experiment with genetic strains, with feeding techniques, with production speeds, with drying systems...They experiment so much that their problem is how to keep track of the experiments and their results, so that the knowledge gained by the solution of problems is not lost and can be used by other people not involved with the experiment.

And we're not discounting the possibility of *virtual experiments*. The 'what if?' technique is a technique of experimentation, achievable through a simple spreadsheet. If they were documented and filed, the spreadsheets existing in many companies would be an excellent resource to help in problem-solving.

10. We should be aggressive and bold, but honest

There are many people who are politically correct or who shrivel up when the boss contradicts them; far too many. Of course, there are also bosses who don't let people contradict them which means (since he's the boss) that people don't. Is this bad? We think that it is not only bad but also wicked because we lose talent. He who keeps quiet, despite knowing that something isn't right, is harmful. He should be fined for putting those around him at risk. But the boss who gets annoyed by contradiction should be thrown out for being the cause of losing talent.

Human respect sometimes leads us to be too political (although not prudent) in our way of speaking. Circumlocution is a waste of time and muddies the waters in problem definition, and a problem that is not clearly defined is much more difficult to solve than one that is.

In the theatre world, clarity is imperative. They tend to say things clearly. 'This doesn't work. It doesn't fit...let's try again.' We have rarely seen them hide the situation behind ambiguous words. One of the protagonists told us that there are times in the theatre when the artistic directors cause great hilarity with their proposals. This hilarity is probably due in part to the clash between the conceptual proposal and the real context in which it's made. The relationship between the two worlds is so absurd that it's laughable.

We're sure that the reader has experienced the same situation. We've all seen 'Brainstorming' on meeting agendas. Brainstorming is a well-known creative technique that essentially consists of speaking before thinking. Fine, we like this, although we know that it doesn't work like that in reality. In front of the boss, nobody will dare to speak without thinking. So we begin, the ideas start appearing, and the majority are variations on a couple of common sense ideas, with very little creativity at this stage. Suddenly someone says something stupid and we all have a great laugh, even the person who made the stupid suggestion, although he or she usually appears a little redder than before.

Be careful though, this 'something stupid' is probably the most interesting idea proposed in the whole session. We advise the reader to take note each time something provokes a guffaw and later perform a detailed dissection of the 'stupid' proposal, trying to find the significance behind it. Using this technique, we've seen many creative ideas appear.

11. We work on facts, not on opinions

Too many organisations devour people. We know a company that specialises in getting rid of its most brilliant talent. Why? Because it doesn't provide them with any type of *information* about what is happening in and around the organisation. If they're not selling product in Barcelona, let's say, nobody does any kind of information collection nor supports any initiative to find out the possible objective causes of the situation. The result is that people take decisions based on the only thing they have: their own *opinions*. If they guess correctly, they get praise; if they get it wrong, they get criticism.

It is impossible to hope that one person will always have good judgement in things if they cannot collect and analyse the *facts*. Company logic is not mathematical or physical logic. In physics, it is sometimes unnecessary to observe the real world. A process of introspection may discover the facts. Of course, one would have to be very clever, impossibly so, to discover all the mathematic facts and have them all at one's disposal to be able to use them in reasoning. A mathematic fact is that $\sin(2\alpha) = 2\cos(\alpha)\sin(\alpha)$. For some of our readers, perhaps very few, this is a trivial fact, but it is a sure thing that the majority of people do not need these facts immediately available, even though they may be arrived at through reason, without the need for experiment.

In corporate situations, this is much more complicated. Nevertheless, 'it seems to me...', continues to be one of the most widely used techniques. Of course, there are times when there is no alternative, but it is as wrong to use it when you shouldn't as it is to not use it when you must. Conclusion: as far as possible, base reasoning on *facts*, not *opinions*. Keep the opinions for those times when getting the facts is too difficult or expensive, or when they are simply not *observable*.

12. In order for improvements to work, everybody involved must benefit (a win-win situation)

This is the famous principle of selfishness that we've used ad nauseam. Companies must be ruled by egoism, of a type that is well understood. 'Well understood' egoism is a politically correct form of egoism that does not have stabilising power because it is a variety of *altruism*. Altruism must be exiled from companies because it leads to giving, to making concessions in which one party ends up losing to achieve a positive result for the rest. Think of the end-of-year bonuses; the company, generously, gives more money to its employees as a reward. But this reduces its profits. No problem; this year has been profitable and the bonuses only amount to 5 per cent of the total profit. Fine. But now, think what would happen in a year when the profits were not so good, and the same bonuses would represent 60 per cent of the profits. Would anyone be willing to bet that the bonuses wouldn't be smaller, or even non-existent? What would the effect on the people be? Probably worse than if the company had never handed out any bonuses at all.

Altruism is *unstable*, and this instability comes about because one of the parties loses something and the other party gains it. How can we stabilise these situations? Very simple, we have to make everybody win. In the case of the distributor of the bonuses, they must be clearly and measurably the profits that for the company represent the bonuses. Increase the production for it? The motivation? The result of the bonus must be an increase in the satisfaction of the person who receives it, an increase that would be destroyed if it wasn't given out one year. And if this is not possible, then it is better to give nothing. The decision should be implemented only if it is demonstrable that the result compensates the cost of its implementation, even in moments of crisis.

Never, in no time or place, will anybody do anything stable in which there is no long-term gain. It is our responsibility to ensure that this happens in all the decisions that we have to take.

13. To attain World-Class Operations you have to have talent and give it room to flourish

This is the key to being a leading company, a world-class company – you have to have talent and give it room to act. As we saw in Chapter XX, you have to 'wring out' the talent. The exploiter wins because he collects the fruits of the talent's labour. But the exploited wins because he increases his own capital. With work he learns, and this learning makes him more worthy for society and thus is in a better position to sell his own knowledge to whoever needs it. This is a marvellous property of knowledge – its use produces results, but at the same time, it produces learning.

The theatre supports its talent. The soloists, the Stage Director, the lighting people, stage managers and so on. All of them are talented people. Companies, too, are full of talented people. Talent is then a consequence of the existence of trained people and the selection process of companies. Companies look for talent.

A friend of ours, a branch manager of a bank, told us a little while ago that he has seven people working at his branch. Seven of them have a degree, and one has two. He said 'I put the one who has two degrees in the archive, to see if I can get more out of him.' Of course, the other six do all sorts of routine administrative jobs. He was failing the seventh because he wasn't *giving him a chance*, because if it's a question of having talent, he certainly had it.

Giving talent a chance is an indispensable condition for making the most of it. Daniel has lots of talent at the Teatro Real. The theatre itself is based on talent. Now the problem is to set it in motion. How to do this? It's not easy, but by now we've managed almost an entire book dealing with it.

14. A good manager must deal out the cards

Daniel tells us that he 'deals out the cards' in the Wednesday meetings. Dealing the cards means helping to anticipate what the critical issues of the week are going to be, their interactions with everything else, and the problems that will have to be solved to overcome the situation. As we saw, Daniel turns up at the meeting with a wad of printed papers, in which he has outlined how he has anticipated events for the period in question, and he hands these out to each of his assistants. To make the analogy of a croupier, he speaks of 'dealing out the cards'.

The 'cards' are not lists of *instructions* to follow, nor are they procedures. To use them in that way would be to return to the arcane Operational Culture of 'manpower', telling each person what he has to do and how. The dual function of the carts is, first, to alert people to the possible *interactions* between the departments, thus providing a *global vision* of the work to be done, and second to ease the *diagnosis* of problems, alerting people to their possible appearance before it actually happens (while always taking into account advice number 8).

The participants retain the initiative. They are the ones who will be responsible for diagnosing the problem and identifying it if it appears and in what form, to then solve it. And they're going to have to consider their specific actions from the point of view of all the other participants in the situation.

The reader must be conscious of the power of these types of actions. Sometimes it seems enough simply to work together, and that talking to each other is enough to be able to work as a team. But nothing could be further from the truth. Meetings are an extremely effective way to waste time. A lot of energy is spent talking in an unstructured way and with mediocre results. Meetings do not guarantee teamwork. Teamwork is about solving problems in a global manner, taking into account the impact on everyone else, the available shared resources and the knowledge base of the entire group. Teamwork requires methodology, and dealing the cards is an interesting one.

Dealing the cards requires an exhaustive analysis by the dealer. He or she has to determine the interactions and anticipate the problem areas, without giving rules for their resolution even if these seem obvious. This demands a mental model of the situation and of the role of the agents. The development of this model continues day-by-day, because it changes constantly. The burden this represents for the dealer is considerable, but at the same time, it is one of the key techniques in *motivating others to 'do'*.

In an industrial company we have worked with, the logistics have always been done by the logistics department working in isolation. The other departments, specifically Operations, limit themselves to delivering the merchandise and logistics looks after everything else. To achieve co-operation between the departments, they created a cross-department work group but didn't set this group any mission. They were limited to meeting once per week, and one of the current authors 'dealt the cards'. In preparation for this, we had previously worked with management on the different aspects of the problem and had proposed the cards to be dealt. After a couple of months, we withdrew from the team, leaving management the task that we'd begun. The success was spectacular. People learned to work together and the weekly meeting is now being seen as a key method to achieve synergies between the departments. Management has learned to manage and the process functions very smoothly.

Unity

15. You should not 'do', but have others 'do'

This is the cornerstone of the new culture, even more so than 'don't bring me problems...' But it is fundamentally about the work of management. The manager who wants talent to flourish, in the form of better solutions to problems and the simultaneous creation of knowledge, must think that he or she alone, isolated, cannot do anything. Therefore, the only thing that he or she can do is to get other people to do.

No matter how clever the reader may be, we're fairly certain that he or she only has one brain and no more than two hands. And working at full capacity he or she will still, at best, use 110 per cent of his brain and 120 per cent of his hands. In total, that's worth the same as 1.15 people. A pittance! What we need to achieve is that the, say, 100 people who work on one directive think and act 100 times more than one person on their own.

This looks easy. The industrial revolution wanted to do this with hands, sharing out the work. Tell each person what he or she has to do and bye, bye. But this only works when we know exactly how to do the job, that is, when we know exactly how to solve the problem, and we can reduce it to operational procedures. We can then break it down, assign it and control it, and then we have our nineteenth-century factory working at full capacity.

Imagine this process in the Teatro Real. We might be able to do this for some things, but it's doubtful. But if the environment is random and flexible we'll have a problem of specification. There is no way to define precisely the complete content of the job. Think of the *tops* system; what is this for? Is it an assembly line? No, clearly not. It is just a way of synchronising the solutions to problems. What the person receiving the *top* has to do is only partially specified, and it is supposed that they have to be capable of filling in the details to reach the desired effect, which is in effect the content of the *top*. *Top 36*, smoke. But how should this be done? Because, as we've said, smoke depends on unpredictable factors such as humidity, the number of people and so on. Conclusion: The *tops* are the elements of co-ordination in the action, not signals of a production line.

The theatre specifies the desired result. It is confident that, with the right rehearsals and training, the operator will be able to solve the problem, of obtaining the result even when the elements seem to be working against him. When we attended *La Dolores* we saw an example. After the party in the second Act, some poles that had fallen off one of the carts were left on stage. Someone who looked like an extra picked them up and took them off. Was this foreseen? We know that it wasn't. But we also know that the person responsible improvised a solution so that the poles weren't left there, creating a danger for the actors.

Getting people to 'do' must be the obsession of every manager. One of the current authors heard this for the first time from the mouth of a high-level manager of Hughes Aircraft in El Segundo, California. Talking with this gentleman, in charge of the aerospace design area with more than 2000 people reporting to him, we asked him about his timetable. He replied 'I go home at five, and I make sure nobody is left here. Similarly, I want absolutely everyone here at eight in the morning and ready to work at full capacity during the day. And, he added, 'my work consists of getting them to do things during the day with the maximum efficiency. I am only one small piece in this machine.' Lesson learned.

16. I'm here for you, if there is something you can't solve

This is the subsidiarity principle applied to management. We have placed great emphasis on *getting people to do* and on each person having to solve problems. But in practice there are situations in which it is impossible for one person to have access to all the resources that would permit him to solve the problem. For example, because it needs an investment whose size exceeds his powers, or because it affects internal or external elements of the Operations. Just because the props manager decides that he's going to build the Rolls-Royces in *Don Giovanni* does not necessarily mean that he has sufficient power to sub-contract the necessary work, or sufficient budget to pay for it. But, and this is crucial, the problem is still essentially his. What happens is that there are parts of the structure that fall outside of his area of action. Simply that.

This is where the higher-ups come to the rescue. One of the current authors in her life as a senior manager, used to tell her subordinates

> I only need three things from you. First, that you train your people. Second, that you look after the resources assigned to you so they are not squandered. And third, that you reach where your people cannot, for which you need to know precisely where they need to reach.

Indeed, a lot of the work of Operations management would be better done if it were limited to these three principles, instead of trying to meddle in the operation that the subordinates normally run perfectly well anyway.

17. A good manager knows how to get the best out of his people

We have arrived at the last four rules that essentially define the PDM management style. The first obligation for all managers is to know your people and know where they can reach. In more formal terms, we'd say that you have to know their knowledge profile and their ability to absorb challenges. From a knowledge point of view, this determines the problems that can be solved, and his or her capacity to face new situations. Every problem is a challenge for the person, and this challenge depends on the knowledge that he or she possesses.

Innovation being one of the key variables, the combination of challenge and stock of knowledge determines the degree and type of innovation that our people can stand before collapsing. In the theatre, Daniel talks of theatrical common sense to denote the constants of knowledge, the knowledge that is common to all the people, and that form a base upon which innovation management could be made more efficient. At the Teatro Real there are many new things, but the majority of them do not alter the basic principles. All of them are platforms that go up and down, step motors, lights that focus, and sets that are constructed with socket drives. Nobody is going to appreciate a challenge in this area.

A manager must ensure that his people grow in the desired direction, to prepare them to provide the maximum contribution to the well-being of the group. Setting aside the knowledge of his people, the manager must identify where he wants to arrive with each one, how to achieve that, what their distinctive competencies are and to what point they may be developed. This identified set will provide him with the innovations and challenges that should be proposed to each one to exploit the individual talent. And, as a by-product, talent learns.

18. We work in plural

In the theatre, nothing that is important can be done by only one person; everything requires the participation of others, not necessarily in an explicit form, of course, but certainly inherently. This is not frequently found in companies. Traditionally, the company divides the work so that all can do their things on their own, without the help of others. Help is considered to be a waste of time and effort.

However, we have to take into account the effect that things done 'in plural' has on Attractiveness and Unity. In particular, the degree resulting from the collaboration, to which the people integrate and identify with the mission of the company. When the stage manager works with the lighting people, it is probably certain that the lighting people could do their work alone, but they would lose the sensation of shared work, of a joint collaboration in the creation of a scenic work of art.

This is not teamwork, though; teamwork was defined earlier as a variety of work based on talent. The 'plural' to which we refer is the integration of everyone in the ensemble of the show, of the product; the sensation that we're dealing with a combined job, not the sum of the isolated jobs of the participants.

It is the duty of management to ensure that the benefits of working in plural are not outweighed by the inconveniences. As in teamwork, working in plural requires methodology. In the first place, everybody has to know the purpose of the things they are doing. If we are setting up a mobile platform for *La Bohème*, we must know that the chorus will be on that platform and that a large part of the second Act will take place there. This is an issue related to the relevance that we analysed in Chapter XIX. It is part of the implementation of relevance. If we manage to organise this plural work, we will have taken important steps in achieving this characteristic.

Later we'll have that sensation of a job well done that comes from seeing how all the elements link up to provide a spectacular result, in such a way that what we ourselves have done is not noticeable. In a company of talent, it is important to eliminate the ownership, typical in industry, of 'this piece was made by John'. The true scale of working in plural is found in the disappearance of 'this is my work' and the emergence of 'this is the result of *our* work'.

19. To manage is to serve

To direct is not the same as to order or command. If the reader has had the patience to read this entire Icosalogue (well, even if he or she has only read half) then he or she will have noticed that the management style underpinning this advice is very far from the concept of giving orders. Nor is it about taking decisions. One of the current authors maintains that there are no decisions,[3] in reality there are only alternatives. It's always clear what needs to be done ... when it's clear what needs to be done.

Let's explain that. In the Teatro Real there are no alternatives around the creation of a determined set. There is a way to obtain the correct result, but nobody tries to look for and choose other ways. In the first place, this is because, as they're problems with a high-exploratory content, we know well that the difficulty is in finding one and only one way of arriving at the desired result. Creativity is focused on finding a feasible solution, not in choosing between various. This is the basic property of exploratory problems. Formulating corporate strategy does not consist of choosing between various. How many more would we want? What is fundamental is being capable of finding one that takes us to the desired result.

So, what do we mean by 'to direct'? Well, it's a bit of everything. To scan the horizon, to be able to see what nobody else has seen, to be able to help others to create an action plan, to develop them so they reach the furthest possible, to ensure learning, to get people to 'do' ... this is fundamentally a *service* to all those who work in the company. They must obtain the best *result*. Our role as managers is to create an environment where all this is *possible*. This is fundamentally *to serve*. Not to order. To be at the disposal of others to make them go places where nobody has gone before.

20. To manage is to educate
We have arrived at our last point and, as a final point, it is also the most difficult; to become an educator. What does it mean to become an *educating manager*? It means to support the development of knowledge and experience; to guide others in their problem-solving process, providing vision to the group; to rehearse.

And this is very hard. As a manager said to us 'This is the hardest thing I've ever done in my life.' And that's logical; to order is easy, but to get someone to understand is very difficult. So difficult that it is a profession. But professions can be learned.

When we manage highly qualified people, the conventional models are unsuitable and require another Operational Culture. But the person who is most questioned is the manager. And not for who he is, but for how he acts. People value managers who take the time to be with them, supporting them, showing them ways to act or revealing sources of knowledge. The more prepared people are, the greater the need to manage by educating. We have seen some people do this innately, but the majority feel lost in the face of this new management challenge.

The big problem is that nobody *teaches* managers how to *educate*. But it isn't complicated. *Patience and knowledge* are the key points. It is about *letting people do* while providing *knowledge, shaping* their *way of thinking*. And the way to do this is simple; it's simply a matter of *working side by side*.

---

[3] And this infuriates the other author, who spends her life deciding.

There are business schools giving courses specifically on how to become an educating manager. We don't think this is necessary. Our advice is that if the style of this new Operational Culture is in line with your ideas, then start implementing it. Be humble and recognise that there are things you don't know how to do, but that you're going to try to do them. Nobody expects you to be super-human; we're only asking you to work with perseverance. To become an educator is to understand that one wants to *teach*. It is to assume that the earth is moving beneath your feet and you have to adopt new ways of working. Don't take courses; tell your people 'here I am, ready and willing to *support you* and to convey what I know. But I am also willing to learn, because there is nothing that increases one's own knowledge more than *teaching* others'.

Conclusions

In this final chapter, we have summarised the basic ideas of our Operational Culture proposal. PDM can be summarised in these twenty aphorisms that we have divided between the three dimensions of the Golden Triad. Perhaps the reader might consider this summary to be a bit folkloric, but after so many years trying to teach, we have reached the conclusion that the best way is through simple and clear messages. That is the objective of this Icosalogue. Twenty maxims that can serve as a guide to apply the ideas expounded in this book.

Annexe

Self-evaluation questionnaire

We present here a small self-evaluation exercise to help the reader analyse his or her management style, seen through the Operational Culture that we propose. The exercise is very simple; it consists of completing the table below in an intuitive way, without worrying about being too precise – it's more important to obtain a relative position in each issue, rather than exact percentages. If you prefer you can substitute percentage with 'Degree', as we've done in some questions, and use a response scale of one to five (from 1 being Very High, through High, Medium, Low to 5 being Very Low).

The table has the following structure. In the first column, we place sentences from the Icosalogue. In the second, we give an example of the type of question that could be asked to specify its use in the management of your company. The third column is an example indicator that may help to evaluate the implementation of an idea. The fourth and last column is left blank for you to complete with an estimation of the 'score' of the example indicator, or the degree to which you recognise the sign.

Using this table, it is possible to obtain a snapshot of the degree of implementation of the new Operational Culture.

	Example	Example indicators	Score
EFFICIENCY			
1. We are 'Yes' Operations, not 'No' Operations.	What do I do to achieve a positive attitude in the face of a problem?	The percentage of times that people tell me 'No it can't be done' without having carefully analysed it.	
2. Keep it simple.	What things are complicated to do? Where do I have confusions?	The percentage of time my colleagues spend solving or fixing complications.	
3. The sense of Operations: 'Why?'	How can I get people to think about the causes of things that happen?	The percentage of time that I spend explaining to people so they understand what is happening.	
4. We don't want one million-Euro improvement; we want one thousand thousand-Euro improvements.	What can I do to find one thousand-Euro improvements?	The number of smaller improvement actions presented or approved during last month.	
5. Everything is questionable, until we reach an agreement.	Must we always go back to the same problems? What can I do to settle issues?	The percentage of meetings where questions are asked again about issues previously solved.	
6. Everyone needs to be 'stuck to Operations'.	Am I in daily contact with the reality of our service?	The percentage of time during which I am in direct contact with the company's Operations.	
7. You can be General Manager, from 0800 to 0805 each day.	Do we waste a lot of time in meetings questioning where the company is going?	The percentage of meetings in which the strategy of the company is questioned.	
8. Five minutes in advance.	How do I get my people to anticipate problems and to be prepared to solve them? Am I blaming anyone?	The percentage of problems that have been made worse by not dealing with them sooner.	

(Continued)

	Example	Example indicators	Score
ATTRACTIVENESS			
9. Don't bring me problems, bring me solutions.	How can I develop my peoples' problem-solving capacity? How can I identify the gaps in their knowledge?	The percentage of my time spent with people coming to me with problems.	
10. We should be aggressive and bold, but honest.	Do I create a climate of honesty? Do I recognise when I'm mistaken? Do I allow my people to contradict me?	The number of times that my people have corrected me in the last month.	
11. We work on facts, not on opinions.	Do we work with methods based on facts? Do we go with gut reactions? Do we have analysis methodologies?	The percentage of data relevant to the company's problems that are systematically collected and analysed.	
12. In order for improvements to work, everybody involved must benefit (a win-win situation).	Do I know what each person in my team wants?	The degree to which I know the personal objectives of each member of my team.	
13. To attain World-Class Operations you have to have talent and give it room to flourish.	How do I manage these 'brains'? Do I clarify my service priorities? Am I consistent between what I do and what I say?	The degree to which I give instructions instead of leaving my collaborators to give their opinions.	
14. A good manager must deal out the cards.	Do I foresee problems?	The percentage of problems that are detected because somebody alerted the others of the existence of those problems.	
UNITY			
15. You should not 'do', but rather have others 'do'.	Do I get bogged down in detail? Do I give people the liberty to take decisions? Do I accompany them in their decisions?	The percentage of my time that I dedicate to solving problems that others could solve.	

(Continued)

	Example	Example indicators	Score
16. I'm here for you if there is something you can't solve.	Am I at the disposal of my collaborators so that they come to me when they need to? Can I provide them with help?	The number of requests received in the last month asking for help in overcoming organisational barriers.	
17. A good manager knows how to get the best out of his people.	Do I obsess over the future of my people in the company? Do I stimulate their growth? Do I support them to 'fill in' their knowledge-gaps?	The percentage of time that I dedicate to support, orientate or develop behaviours, instead of correcting, specifying, controlling or ordering.	
18. We work in plural.	Do we take decisions by consensus? Do we respect the opinion of the specialist?	The percentage of problems that are solved by group consensus.	
19. To manage is to serve.	Do I create the right environment where people will share their problems with me? Do I support them when they've made a mistake?	The percentage of time that I dedicate to helping my collaborators.	
20. To manage is to educate.	Do I search for ways in which people can learn? Do I understand their individual differences? Do I adjust their challenges to the level of their knowledge? Do I introduce innovations to help them learn?	The percentage of time that I personally dedicate to educate my collaborators.	

Epilogue

Conversation with maestro Jesús López Cobos

We end this book in conversation with maestro Jesús López Cobos. López Cobos is a client of the Technical department of the Teatro Real. His extensive experience of many opera theatres helps us to have a more objective view of the service that he receives. He is a demanding client, and with his help we submitted the Teatro Real to scrutiny ... and we believe the Teatro Real passed the test with flying colours.

It is perhaps unnecessary to introduce maestro López Cobos. He is known throughout the world, and we are privileged to have him put his 'Midas touch' to the end of this book. He is the ideal person, having worked with innumerable opera theatres, to explain to us what the Operations department of the Teatro Real has provided him with.

Maestro López Cobos: The theatre has always fascinated me. I practically started my career in the theatre. When I started I was in Venice and then two years later I went to the Berlin opera. I knew that theatre for 19 years; a show every day, 50 different operas each year. I think, therefore, I've seen just how much it is fascinating for me always to have a show prepared and ready to go.

I think that raising the curtain is a miracle, an everyday miracle. Here it's a miracle every 15 days, but there it was every day. It's incredible, the capacity that an organisation must have in order for the technical part, the musical part, the artistic; all the organisation comes together in such a way that at a pre-determined moment, at eight o'clock on the dot, the curtain goes up and everything works. I have always found this fascinating, and I continue to do so to this day.

For a theatre to function, it is fundamental that there is organisation and continual communication between departments. We are all dependent upon one another. The Artistic Director can have ideas, but perhaps they're not realistic if they can't be put into practice with the techniques and resources available. It is fundamental that the theatre recognises its own limitations and qualities, and how far it can go. The theatre tends to be conservative by nature, preferring not to risk raising the curtain and finding itself with unforeseen problems.

We are often afraid in the theatre of offering all our possibilities, both technical and musical, for fear of failure. I have seen theatres risking everything to the limit, believing that it would work, and the result has not been positive. Other theatres have never reached the limit of their possibilities. For example, the technical possibilities of this theatre have been seen in the odd production, but not in all of them. This is one of the problems of co-production. Theatres tend to co-produce to reduce costs, but not all of them can do it so well because the level is not the same. The levels are often different; perhaps they are the same on the artistic side but not on the technical. You take a production that you want to stage here and perhaps it doesn't make the most of the theatre's possibilities. That's why you have to sometimes do new productions, to show the exceptional possibilities of this theatre.

From the musical point of view, is the increasingly technological nature of theatres a little disconcerting?

Yes, there needs to be a balance. From my point of view, we musicians often have the sensation that these days we're the lowest in the theatrical pecking order. The technical side, the staging, is what counts, what sets the guidelines. For us, this relationship is always negative, a point of friction. We Musical Directors are always trying to defend our territory so that the music doesn't end up relegated to last place.

In this respect, until now I've always felt very comfortable in the Teatro Real, because they are implementing a philosophy I like, that I learned in Germany. You'll remember that there they don't call it opera, but 'musical theatre'. The two words, 'theatre' and 'musical' are of equal importance. They always say in Germany that the quality of a performance starts and ends with the chorus and the orchestra. And they're completely right. I'm trying to instil the idea in this theatre that the chorus and the orchestra are fundamental. Of course, that all depends on being lucky enough to have a good Stage Director and good singers.

Do Stage Directors nowadays tend to be 'prima donnas'?

They have become so somewhat through the media. A lot of emphasis is placed on the staging. They have also created the myth of the rebel director, who wants to change everything. From the curiosity point of view, it can be interesting to see what a Stage Director might think of doing with *La Bohème* or *La Traviata*. But the Stage Directors are also a victim of themselves. They associate themselves with the image of an innovative director, and then of course they always have to do something new.

And can musicians put an end to this?

There is always a way out, which is not to do it. The best is to prepare and anticipate. When I've done new productions, I've always tried to get involved as early as possible by talking to the Stage Director to know what he's thinking of doing. So far, I've been lucky. I have done things in Germany that have been quite controversial. I worked in the time in which Friedrich Tuve was General Musical Manager, a great professional, with a modern but fantastic vision of opera. I had some contact with 'mad' things but here, so far, I've never had to say 'I'm not doing this.' But if that time comes, I will. Everything depends on who the Stage Director is and this is the work of the

Artistic Director, to not only choose which productions we do, but also to say to which artist and to which singer(s) we give the role.

We've been very interested by how much people in the Teatro Real get involved in the project, through the service they provide. Is this universal? Are people so integrated in other theatres?

No, no, not at all. There are theatres in which, when you ask questions, you realise that nobody even knows, for example, who's in charge of the audio-visuals. They just don't appear; you don't know who's who, nobody to ask, you have to call them and tell them to please come along. Here everybody is very involved in the production. During the rehearsals absolutely everybody is here: the audio people, the stage management, the Operations Director... right the way up to the artistic management, there is always someone there. They keep a close eye on the day to day, how the show's working, how it's being set up... I think that's fundamental, above all in our system, because each production lasts a short time and, when it's over, you have to quickly go to the next. In Germany, for example, it's much more clinical, because it functions from one day to the next, or in the New York Metropolitan, or the Chicago Opera, where I directed recently.

What are the differences you notice between, for example, the Metropolitan and the Teatro Real?

The Metropolitan is a seasonal theatre with a huge repertoire. The difference is that they, for example, have a very simple stage, much older, and so they don't have the same technical possibilities that we do here. Also, the shows in the United States are much more conservative than here. Our productions are much more modern, and in this aspect I believe that our theatre is more advanced.

Practically the same thing happens in the Bastille Opera. The architects didn't design the new Bastille theatre 'humanely' – they put the auditorium on top, and everything else below. When directors come here, they're surprised to see, for example, natural light. All the singers who come here say the same. In the Liceo, which was recently renovated, the orchestra's rehearsal room is tiny, and it's really difficult to work in there. All of this greatly reduces peoples' performance. You always have to think how to get the best out of people who are working every day in a theatre.

When 'lay' people talk of the Teatro Real, they all say 'Ah yes, but the best X is at the Metropolitan or the Bastille has the best Y.' Very few know these things about the Teatro Real. Do they know these things in the world of opera?

Yes, all the singers say it; all of them. When they come to work here, they say 'Wow, it's fantastic to work in this theatre. I love coming to rehearse here,' and about other theatres they'll say 'Hmm, that's nothing like it. They have a lot of money and put on star-studded shows with big names, and the objective work conditions in these theatres was very good maybe 30 or 40 years ago, but not now – they're just old-fashioned.'

We've been to various rehearsals of *Don Giovanni* and, at the time scheduled for the end of rehearsal, the musicians put down their instruments and leave

That's the same all over, despite us having flexible times. In the United States, it's incredible – there they have rigid, fixed rehearsal schedules, including breaks and everything, and you can't change them. Our orchestra is private, and they're incredibly flexible. I can decide at the beginning of a four-hour rehearsal how I'm going to use those hours, according to the technical needs. I can organise the four rehearsal hours according to the set changes and how long it takes to do them. Typically, we'll follow a standard timetable. We'll do an hour and ten minutes, then a twenty-minute break, another hour and ten, another break, and finally an hour. But if, for example, we start with an hour and twenty, later we'll do an hour, then another hour and twenty, then a twenty-minute break, then a final half hour. This could never happen in the United States; you have to start and stop by the clock, regardless of where you are in the rehearsal. And if the break fits with the set change, fantastic, but if not then you just have to put up with it.

Logically, we have a timetable. And people stop at the end of it, because you have to respect the contracts. If the rehearsal is four hours' long, then it must be four hours. You can't say 'today we're going to do ten minutes more'. Well, that has happened here occasionally, but nobody tends to say anything because it works the other way too – the other day I let them out early. But normally we stick to the timetable.

And the management of the technical operations?

From the musical point of view we don't get quite so involved in how it works. But what I do know is that, here, when something has to be changed on the fly, for example during the rehearsals, they are incredibly effective; they're so fast. You say to them 'Excuse me, sorry, but that doesn't work for me here; could you give me a monitor speaker for when they're singing on the stage?' The technical possibilities here are so fantastic that you don't even have to wait until the next rehearsal. They'll do it there and then. They say 'No problem, you'll have it in five minutes.' This demonstrates the operational capacity of the theatre; that you don't have to wait until the following week.

It's true; the operations people truly care about contributing their service towards the result. There is none of that 'we'll put the set up and from there you're on your own'. Here I always find great support and this helps facilitate many things. For example, for *La Bohème* we're doing this year, which is so complicated, we have only rehearsed three days with the orchestra. That's all. We're talking about a production that was prepared five years ago! And we've such a high degree of precision that, from the first rehearsal, all the set changes have gone perfectly. If that's not the case, you really suffer, because as a musician you can't help but think 'Let's see what'll happen; I wonder if this is going to work.' When you see everything running like clockwork, you're much calmer and can concentrate on the music. If not, you're always dependent upon what's going to happen.

From the moment the curtain rises you're calm, because they're there with their *tops*...

Ah yes, and you realise that they know it perfectly well. One thing we really like is that when you stop in the orchestral rehearsals you don't even need to say what bar you're at in the score, nor the associated *top*. You say 'Let's jump to this bar or that' and everybody knows exactly where you are; they know the book because the stage manager has the annotated score. You realise that they know the opera perfectly – the book as well as the music – and this really helps the rehearsals to go smoothly.

To what do you attribute all of this? To the people being new, being young?

To the fact that we have not had a tradition of opera. We've done everything from scratch. And when you start a theatre from zero, there are times when you'll be lucky, and there are things that get set up well and later work well. I think the technical department of this theatre was set up very well.

We were lucky, and the fact that there is no permanent orchestra means that this didn't prejudice things from the outset. If you have a national orchestra, an orchestra of 'civil servants' almost, then there's really nobody who can alter things; there's no way to change it or improve it. In this respect, I think it was a real innovation here. In fact, this is the real reason why I accepted the offer to come here to the Teatro Real.

I've immersed myself in opera for the past 20 years, although I've always loved it. I spent ten years not doing any opera, but in 2000, I decided I'd return to it, and I started again at the Bastille. But my idea was to be there as an invited artist, to do one production in a good theatre and nothing else.

When they spoke to me about the Teatro Real, my reaction was 'Oh...the theatre again, and a permanent position.' But when I came here the first time as a guest director, in 2001, and I saw the work I said to myself 'Well, it seems to me that this theatre is actually worth working at.' And I then took a very special decision, because I'd spent almost all my life abroad, and the three or four years I was in the National Orchestra were not very pleasant. Of course, to return to my country, to return to work and give a bit of my experience back to my own country, well, that seduced me. But before then I'd never really thought of returning, especially not to opera, because opera is far more complicated than orchestra. It has been a wonderful experience for me. I never thought I was going to be able to work and live in a theatre at the incredibly high level that you can work at here.

Bibliography

Boden, Margaret, *The Creative Mind: Myths and Mechanisms.* Routledge: London 2004.

Finke, R.A., Ward, T.B. and Smith, S.M., *Creative Cognition. Theory Research and Application,* MIT Press: Cambridge, Mass., 1992.

Heskett, J.L., Sasser, W.E. and Hart, C.W., *Service Breakthroughs. Changing the Rules of the Game,* Free Press: New York, 1990.

Muñoz-Seca, B. and Riverola J., *Del buen pensar y mejor hacer.* MacGraw-Hill: Madrid, 2003.

Muñoz-Seca, B. and Riverola J., *Problem Driven Management.* Palgrave: London, 2004.

Pérez López, J.A., *Teoría de la Acción Humana en la Organizaciones: la acción personal.* Rialp: Madrid, 1991.

Index